THE DYSFUNCTIONAL LIBRARY

THE DYSFUNCTIONAL LIBRARY

CHALLENGES AND SOLUTIONS TO WORKPLACE RELATIONSHIPS

JO HENRY | JOE ESHLEMAN | RICHARD MONIZ

ALA Editions

AN IMPRINT OF THE AMERICAN LIBRARY ASSOCIATION
CHICAGO | 2018

Extensive effort has gone into ensuring the reliability of the information in this book; however, the publisher makes no warranty, express or implied, with respect to the material contained herein.

ISBNs
978-0-8389-1623-0 (paper)
978-0-8389-1671-1 (PDF)
978-0-8389-1670-4 (ePub)
978-0-8389-1672-8 (Kindle)

Library of Congress Cataloging-in-Publication Data

Names: Henry, Jo, author. | Eshleman, Joe, author. | Moniz, Richard, author.
Title: The dysfunctional library : challenges and solutions to workplace relationships / Jo Henry, Joe Eshleman, Richard Moniz.
Description: First edition. | Chicago : ALA Editions, an imprint of the American Library Association, 2018. | Includes index.
Identifiers: LCCN 2017031305| ISBN 9780838916230 (pbk. : alk. paper) | ISBN 9780838916704 (ePub) | ISBN 9780838916711 (PDF) | ISBN 9780838916728 (Kindle)
Subjects: LCSH: Library personnel management. | Communication in library administration. | Library employees—Psychology. | Team librarianship. | Conflict management. | Organizational behavior.
Classification: LCC Z682 .H495 2018 | DDC 023—dc23
LC record available at https://lccn.loc.gov/2017031305

Cover design by Karen Sheets de Gracia.
Book design by Alejandra Diaz in the Questa, Ingra, and Rift typefaces.

♾ This paper meets the requirements of ANSI/NISO Z39.48–1992 (Permanence of Paper).
Printed in the United States of America

22 21 20 19 18   5 4 3 2 1

We would like to dedicate this book in memory of
CHRIS RHODES, EDITOR EXTRAORDINAIRE.

CONTENTS

ACKNOWLEDGMENTS

We would like to thank ALA's editorial board for its overwhelming support of our book. We especially want to say a huge "thank you" to our editor Jamie Santoro for all her support with this project. As with our other books, she has provided invaluable feedback and guidance throughout the process. We would also like to thank all the other members of the ALA Editions-ALA Neal Schuman team who work behind the scenes with great success. Thanks to marketing manager Jill Hillemeyer, marketing coordinator Rob Christopher, and their staff. Rob not only assisted with marketing for our book but with review and distribution of our incivility survey, which provided supporting evidence for our text on incivility issues within library organizations. We would also like to recognize Angela Gwizdala, director of editing, design, and production, her editorial staff, and copy editor Helayne Beavers for seeing us through the final stages of publication.

Additionally, we would like to thank all those who replied to our 2017 incivility survey. You provided valuable feedback and supporting evidence for the text. We read every comment from the over 4,100 respondents. You know who you are! We hope many of you will find both validation and hope for an improved work environment through our work.

As in all our writing projects, the support of spouses, family, and friends is invaluable. They too sacrifice as we take time away from them for research and writing. Without their continuous support, our work would not be possible. Finally, we would like to acknowledge our parents, who played a vital role in shaping us into the individuals we are today and giving us the opportunities and wisdom to be able to complete a project like this.

INTRODUCTION

When we first began this project, our discussions ranged from successes to challenges to managerial methods we had encountered during our nearly fifty years of collective managerial experience. Inevitably, the challenges left the deepest impressions, which steered us towards the topic of workplace dysfunction. Instead of writing another how-to book about library management, we focused on this concept. At the time, we did not know our exploration of dysfunction would lead us to information that was valuable not only to managers, but to anyone working in a library organization. It was not surprising that much of what we found echoed managerial and staff challenges we had experienced. Many have asked us if this is a "tell-all" book about our experiences. It is not. Instead, we chose to approach the topic from an academic viewpoint and draw our final conclusions from available evidence. Our work led us to define and categorize dysfunctional behaviors and to look at potential solutions.

When discussing this project with friends and peers, nearly every conversation produced a story about a problem with a coworker or manager. Even years later, many of the stories were emotionally charged. We would later discover that this long-lasting impact is not uncommon. Many people we talked with asked us to include their specific issue because they wanted to prevent others from encountering similar negative experiences in the future. However, because the range of individual dysfunctions is extensive, we could not address them all. We were, however, able to address many, and we believe everyone who reads this book will be able to personally relate to this work. One of the goals in writing this book was to inspire discussion about dysfunction in the library workplace. Another was to provide practical and useful solutions for these challenging situations. It is our hope that we have accomplished both goals.

Although many of the topics of individual chapters could be the subject of entire books, we strove to provide an overview of various dysfunctions found in many organizations, including libraries. Our focus was on the library work environment rather than interactions with students or patrons. Because there was limited research specific to the topic, we conducted our own survey of 4,186 library workers. Many of the study results have been included in the text. Not surprisingly, our library-specific survey results on dysfunction were similar to studies of other industries and organizations. Although libraries are unique in many ways from other organizational environments, they face similar challenges from workplace dysfunction.

This journey into workplace dysfunction cannot begin without self-examination. Chapter one examines the importance of understanding our relationship to the library workplace and identifies library specific attributes that foster personal achievement. This chapter also addresses the important role emotional intelligence plays in an individual's success as a functioning contributor to the library workplace, while acknowledging that psychological disorders and burnout are significant elements with which library staff must deal. It also offers examples of dysfunction and remedies for library-specific problems.

Whereas chapter one focuses on the self, chapter two probes how organizational culture can be a potential source of dysfunction. Dysfunction stemming from the organizational level is often rooted in poor communication and lack of employee engagement, although we know the critical factor of trust is enhanced through "more effective internal communication."[1] The chapter explores how silos within the organizational structure negatively impact communication. Overbearing bureaucracies create a culture of dysfunction by stifling workers' voices and creativity. Worst of all, poor leadership, especially when it ignores bad behavior, can be corrosive to a library's culture. Finally, the chapter reflects on other potential causes and impacts a dysfunctional organizational culture can create.

Chapter three is the first of two chapters dealing with individual deviant behaviors that are based on interpersonal relationships. The minor deviant behaviors are reviewed in this chapter. Incivility is present in all work organizations, libraries included. We investigate findings of the library-specific incivility survey, which documented the prevalence of rude behaviors in library work environments. This kind of dysfunction (which is experienced more often among the younger generations) is on the rise. The chapter goes on to review its causes and effects and explores solutions for workplace incivility.

The more disturbing and toxic work behaviors displayed by staff are addressed in chapter four. A lengthy examination of bullying and mobbing in the workplace reveals both the prevalence and severity of such toxic behaviors on individual workers and the organization. Solutions to help individuals and the organization counter these behaviors are presented. Other behaviors potentially toxic to the workplace are reviewed, including passive-aggressive and counterproductive work behaviors. As in chapter three, we have included library-specific survey data gathered on toxic workplace experiences.

The impact on organizations of dysfunctional behaviors that affect property and create political deviations is addressed in chapter five. Employees act out in ways that negatively impact the organization. This chapter addresses causes, results, and potential solutions for cyberloafing, fraud, theft, and sabotage. It also investigates gossip's impact on the organization and workplace, in addition to the fallout from rankism, bias, and individual lobbying in the library organization.

Chapter six focuses on challenges in communication. It begins with a review of communication channels, and addresses challenges that originate in the library's organizational structure, such as limited or distorted information. This chapter also looks at the impact of individuals who have communication apprehension or introverted personalities. The effect of other barriers such as passive listening, dismissive communication, and a lack of empathy are explored. Finally, some of the negative impacts on the library organizations resulting from poor communication are considered.

Chapter seven covers conflict management. Conflict occurs in all organizations, and though certain types of conflict can be healthy, much is not. A variety of conflict management approaches are reviewed. In addition to addressing the wider scope of conflict management, the chapter discusses situational conflict and how to identify the managerial skills needed to handle these challenging situations.

The impact of ineffective collaboration dominates chapter eight. First, we identify some of the general barriers to collaboration among individuals in the library workplace. These include the general culture; attitudes of group members; lack of trust; distance; poor synchronization; and stress. The chapter notes how organized and productive meetings contribute to successful collaboration. The importance of workplace design on collaboration, as well as the insufficient attention devoted to this topic, are also addressed. Finally, chapter eight discusses how staff's resistance to change and to participate in collaborative activities can impact a library.

It is the rare librarian who does not find herself in workplace situations where she is required to be part of a team. Chapter nine focuses primarily on team composition and how managers can build functional and productive teams. To help consider how to design teams, we present ideas that help to reconcile the tension between the goals of teamwork and individual personalities, strengths, and weaknesses. Sometimes there is a failure to acknowledge the number of teams in which librarians participate, and that they may not give enough attention to their team roles.

In chapter ten, the influence of functional leadership (or lack thereof) in libraries is addressed. The present consists of, and the future will be, challenging times for library leaders. In a world that demands agile and forward-thinking leaders, librarians are often at a disadvantage because of budgetary constraints, the constant need to prove value, and the need to provide guidance to the employees they supervise. In addition to the issues that can contribute to dysfunctional libraries, there is the added dimension of recognizing and alleviating all the individual dysfunctions documented in this book. Because the future of libraries depends upon providing support and information access to their communities, this chapter sounds a clarion call to those who have a passion to lead libraries forward.

It is our hope that the readers will find topics they relate to in every chapter of this book. While we encourage readers to start with chapter one and begin their journeys by reflecting upon the self, each chapter focuses on a specific area of dysfunction and can be read on its own. The only recommendation we would offer would be to read the two chapters on individual dysfunctional behaviors (chapters 3 and 4) in sequence as the first addresses lower-level behaviors and the second explores more toxic and disruptive ones. Otherwise, let the page turn and the exploration of library workplace dysfunction begin.

NOTE

1. Karen Mishra, Lois Boynton, and Aneil Mishra, "Driving Employee Engagement: The Expanded Role of Internal Communications," *International Journal of Business Communication* 51, no. 2 (April 2014): 199.

THE DYSFUNCTIONAL SELF

t is human nature for individuals to blame the problems that they see in the world and in the library workplace on someone or something other than themselves. As this book will indicate, there are often good reasons to look for external validation of why dysfunctional systems and situations exist. This chapter could have been put at the end of this book, but there is a reason for its placement at the beginning. It may seem cliché, but if librarians and administrative staff really hope to improve their respective libraries and the work that is done in them, it *starts with improving themselves*. The intent of this book is to deal with dysfunctional issues and problems, and this chapter is no exception. It is, however, worth noting that while library staff may not exhibit a major degree of dysfunctional behavior, none are not entirely immune. As humans and as librarians, all of us are essentially works in progress. Ronald Wheeler, the director of the Fineman and Pappas Law Libraries and an associate professor of law and legal research at Boston University, bravely declared, "I had to admit to myself that I was the source of the problem and that I had to work on my own internal issues in order to function appropriately in the workplace and elsewhere." Jamie Watson, Collection Development Coordinator for the Baltimore County Public Library, writes that "sometimes in a busy work day, you (and others) make knee-jerk decisions." As a recent study by the authors of this book revealed, workload and frequent interruptions—just to name a couple of external challenges—can be constant hurdles for many librarians. This chapter will examine individual attributes that have been identified as critical or in some cases dysfunctional. It will then explore the topic of emotional intelligence and its applicability to libraries and librarians; briefly touch on the relative prevalence and effect of psychological disorders in the library workplace (especially if they pertain to us personally); and, finally consider anecdotally how these relate to a handful of specific library roles.[1]

LIBRARIAN TRAITS AND ATTRIBUTES IN GENERAL

It is the authors' contention that emotional intelligence, or a lack thereof, plays a central role in dysfunctional decision-making and behavior in the library workplace. As such, much of this chapter targets emotional intelligence and how it can be built, encouraged, and repaired. Other relevant factors to consider include key traits that experts have identified as pertinent for workplace success. For example, in citing several other authors, Helen Partridge, Julie Lee, and Carrie Munro state that all librarians must be willing to experiment and accept that change will, at times, entail mistakes.[2]

Partridge, Lee, and Munro also note the work of Cheryl Peltier-Davis, associate cataloging librarian at the Alvin Sherman Library at Nova Southeastern University in Florida, who outlines a long list of the traits or attributes that individuals should look for and foster in themselves. They must

- have the capacity to learn constantly and quickly
- monitor new ways of organizing and accessing resources
- keep abreast of trends in technology
- possess the temperament to work independently as well as work on a team
- have the propensity to take risks and to work under pressure
- be service- and user-oriented
- be skillful at enabling and fostering change
- have a sense of humor (most important!)
- be committed to continuing formal and informal education . . .
- conduct research and publish results
- read professional literature, especially outside the field
- become actively and, in some instances brazenly, involved in ILS design and usability studies

- support cooperation and collaboration among the global community of librarians
- advocate for the profession by marketing the value of web 2.0, library 2.0, and librarian 2.0 to decision-makers.[3]

This is a daunting list, but extremely pertinent to our desire to avoid dysfunction and be as productive as we can be. It is worth noting that Partridge, Lee, and Munro conclude their study on attributes of librarians by stating that "librarian 2.0 is less to do with technology and more about quality transferable skills and interpersonal abilities." Of greater importance is the study's discovery that librarian 2.0 is more about changing attitudes and ways of thinking than anything else.[4]

When exploring individual traits, it is interesting to look at how they can change under specific circumstances and over time. Patrick Kyllonen discusses how particular events in our lives seem to be associated with significant changes in personality: Successful careers are associated with increases in emotional stability and conscientiousness, remarriage is associated with a reduction in neuroticism, just as numerous other such life events can correlate with change. Any number of events that affect individual lives can have profound or subtle impacts. Kyllonen also describes an additional study that indicated that "self-confidence, warmth, self-control, and emotional stability all tend to increase with age." This is a hopeful sign. Perhaps time, coupled with greater awareness, can boost this process.[5]

Before moving on to a more detailed treatment of emotional intelligence, it is worth touching on the importance of grit and resilience. Dysfunction might come from a tendency to give up at the first sign of adversity instead of applying a reasonable amount of perseverance. Grit is a known quality or attribute that helps us to persevere. Although the authors' focus here is on librarians, it is worth noting that many institutions of higher education have in recent years developed programs to encourage students to assess their own grit and resilience. For example, the Educational Testing Service recently created the Personal Potential Index (PPI), which, among other attributes, measures just these traits.[6]

At Johnson & Wales University in Charlotte, NC, new-student orientations have taken on the task of introducing students to the concept of having a growth mindset and the importance of grit and resilience as masterfully discussed by Carol Dweck in her book *Mindset: The New Psychology of Success*:

> Sometimes we don't want to change ourselves very much. We just want
> to be able to drop some pounds and keep them off. Or stop smoking.
> Or control our anger. Some people think about this in a fixed mindset
> way. . . Some people think about losing weight or controlling their anger
> in a growth mindset way. They realize that to succeed, they'll need to
> learn and practice strategies that work for them.[7]

This book focuses on workplace-related thoughts and behaviors. Adopting a growth mindset is a critical element of improving or reducing dysfunction, and it goes hand-in-hand with the concept of emotional intelligence.

EMOTIONAL INTELLIGENCE

After this brief exploration of traits and mindset, it is important to consider just how central emotional intelligence can be in defining the successful or dysfunctional library workplace. Why is emotional intelligence so critical when considering dysfunction on a personal level? In a nutshell, multiple studies have indicated that individuals who score high in emotional intelligence have better job performance and tend to be associated with high-performing teams and organizational effectiveness. Daniel Goleman, the foremost scholar associated with the concept of emotional intelligence, broke emotional intelligence down into five separate areas: "self-awareness, self-management, self-motivation, empathy, and social skills." According to Goleman, "at best, IQ contributes about 20 percent to the factors that lead to life success." Although scholars and researchers continue to debate this exact percentage, it is widely accepted that cognitive ability alone is not sufficient for workplace success. In fact, dysfunction in our behavior and success could be the result of an overreliance on developing cognitive capacities at the expense of other equally or more important skills. It is necessary to break down each of these in turn, consider where we fall on the spectrum of functional to dysfunctional, and determine what we can do to play to individual strengths and repair or nurture areas of weakness. While there is some debate within the literature as to how to effectively measure emotional intelligence (e.g., by employing self-report, observed skills, or problem-solving), and there is also debate about how much people can improve, it is generally agreed that most people can benefit from training and awareness. Most authors concur that, while variance exists, nearly everyone is able to improve to some extent. Finally, when working in a field that is experiencing rapid change, it is important not to minimize the challenges that are at the very core of self-perception.[8]

In her exploration of the professional identity with which librarians identify, Suzanne Stauffer concludes that

> Inherent in this construction of the professions as a source of identity is the recognition that changes in a profession are more than simple changes in the functions or structures of duties, responsibilities, or institutions. They are changes in the *identity which professionals derive from their membership in the profession.* [emphasis added] . . . When such changes are imposed suddenly from outside the profession or by an influx of members whose identities are radically different, such changes become challenges, even threats, to the identity which members derive from their professional role . . . The resistance of many librarians to changes in the profession over the past several decades . . . is now understood as a reaction against the imposition of an alien identity which rejects, degrades, and devalues the identity which they derive from their profession.[9]

When moving forward and considering the challenges associated with developing emotional intelligence, do not forget the context of librarianship and the special burdens that are placed on individuals who connect their personal identities with their professions. Indeed, library professionals may have opportunities to reframe some of the big picture. As Simon Lord observes, "Rather than perceive these changes as a threat to the profession, information professionals should be willing to adapt and recognize that, with the right response, these changing forces can become an opportunity to evolve and enhance their roles—from gatherer and supplier to analyst, educator and indispensable guide."[10]

The Elements of Emotional Intelligence

- self-awareness
- self-management
- self-motivation
- empathy
- social skills

Self-Awareness

When considering the topic of emotional intelligence, begin with self-awareness. Without self-awareness, the other elements of emotional intelligence are, for all practical purposes, unattainable. According to Ronald Wheeler, "being self-aware means knowing what you are feeling and why, it means knowing what you are good at and what you are not good at, it means knowing what others think about you, and it means really knowing who you are." Perhaps the most critical element is knowing our strengths and weaknesses. It is likely you have seen examples of dysfunction that have risen out of a lack of self-awareness. For example, supervisors who have anger issues but are not self-aware will have no idea where to begin in terms of correcting their dysfunctions, because taking the first step requires self-awareness. Knowledge of ourselves and our strengths and weaknesses can help us avoid or prepare for dysfunctional responses. Individuals who sometimes respond passive-aggressively might be able to recognize how they act in certain circumstances and determine what they should do to be more assertive or direct. In exploring the literature on emotional intelligence, Rosita Hopper, the dean of academic libraries at Johnson & Wales University, emphasizes the importance of being able to honestly assess oneself, especially when it comes to library leadership. Again, without self-awareness such corrective action would not be possible.[11]

According to Steven Covey,

> We are not our feelings. We are not our moods. We are not even our thoughts. The very fact that we can think about these things separates us from them and the animal world. Self-awareness enables us to stand apart and examine even the way we "see" ourselves—our self-paradigm, the most fundamental paradigm of effectiveness. It affects not only our attitudes and behaviors, but also how we see other people. In fact, until we take how we see ourselves (and how we see others) into account, we will be unable to understand how others see and feel about themselves and their world. Unaware, we will project our intentions on their behavior and call ourselves objective.[12]

Covey's observations, along with the examples provided above, support the notion that it is critically important to be self-aware.

How do we address the lack of self-awareness in ourselves or others? Michael Crumpton's creative approach suggests that we "identify others who are self-aware and demonstrate problem-solving skills in the face of change. Put them in a position of helping others." A related approach that is highly effective is to find a mentor or colleague who can help point out these tendencies when they occur. This should be someone who can hold up a mirror to another's behavior, even if doing so might hurt that person's feelings. Mentors should be people who are trusted and have the individual's best interests at heart. As Crumpton suggests, ideally mentors should possess good problem-solving skills. Finally, individuals who use journaling to reflect on their actions and behaviors might supplement this by touching base with a trusted mentor.[13]

Self-Management

On the surface, self-management refers to the ability to control outward behavior or appearance. However, it is connected more to the relationship individuals have with their own thoughts and feelings. Therefore, it would be a mistake to say that self-management is the act of *controlling* thoughts and behaviors. It would be better to consider it in terms of how we use awareness of inner thoughts to behave or respond in a certain way in a given situation. Dysfunction can arise even when we try to control our own thoughts. At its highest level of functionality, self-management includes a healthy ability to recognize when we are angry, sad, frustrated, or tired. Its goal is not to suppress, but rather to become more acutely aware of our emotions.

According to Kavita Singh,

> Recent research on "mindfulness" training—an emotional self-regulation strategy—has shown that with the help on appropriate training the brain centers that regulate the positive and negative emotions can be changed. This training helps people keep their anxieties and tensions at a distance and maintain their emotional calm at the time of crises. We should step back from everyday focus on getting extra work done and take out time to indulge in activities that seem unaffordable. Only the most emotionally intelligent people will have the determination to do it.[14]

Perhaps the most comprehensive book written on the topic as it relates to librarians, *The Mindful Librarian: Connecting the Practice of Mindfulness to Librarianship,* is a comprehensive text that discusses the history and context of mindfulness, how it applies in different library situations and roles, and how it can improve health and workplace performance. It provides practical and immediate solutions that can help with self-regulation or self-management. One of the key elements to achieve this is to cultivate the ability to act less impulsively. To one degree or another, everyone makes impulsive actions. Sometimes the consequences of doing so are minimal or nonexistent. At other times, especially when critical decisions need to be made, impulsivity can have dire consequences.[15]

Covey provides a masterful explanation of this concept:

> Reactive people are often affected by their physical environment. If the weather is good, they feel good. If it isn't, it affects their attitude and their performance. Proactive people can carry their own weather with them . . . Reactive people are also affected when their social environment, by the "social weather." . . . The ability to subordinate an impulse to a value is the essence of the proactive person.[16]

Covey continues, "Proactive people are still influenced by external stimuli, whether physical, social, or psychological. But their response to the stimuli, conscious or unconscious, is a value-based choice or response." The most important component of Covey's reasoning is that whether or not we realize it, between an action and a reaction there is always an opportunity to choose. Mindfulness-based instruction in meditation, among other techniques, is intended to help us create that pause, which in turn allows us to avoid making a dysfunctional decision or taking the wrong action in a particular circumstance. Kathryn Thory discusses a recent study that "reported that police officers' skills in emotion regulation were improved significantly after intensive emotion regulation training. Strategies taught included muscle and breathing relaxation, non-judgmental perception of emotions, mood repair strategies and modification of emotions." On a practical level, role-playing, simulations, and even carefully constructed games have been shown to improve self-regulation. Therefore, we might seek out a mentor or a trusted colleague to "practice" tough situations.[17]

Self-Motivation

Librarianship is a profession full of self-motivated individuals. That is the good news. The bad news is that this is not *always* the case and everyone will face potential lapses in self-motivation. To be clear, self-motivation is motivation that comes from an internal drive to do better, create something, and assist others. As far as motivation is concerned, salary has little to do with emotional intelligence.

So how can we improve self-motivation? Lori Freifield suggests setting goals or helping others set their own goals (which, of course, should align with institutional goals). It is important for people to have a personal level of buy-in if they are to be self-motivated. Self-motivation requires a measure of grit and resilience. Part of motivation is just sticking with goals in the face of failure or difficult situations. Paul Werlin highlights the importance of setting up a timeline and rewarding ourselves when we reach points along the way. He also suggests having fun: "Finally, enjoy yourself. While this may seem more obvious than other self-motivational tips, it's essential. If you're not having any fun, you will lose motivation and stop caring about your goals." This is not always easy to do, but hopefully everyone finds some aspects of librarianship enjoyable and can focus on those.[18]

Empathy

According to Singh, "Empathy is an essential component to enhance altruism and compassion. These tendencies may go a long way to promote and foster ethical outlook in organizations." On an institutional level, the value of empathy is obvious. Value also exists at the individual level in a practical sense. For example, Brandi Porter, the director of the library at Mt. Aloysius College adds, "As a library director I have found EI critical in building staff relationships . . . EI has enabled me to understand the feelings of my employees and how they are likely to respond in a given situation." On a managerial level, the ability to empathize is crucial. It truly cuts across all areas of the library. Lynne Maxwell, writing in *Law Library Journal,* states, "Sensitivity and empathy are traits well worth cultivating in the library environment, where a strong service orientation is crucial."[19]

What happens in a dysfunctional situation or if there is a lack of empathy in the workplace? This can lead to unhealthy situations that negatively affect communication and productivity. Therefore, it is important to cultivate empathy not only in organizations, but also in the self. One study of medical students found that reflective writing can help considerably. A study of nurses indicated that experiential learning and role-playing can be effective in building empathy. A similar approach could work with librarians. If library staff can imagine the perspective of colleagues and patrons, undoubtedly there would be some degree of increased empathy. Writing in *School Library Journal,* Karen Jensen describes how to create a culture of empathy. It is not a quick fix, but rather entails developing a deeper understanding of specific problems and challenges that library patrons face. This can apply just as readily to our colleagues.[20]

Social Skills

Although other characteristics like self-awareness and empathy are necessary precursors to social skills, it is probably the latter that most frequently comes to mind when thinking about dysfunction in the library workplace. Much of this book will deal in detail with issues such as workplace culture and civility. But even in terms of basic or core social skills, it is worth stating that these are critical within the profession of librarianship. In a study that explored the text of job postings to determine the importance of social skills in librarianship, Reeves and Hahn "reported that 'social skills' (including communication, collaboration and cooperation, and team capabilities) was the highest category in the emotional intelligence traits they examined; over 57 percent of the advertisements mentioned these attributes." Maxwell notes that Goleman frequently defines social skills to include "influence, communication, conflict management, leadership, catalyzing change, building bonds, collaboration and cooperation, and team capabilities."[21]

Whether in the library or elsewhere, most individuals have engaged in interactions with people who lack social skills. For example, we may have interacted with a colleague who is extremely shy or not a forthcoming communicator. More common dysfunctional examples include people who make rude, inappropriate, or unprofessional gestures or comments. Here too context and situation are extremely important. For instance, a conversation that is acceptable with another member of library staff might be inappropriate with a patron. The constellation of social skills includes the ability to communicate and understand body language, tone, intent, and numerous other variables. Many of us take this for granted, but these should not be underestimated as a critically important skill.

Luckily, social skills can be easier to develop than some other skill sets associated with emotional intelligence. That is not to say that this cannot be difficult for some people (an extreme example might be someone on the autism spectrum). However, practice can help. Having more opportunities to interact while consciously seeking to improve one's social skills can lead to development in this area. Participating in the profession more fully by attending social events and conferences is a good way to accomplish this.

When thinking about social skills, consider the related concept of self-ef-ficacy. Although self-efficacy can apply to many circumstances, it also applies to social skills. Beverley Kirk, Nicola Schutte, and Donald W. Hine, in a discussion of the work of noted scholar Albert Bandura, write "*Self-efficacy consists of an individual's beliefs about his or her ability to show a certain level of performance.*" Practice and learning by watching good role models are two of the best ways to improve social skills.[22]

DEALING WITH PSYCHOLOGICAL DISORDERS IN THE WORKPLACE

Although individuals may deal with a wide variety of their own and others' personal issues, in terms of possible dysfunction, psychological disorders present an entirely different level of complexity. The American Psychiatric Association defines personality disorders as "an enduring pattern of inner experience and behavior that deviates markedly from the expectations of the individual's culture, is pervasive and inflexible, has an onset in ado-lescence or early adulthood, is stable over time, and leads to distress or impairment." One study indicated that in the United States somewhere between 6 to 9 percent of adults have a personality disorder. Another study puts this figure higher, at 18 percent for men and 16 percent for women. These types of disorders may be broken down into three clusters. Cluster A includes cognitive problems or ailments such as paranoia and schizophrenia. Cluster B incorporates people who may regularly act out in narcissistic or dramatic behavior. Cluster C concerns those who may be overly anxious or experience fear of social interaction. According to researchers Susan L. Ettner, Johanna Catherine Maclean, and Michael T. French, "While most individuals are likely to exhibit at least a few of these traits at some point in their lifetime, it is the constellation, severity, and stability of a particular set of personality traits that constitute a diagnosable disorder."[23]

It almost goes without saying that a wide variety of dysfunction can be exhibited, depending on an individual's diagnosis. Some tend to lash out or externalize blame. They might not be able to work within parameters that require satisficing (especially if they have OCD). They might even pose a serious physical threat to others in the library. Studies have indicated that personality disorders can wreak havoc on careers. According to one group of authors, "Paranoid, antisocial, and obsessive-compulsive [personality disorders] were the conditions most often associated with adverse work outcomes such as being fired, laid off, or chronically unemployed, or expe-riencing problems in interactions with coworkers and bosses."[24]

Unfortunately, there is not a great deal we can do in some of these more extreme cases other than document and report issues as appropriate. For those suffering from one of these disorders, relief may come from a variety of remedies, which can include mindfulness practice and exercise, but may also require medication and therapy. As most sources point out, every library should have access to an Employee Assistance Program (EAP). Individuals can contact their EAP, learn what benefits exist, and get the treatment they need to become successful in the library workplace.[25]

BURNOUT

Burnout is neither a small problem nor one that is likely to go away soon. It can create major problems in the library workplace. According to one study conducted outside librarianship, "burnt out executives lacked emotional sensitivity." It is easy to imagine a similar effect among librarians. Similar studies have found significant effects on health and quality of life as well. Miriam Matteson, Sharon Chittock, and David Mease observe that "emotional labor, which is the effort required to manage one's emotions to meet organizational expectations, is a particularly salient construct in librarianship, and that this is especially true in any service occupation." According to Linda Christian, "in recent decades, libraries worldwide have experienced profound change. The need for expertise within the field has presented new challenges and hazards, and forced the occupation to compete for limited resources in the organizational chain." She states that stress is caused primarily by these two factors of change and limited resources, which often create an incredible workload for librarians. A recent study conducted by the authors of this text concurs with this assessment as the greatest stressor among librarians by far appears to be overall workload.[26]

Some Possible Effects of Burnout

- less enthusiasm for work
- less engagement and productivity
- increased absenteeism
- workplace accidents
- poor customer service[27]

As discussed throughout this book, mindfulness is a welcome antidote for burnout. It includes meditation and other practices. Other recommendations would include a renewed focus on time management. This might involve a mix of these skills in both personal and professional life. In a chapter entitled "Don't Get Stuck in a Rut!" in the book *Mid-Career Library and Information Professionals,* Richard Moniz notes the following ways to handle burnout: engage in professional development through conferences and workshops, develop trusting and caring relationships with colleagues, assess the library's environment from a variety of perspectives, do not be afraid to pull in ideas from outside the library, read widely, try new things, and interact with new librarians (who tend to be enthusiastic and passionate about the profession). Finally, one author suggests having candid discussions about workload to address interruptions, which many librarians face. Scheduling staff to allow them to be more centrally focused on a single task or cluster of tasks would go a long way towards alleviating burnout.[28]

Roles and Dysfunction

The following list is not intended to be exhaustive but rather to inspire the reader. What is your role? How would you describe it as functional? How would you describe it being dysfunctional? What can you do about the latter?

Role	Functional	Possible Dysfunction	Possible Remedies
Library Director or Administrator	Provides vision and guidance for staff, self-motivated and trusting, connects the library's vision to the community or institution and collaborates with other areas	Burnt out, distrustful of staff, works in a silo, micromanages staff, anger-management issues	Attend and present at conferences, read more about changes in the field, have conversations with staff, support staff development, collaborate outside the library with key constituencies, practice mindfulness
Reference Librarian	Provides excellent-quality reference service to patrons utilizing wide depth and breadth of knowledge of resources/tools and applying RUSA's Behavioral Guidelines for Reference Interviews	Burnt out, not ready to listen and engage with patrons, not knowledgeable about new or changed resources	Play with the resources, attend and present at a conference, practice mindfulness, look for new challenges

Role	Functional	Possible Dysfunction	Possible Remedies
Cataloger	Pays close attention to detail, cares about materials or resources, understands the value added by catalogers assisting patrons, attempts to build bridges to other areas of the library and beyond	Feels and acts threatened by the changes in libraries as physical materials are displaced, unwilling to be flexible in applying new approaches and standards for reaching patrons, not interested in venturing beyond his or her own department	Attend and present at conference, receive and provide training in the use of new cataloging or cataloging-related resources, attend meetings outside technical services or even the library
Instruction Librarian	Considers and implements the most effective instruction based on the patrons served. Keeps abreast of changes to information literacy standards at all levels	Allows overload to cause frustration and burnout, not willing to delegate workload, using old or ineffective instructional approaches	Attend or present at a conference, find a teaching mentor and ask for constant feedback, experiment with new approaches for teaching patrons how to access and utilize information resources, collaborate with areas outside the library

CONCLUSION

There are many things that we can do for ourselves to become better librarians and human beings. Being actively engaged in the library community and staying current with library trends fosters positive growth and helps dispel job-related burnout. Improving our emotional intelligence can play a central role in minimizing dysfunction. Library workers also need to recognize that personal lives and library work can be challenging, and therefore resilience and grit must be exhibited. Finally, individuals must take care of themselves through exercise, meditation, therapy, or whatever else may be required in each specific case. Avoiding dysfunction in the library starts with the self.

NOTES

1. Ronald Wheeler, "Soft Skills: The Importance of Cultivating Emotional Intelligence," *AALL Spectrum* (January/February 2016): 30; Jamie Watson, "Be a Leader by Knowing Yourself," *Young Adult Library Services* 12, no. 2 (Winter 2014): 4.
2. Helen Partridge, Julie Lee, and Carrie Munro, "Becoming 'Librarian 2.0': The Skills, Knowledge, and Attributes Required by Library and Information Science Professionals in a Web 2.0 World (and Beyond)," *Library Trends* 59, no. 1–2: 317.

3. Cheryl Peltier-Davis, "Web 2.0, Library 2.0, Library User 2.0, Librarian 2.0: Innovative Services for Sustainable Libraries," *Computers in Libraries* 29, no. 10, (2009): 20.

4. Partridge, Lee, and Munro, "Becoming 'Librarian 2.0'."

5. Patrick Kyllonen, "Soft Skills for the Workplace," *Change: The Magazine of Higher Learning* 45, no. 6 (2013): 20.

6. Ibid.

7. Carol S. Dweck, *Mindset: The New Psychology of Success,* (New York, NY: Ballantine Books, 2008), 239–40.

8. Nivedita Srivastava and Shreekumar K. Nair, "Emotional Intelligence and Managerial Effectiveness: Role of Rational Emotive Behaviour," *Indian Journal of Industrial Relations* 46, no. 2 (October 2010): 316; Wheeler, "Soft Skills"; Daniel Goleman, *Emotional Intelligence,* (New York, NY: Bantam Books, 1997), 34.

9. Suzanne M. Stauffer, "The Intelligent, Thoughtful Personality: Librarianship as a Process of Identity Formation," *Library and Information History* 30, no. 4 (November 2014): 267–68.

10. Simon Lord, "Closing the Gap: The Five Essential Attributes of the Modern Information Professional," *Legal Information Management* 14, no. 4 (2014): 258–65.

11. Wheeler, "Soft Skills"; Rosita Hopper, "Emotional Intelligence in Academic Library Leadership," *Library Staff Publications,* 11, http://scholarsarchive.jwu.edu/staff_pub/1.

12. Steven Covey, *The Seven Habits of Highly Effective People* (NY: Free Press, 2004), 66–67.

13. Michael Crumpton, "Keeping the Motivation Going," *The Bottom Line: Managing Library Finances* 26, no. 4 (2013): 144.

14. Kavita Singh, "Enhancing Ethics at Workplace through Emotional Intelligence: An Exploratory Study on Business Organizations in India," *International Journal of Business and Management* 4, no. 1 (2011): 69.

15. Richard Moniz, Joe Eshleman, Jo Henry, Howard Slutzky, and Lisa Moniz, *The Mindful Librarian: Connecting the Practice of Mindfulness to Librarianship* (Waltham, MA: Chandos-Elsevier, 2016).

16. Covey, *Seven Habits,* 72.

17. Covey, *Seven Habits*; Kathryn Thory, "Teaching Managers to Regulate Their Emotions Better: Insights from Emotional Intelligence Training and Work-Based Application"; *Human Resource Development International* 16, no. 1 (February 2013): 6; Sarvesh Satija and Waheeda Khan, "Emotional Intelligence as Predictor of Occupational Stress among Working Professionals," *Aweshkar Research Journal* 15, no. 1 (March 2013): 89; Priti Suman Mishra and A. K. Das Mohapatra, "Relevance of Emotional Intelligence for Effective Job Performance: An Empirical Study," *Vikalpa: The Journal for Decision-makers* 35, no. 1 (January 2010): 60.

18. Lorri Freifield, "Why Cash Doesn't Motivate. . . ." *Training* 48, no. 4 (July 2011): 22; Paul Werlin, "Seven Keys to Self-Motivation," *Bank Investment Consultant* 18, no. 8 (August 2010): 26.

19. Singh, "Enhancing Ethics," 69; Brandi Porter, "Managing with Emotional Intelligence," *Library Leadership and Management* 24, no. 4 (2010): 200; Lynne F. Maxwell, "Emotional Intelligence: What Works at Work," *Law Library Journal* 102, no. 1 (2010): 158.

20. Anita D. Misra-Hebert, J. Harry Isaacson, Martin Kohn, Alan L. Hull, Mohammadreza Hojat, Klara K. Papp, and Leonard Calabrese, "Improving Empathy of Physicians Through Guided Reflective Writing," *International Journal of Medical Education* 3 (2012): 77; Scott Brunero, Scott Lamont, and Melissa Coates, "A Review of Empathy Education in Nursing," *Nursing Inquiry* 17, no. 1 (March 2010): 73; Karen Jensen, "A Culture of Empathy," *School Library Journal* 61, no. 11 (November 2015): 40–43.

21. Gaby Haddow, "Knowledge, Skills, and Attributes for Academic Reference Librarians," *Australian Academic and Research Libraries* 43, no. 3 (September 2012): 234; Maxwell, "Emotional Intelligence: What Works at Work," 157.

22. Beverley A. Kirk, Nicola S. Schutte, and Donald W. Hine, "The Effect of an Expressive-Writing Intervention for Employees on Emotional Self-Efficacy, Emotional Intelligence, Affect, and Workplace Incivility," *Journal of Applied Social Psychology* 41, no. 1 (2011): 180.

23. Robert C. Abrams and Chaim E. Bromberg, "Personality Disorders in the Elderly," in *Encyclopedia of Elder Care: The Comprehensive Resource on Geriatric Health and Social Care,* ed. Elizabeth Capezuti (New York, NY: Springer Publishing Company, 2013); Susan L. Ettner, Johanna Catherine Maclean, and Michael T. French, "Does Having a Dysfunctional Personality Hurt Your Career? Axis II Personality Disorders and Labor Market Outcomes," *Industrial Relations: A Journal of Economy and Society* 50, no. 1 (2011): 149; Stuart D. Sidle, "Personality Disorders and Dysfunctional Employee Behavior: How Can Managers Cope?" *Academy of Management Perspectives* 25, no. 2 (2011): 76.

24. Ettner, Maclean, and French, "Does Having a Dysfunctional Personality Hurt Your Career?" 167.

25. Sidle, "Personality Disorders and Dysfunctional Employee Behavior," 77.

26. Radha R. Sharma, "An Empirical Investigation into the Role of EQ/Emotional Intelligence Competencies in Mental Well-Being," *Vision* 15, no. 2 (June 2011): 179; Miriam L. Matteson, Sharon Chittock, and David Mease, "In Their Own Words: Stories of Emotional Labor from the Library Workforce," *Library Quarterly* 85, no. 1 (2015): 85, 102; Linda A. Christian, "A Passion Deficit: Occupational Burnout and the New Librarian: A Recommendation Report," *Southeastern Librarian* 62, no. 4 (2015): 2.

27. Christian, "A Passion Deficit."

28. Richard Moniz, "Don't Get Stuck in a Rut!" in *Mid-Career Library and Information Professionals: A Primer,* ed. Dawn Lowe-Wincensten and Linda Crook (Oxford, United Kingdom: Chandos, 2011): 137–50; Mary Wilkins Jordan, "All Stressed Out, But Does Anyone Notice? Stressors Affecting Public Libraries," *Journal of Library Administration* 54, no. 4 (2014): 304.

2

DYSFUNCTIONAL
ORGANIZATIONAL CULTURE

An organization's culture has a profound impact on whether it succeeds or fails in both small and large ways and the short- and long-term pursuits of its mission and goals. Libraries are no exception. Although it has been studied from countless angles, organizational culture has often been boiled down to "the way we do things here." Perhaps the foremost scholar of organizational culture is Edgar Schein. According to Schein, organizational culture can be derived from three sources: "(1) the beliefs, values, and assumptions of founders of organizations; (2) the learning experiences of group members as their organization evolves; (3) new beliefs, values, and assumptions brought in by new members and leaders." This constitutes a wide variety of possibilities within libraries if we consider not just libraries themselves but also the communities, institutions, schools, or businesses (in the case of special libraries) within which they have been created and evolved. It hints at the different influences that history, changes over time, and individuals can play in crafting a culture. For the purposes of this book, although the implication is that culture is rooted, it can also be changed by *individuals*. In the case of a library workplace that exhibits elements of dysfunction this should provide some hope that individuals can influence and create change.[1]

For practical purposes, Schein elucidates the typical ways that sub-cultures (in our case, the library, or even divisions of larger libraries) are broken down:

- functional/occupational differentiation
- geographical decentralization
- differentiation by product, market or technology
- divisionalization
- distinction by hierarchy[2]

As this chapter explores the topic, consider how your specific library fits into this scheme. Librarians and libraries have obvious functional or occupational differences that often set them apart from the university, college, school, community, or larger institution which they serve. In a study exploring the organizational culture of the profession, Deborah Hicks states:

> The service repertoire was found in the text and speech of librarians throughout the data set. Service, broadly defined, was often considered to be the essence of librarianship. Service included activities such as public services (for instance, reference, instruction, and reader's advisory), technology services (from helping people with e-readers to providing public-access computers), the organization of information (from cataloguing to knowing how information on the Web is organized), provision of access to information (books, journals, DVDs, specialized databases, and the Internet), and professional service (such as publishing in journals, association membership and participation, and mentoring of other professionals). Service was described as a core value, the ethos and purpose of librarianship.[3]

When thinking about what contributed to a healthy library culture, service would be at the forefront. The authors would argue that a healthy library culture includes a love of learning and, to some degree, the desire to help others through the ways library workers organize information and, more importantly, how they teach our patrons about the organization of information, its relative qualities, and how it can be accessed and used. Furthermore, it is the contention of the authors that not just accepting change, but rather embracing change and adaptability is paramount in a healthy library organizational culture. On a fundamental level, an overreliance upon doing things as we always have is one of the key challenges faced in library culture. It is the authors' further contention that this must go past the stage of accepting incremental change and include accepting more fundamental change if libraries are to thrive and be successful.

All four of the other factors espoused by Schein involve elements that will be specific to our own libraries. Many school, academic, and public libraries are part of a larger system that may be spread over large or small geographic areas. This may lead to certain hierarchical arrangements and structures as well as the necessity to meet the needs of a more-or-less distinct population. Some libraries may be loosely tied together and share some overall leadership but work in relative autonomy. On the flip side, a group of libraries may be more hierarchical and centralized. (In the case of larger libraries, this may be even further broken down within a given geographic location.) It can be argued that, while no one method is necessarily better than another, libraries are generally better served by cultures with enough autonomy to meet the needs of local or directly impacted patrons, but which balance autonomy and overall leadership or guidance. In this regard, a dysfunctional culture might be viewed as out of balance, lacking either overall strategic vision and direction or the ability to respond adequately to local needs (because of a stifling hierarchy).

On an individual level, librarians who are new to an organization will undergo a process of acculturation and are thus of critical importance when we contemplate the culture of our libraries. According to Jason Martin, writing in *College and Research Libraries News*:

> Just like the culture of a society, organizational culture influences and controls the behavior of its subjects and colors how they view the world and construct reality . . . Culture is taught to a library's new members both formally through the orientation process and the rites and rituals of the library and informally through one-on-one interaction among librarians and library staff.[4]

The complexities of the socialization process, which are beyond the scope of this book, are best described by John Van Maanen. He has identified seven dimensions that have an impact on how someone does or does not absorb the culture of an organization or library. For libraries, the most important dimension is serial versus disjunctive. Applying this theory, when a new staff member is brought on board, he may be groomed to a lesser or greater degree by existing staff. Therefore, when library workers learn organizational culture from a staff member or, more realistically, multiple staff members, it is critical that the staff convey a balance of organizational values along with an openness to change and innovation. If a new member were to be taught that processes are set in stone, this could allow dysfunction not only to remain, but to become further entrenched. (In extreme circumstances, this could lead to what Vikas Anand, Blake Ashford, and Mahendra Joshi have referred to as "corruption via co-optation.") Empowering new staff to question processes, while keeping in mind professional and institutional values, empowers the organizational culture of the library.[5]

THE DYSFUNCTIONAL ORGANIZATION OR LIBRARY

Although it was necessary to cover some background on organizational culture and hint at how it can be impacted, the intent here is to target dysfunction in library culture and to provide specific perspectives and possible remedies from the literature to address these problems. According to Pierre Balthazard, Robert Cook, and Richard Potter, "The dysfunctional organization, much like a dysfunctional individual, is so characterized because it exhibits markedly lower effectiveness, efficiency, and performance than its peers or in comparison to societal standards." In the words of Stephen Harper, "Most companies have some dysfunctional dimensions that hurt performance and, in many cases, drive very capable people away." It is important to remember that just about any library is going to experience this to some degree. In fact, becoming overly cynical and not responding constructively to the slightest sign of dysfunction might be considered its own dysfunction! Life is messy sometimes. Although the discussion and potential solutions provided below come from a variety of sources and experiences, several were taken from Martin Dandira's "Dysfunctional Leadership: Organizational Cancer." These include poor communication, overbearing bureaucracies or dictatorial leadership, high turnover, lack of collaboration, too much talk with no action, working within silos, micromanaging, inefficient or imbalanced resources, the high stress level of a workplace, and convoluted or destructive organizational politics. Dandira's concise list has been expanded below to include a variety of additional circumstances and situations where a given library's organizational culture can create greater or lesser degrees of dysfunction. When reading through the list, it is important to remember that many of these may be interrelated and thus may contribute even further towards the depth of dysfunction.[6]

Poor Communication

A significant portion of this text addresses dysfunctional communication. That said, a general list of problems associated with communication challenges related to organizational culture is found in the sidebar.

Frank Sonnenberg's Examples of Poor Communication

- reacting too quickly
- reacting to emotional words
- listening without being flexible
- permitting distractions
- avoiding difficult subjects
- using words and phrases with double meaning
- being sarcastic
- responding too emotionally[7]

The greater issue of communication can encompass a wide variety of factors, but for the purposes of this discussion, we will consider the danger of poor communication not just as an attribute of an individual or supervisor, but rather as something pervasive that occurs systemically throughout an organization or library. There are many ways this can happen. If someone were to do a SWOT (strengths, weaknesses, opportunities, and threats) analysis in just about any organization, there would be complaints about communication. Some would say there was too much, and others that there was too little. Undoubtedly, "Reply All" email chains can rear their ugly heads at any time and create frustration. According to Barbara Kaufman, "Used inappropriately, email perpetuates misunderstandings such as mixed messages or overreaction to the perceived tone of an email."[8]

The bigger problem, however, seems to be organizational culture that does not foster regular communication. Authors Karen Mishra, Lois Boynton, and Aneil Mishra write:

> Efforts to build trust with employees through internal communication can provide benefits for both employees and the firm. Employees feel more engaged, build trust with their supervisor and the firm, and are therefore more empowered to build relationships with customers on the firm's behalf. More effective internal communication can enhance this engagement.[9]

Again, the emphasis is on more, as opposed to less, communication. This is especially true in libraries that hope to generate a more collegial atmosphere. That is not to say that the message does not need to be tailored. Rather, messages need to be constructed for the benefit of those who will receive them and consider the receivers' preferred means of communication. Mishra, Boynton, and Mishra continue, "Employees will be more likely to respond and engage when they receive information in a form and channel that they prefer." In the words of noted librarian and author Michael Stephens, the library organization must recognize "the importance of transparency and honest, authentic listening to the folks who keep our libraries going." This is especially true of library management but also true for all internal library relationships.[10]

Overbearing Bureaucracies and Dictatorial Leadership

Although both stifling bureaucracies and excessively top-down management approaches within an organization can choke the very life out of its members, they could also be addressed as separate issues. The decision to couple them here lies in the fact that they both create essentially the same problem: organizational paralysis. Whether through dictates from above or from a rulebook, too-narrow direction can kill an organization's ability to develop and adapt. Seeking a balance is necessary. Some of the literature on organizational culture suggests that appropriate policies and procedures can curb seriously deviant behavior within an organization, such as employee theft. In fact, although the word "bureaucracy" conjures up negative images, it is both necessary and superior to the absence of structure. According to one source, bureaucracies can provide for "effective and accountable" organizations and are "the best known means of preventing public corruption" (or really any type of corruption) within any organization or library. Again, we must use a balanced approach.[11]

Beyond acknowledging that organizational culture often relies on the positive use of bureaucratic accountability, it all too often becomes a straightjacket that inhibits or slows innovation. It can also slow or inhibit the ability to best serve patrons. Most experienced librarians can think of an instance of frustration that resulted from such dictates. Steven Applebaum, Giulio Iaconi, and Albert Matousek contend that such circumstances require "positive deviance" to push back against an organizational culture that prohibits the best application of an organization's highest values. They believe that in such circumstances non-compliance, or even whistle-blowing, may be necessary. There are solutions; however, they are not always easy! Again, dysfunction can be considered on a broad continuum, so there are several questions to be asked. Do the rules or dictates that are in place violate an individual's own ethical interpretation of what is acceptable? Or are they merely inconveniences? What are the potential consequences of fighting the system on a small or large scale? Is there potentially a time in the near future when it would be logical to bring up the negative repercussions of a given dictate or system? For example, if an academic library is experiencing a problem affecting incoming students, will there be a designated debriefing meeting? What kind of data or information might be useful to collect to describe the nature of the problem to interested parties?[12]

Perhaps the most extreme manifestations of dictatorial leadership are not addressed here—that is, when it turns even more abusive and impacts a culture. The authors recognize that, as David Van Fleet and Ricky Griffin note, "such leaders engage in threatening behaviors towards subordinates; display emotional or verbal abuse and bullying; are likely to harass subordinates in one way or another; and may even use physical assault against subordinates." They continue, "Our work suggests that organizational cultures may contribute or detract from dysfunctional behavior in a variety of ways." Because these more extreme examples are important and have a profound impact on organizational culture, they will be addressed at much greater length in chapter four of this book.[13]

Misplaced Reward Structures

It is safe to say that many individuals in different parts of their daily lives have been affected by a reward structure that compensates them based on a motive, or have been part of an organizational culture that encourages employees to make decisions or provide information based more on profit than on the reasonable interests of the customer. A typical example would be the car salesman incentivized to sell unnecessary extras or bake in extra costs when selling an automobile. Another example is the entire subprime mortgage industry, which seems to have taken off prior to the housing collapse in 2008 based on an extraordinarily distorted set of priorities that was twisted further by the banks that packaged these bad loans into credit default swaps. What happened with Enron is yet another modern example where employees were continually encouraged to inflate balance sheets regardless of how this was accomplished. Barrie Litzky, Kimberly Eddleston, and Deborah Kidder state, "It is the link between sales and financial rewards that provides a context for commissioned and gratuity-based employees to rationalize deviant behavior." A final recent example would be the reward structure that warped organizational culture at Wells Fargo. An article by Chris Arnold posted on the National Public Radio (NPR) website on October 4, 2016, reveals that "former employees of Wells Fargo tell NPR that a toxic high-pressure sales culture at the bank drove some workers to deceive customers and open unauthorized accounts—even in the bank's own headquarters building in San Francisco." This type of extreme behavior may seem far removed from libraries, but it can be argued that it is not so far afield as to be entirely irrelevant.[14]

Libraries perpetuate values but, as will be discussed repeatedly in this book, they also perpetuate cultures and procedures or systems. When employees respond to rewards that are linked to outdated procedures, they are responding in less healthy or relatively dysfunctional ways to meet the needs of patrons. It is challenging to find an example that fits every library situation but, for instance, what if a library continued to perpetuate and allocate resources towards a given collection that has become grossly negligent of the needs of the population served (i.e., those resources could be allocated somewhere else)? For example, many of us held on to the practice of collecting materials in formats that were so dated as to be almost useless. In higher education, a particularly pertinent example of the fine line between rewards and culture involves finances and student success. In the twenty-first century, institutions of higher education are increasingly held accountable on measures such as the rising cost of tuition (and resulting student debt), retention (strictly defined as students who matriculate from freshmen to sophomore year) and, to a slightly lesser extent, graduation rates. These factors alone can constitute a significant challenge when weighing punishments and rewards. A culture that rewards passing students through classes is an egregious disservice to all involved. Yet, at the same time, when an institution accepts students, it has a duty to provide whatever reasonable support is necessary for their success. The sudden shutdown of ITT Educational Services in 2016 stands as a stark example of what can happen when an institution over-promises and creates an imbalance in rewards.[15]

When thinking about solutions to these situations or similar examples of misplaced rewards, do not forget that they are often highly entrenched. It will frequently require support from the highest levels of the organization to accomplish change. Furthermore, change that does not comprehensively consider implementation, and lacks input from all levels, may do more harm than good. Creating the right incentives to impact organizational culture positively can require creative thinking, and they are not without risk. For example, many libraries require librarians to maintain statistics and data regarding patron interaction. Although this can be of great value for discovering where change is needed, if the focus is placed on the process of collecting data, then it may be a somewhat dysfunctional misplacement of incentive. On the other hand, it might be that the data collection is the very thing needed to force the realization that change is necessary. This book provides some paths to possible solutions, but they are rarely easy. They require thoughtful consideration of balance; the gumption to try new approaches; and the vigilance to adopt and adjust them as continuous iterative processes (especially regarding reward structure).

Another warning when developing reward structures—it is crucial to know your staff. Although many retail and commercial enterprises place a heavy emphasis on extrinsic rewards, librarianship is very different. When designing reward systems, it has been shown that an overemphasis on extrinsic rewards can undermine properly aligned intrinsic rewards. A recent study of MLIS students revealed that they chose the profession due to a strong drive to become engaged in meaningful work that is intellectually challenging and focuses on assisting others. The same study indicated a desire to work in libraries that foster a culture of trust, respect, and rapport. In libraries, these incentives seem to be more relevant than monetary rewards, which library organizations should consider when they attempt to create solutions.[16]

High Turnover

Often a symptom of dysfunction in other areas, high turnover itself is a problem that can lead to dysfunction. Although our emphasis has been on adaptability and innovation, we cannot discount the critical importance of continuity within an organization. A lack of continuity can result in a culture that is disconnected from core values. It also leads to situations where initiatives must be started from scratch over and over whenever new library staff are brought into the fold. There are, of course, many elements that can lead to high turnover, several of which are discussed in this chapter. In addition to implementing the remedies associated with these, another method to combat turnover is to invest in employees. In a relatively recent article in the *Journal of Financial Planning*, Jamie Bosse suggests creating "a career path for each employee based on his or her personal goals and your overall vision for the firm." In addition to stressing the importance of recognizing impersonal employee goals, another recent study concluded that providing employees with more challenging and less monotonous work is crucial to reducing turnover. Good employees will grow and move on, but organizations and libraries that have turnover due to employees escaping from bad situations, often because the library did not invest in them, will suffer the negative consequences.[17]

Lack of Collaboration or Working in Silos

The authors have written previously about the importance of collaboration. Most notably; *Fundamentals for the Academic Liaison* focused on collaborating with faculty; *The Personal Librarian: Enhancing the Student Experience* explored developing relationships in other academic areas (focused primarily on working directly with students); and *Librarians and Instructional Designers: Collaboration and Innovation* investigated collaboration between the two groups mentioned in the title. Exemplary collaborative efforts are demonstrated at library conferences and individual institutions. That said, librarians frequently complain about the lack of collaboration, both internal and external (although libraries will differ considerably in this regard). In a large academic library, the greatest challenge involves getting different service areas to work together. Externally, the biggest challenge is often developing partnerships—not just with faculty but with other departments that play key support roles as well. In the small academic library, the challenge may be developing the team and/or creating partnerships across campus. In the school library, it might entail working more closely with teachers and administration. In the public library, the problem may be that staff are grouped in departments or different branches and may not always collaborate with other groups or areas. According to Dandira, in dysfunctional cultures "departments will not work together to contribute to the overall vision of the organization." Some solutions would be to reward collaborative efforts, conduct team-building exercises that span library departments or extend beyond the library, and physically move people around to work in different spaces (even if temporarily). The Charlotte Mecklenburg Library has created teams that do different things for all branches (e.g., approving and creating new classes), initiate pod meetings every quarter where divisions of three branches get together and share programming ideas, and hold retreats for each area (adult or child/teen, services, etc.) to share information. It also utilizes an intranet as a communication source. These are all solutions to overcome the silo effect.[18]

Too Much Talk and No Action

Sometimes organizations have cultures that foster a high level of talk and buy-in, which can cause a different kind of dysfunction and paralysis. Many employees have served on committees, task forces, or teams that went around in circles or did not seem to get much accomplished. This may be especially true in libraries. The literature presents many possible solutions for moving past talking and towards doing. For example, Stephan Liozu suggests focusing efforts and prioritizing. Often workers or organizations try to take on too many tasks at once. David Allen has created the GTD (Getting Things Done) methodology, which helps organizational culture to become more action-oriented. It consists of a five-step approach that includes collecting and creating a list of what needs to be accomplished, writing down what should be done next to accomplish each task (and doing it right away if it takes less than two minutes), organizing tasks according to the dates by which they must be accomplished, reviewing items on a regular basis, and focusing energy on what comes next (as opposed to stressing about the big picture).[19]

Staying Focused and Functional

- get past organizational inertia
- create a list
- write down details for each task on the list
- set deadlines
- review the list and deadlines on a regular basis[20]

The High-Stress Library

In 2016, the authors published *The Mindful Librarian: Connecting the Practice of Mindfulness to Librarianship*. Following the book's release, we conducted a follow-up study on mindfulness that had a component that assessed stress within the profession. The survey was completed by 629 librarians working in all types of libraries. When asked to identify the greatest stressor related to their jobs, the following ranked highest. (Unfortunately, the degree to which these negatively impacted individuals was not measured.)

- workload and time management—38 percent
- colleagues—14 percent

- instructional workload—9 percent (due to comments specifying teaching load, we separated this from general workload)
- patrons—8 percent (comments indicated these weren't just any patrons, but rather specific problem patrons)
- supervisors and administrators—7 percent
- short deadlines—7 percent[21]

These results contributed to the authors' decision to write this book. Librarians of all types have been under increasing stress in recent years due to declining budgets. It is highly probable that this economic pressure, and trying to add new services, has much to do with the heavy emphasis on workload. Furthermore, survey comments that indicated issues and challenges related to working with other people such as colleagues, difficult patrons, and some supervisors and administrators led the authors to explore more solutions. *The Mindful Librarian* addresses mindfulness more from an individual perspective, suggesting such activities as short meditations, brief walking breaks, and improved time management. When addressing organizational culture, it is necessary to consider the problem from a slightly different angle. Instead of individual solutions, there must be systemic ones. Pending the improbable return of increased financial and human resources, what stands out is the need to prioritize and make some difficult decisions. Rather than trying to be everything to everyone, staff—with management support—should be allowed to prioritize tasks. This may require significant group discussion and soul-searching to determine what items are of the highest value. It may also need data, which could, in turn, require a survey of patrons or focus groups to find out what is most important or relevant. This is not an easy solution for a staff already pressed for time, but it might be necessary.

The challenges in dealing with other people are another matter altogether. These will be addressed in detail in other chapters of the book. Two key elements will be 1) the need to systematically promote emotional intelligence among staff, and 2) to train and develop staff to deal with challenging interpersonal interactions. That said, it is a step in the right direction to emphasize that staff need to slow down, breathe, and take a couple of moments for themselves when they are overcome by stress.

Micromanaging

Most of us probably have experienced micromanagement or have observed others who have been micromanaged. Whether due to a lack of trust in staff or due to managers' own insecurities, this most often occurs when dealing with management. However, this type of behavior might also be seen laterally, when staff members need to assign tasks or require assistance and lack trust. In their discussion of negative and positive deviance, Applebaum, Iaconi, and Matousek write that empowerment and an "empowered mindset" are key to the healthy function of an organization. Indeed, the ultimate solution to defeat or change micromanagement is to create an atmosphere where staff are empowered. That may seem daunting to anyone who is currently being micromanaged. How can we start to change cultures characterized by micromanagement? In an article entitled "The Micromanagement Disease: Symptoms, Diagnosis, and Cure," Richard White explores this topic in detail. In addition to noting the general need for empowerment, he also states that one solution is to "encourage managers to delegate." As will be discussed later in this book, it is crucial that staff are designated according to their strengths and weaknesses. Some organizations do not emphasize how important this is. It is essential that employees know it is all right to make mistakes from time to time—especially when innovating—to define clearer roles and responsibilities and to encourage mutual trust. This may still be extremely difficult, but if an institution can foster broader discussions (which might even be initiated by frontline employees), this could lead to less dysfunction and more productivity throughout the organization or library.[22]

Destructive Office Politics

Politics are often defined within the context of the pursuit of power. As with many of the issues discussed in this chapter, this requires a balanced approach. According to the authors of one recent study,

> Although we are aware that political tactics are linked to power and conflict and are associated with an unhealthy organizational climate, we in fact demonstrated the opposite: some kinds of politics can be beneficial for the firm. Office politics are often radically affected by those who wield higher levels of authority, however, organizational culture is affected by politics at all levels.[23]

Perhaps the most destructive version is practiced by those who blatantly seek to manipulate people and situations for their own benefit. According to Applebaum, Iaconi, and Matousek, "Machiavellianism is another trait thought to be linked to the likelihood of deviant behavior within individuals and groups." Like bureaucracies, politics are often thought to be negative. Healthy or balanced political conflict and debate can, however, lead to better solutions and outcomes. Although this will be covered in greater detail later in this book, negative office politics needs to be incorporated or at least mentioned in any general discussion of organizational culture. We refer to the Machiavellian approach when politics are used to achieve narrow agendas that do not consider or appropriately prioritize the needs of the organization, library, or those it serves. The literature suggests that another method to combat this is to redirect negative energy or conversations. Yet another method is to harness politics for positive discourse. Edgar Rogelio Ramírez Solís, Verónica Iliàn Baños Monroy, and Margarita Orozco-Gómez conclude that "political strategies should be built with trust, collaboration, ethics and 'win-win' negotiations in view of greater organizational well-being."[24]

Lack of Diversity

Diversity in libraries can be considered within a wide variety of contexts. For example, we might consider ethnic and gender diversity in the context of communities that are in themselves diverse. A Spanish-speaking librarian, for instance, in a community that serves a largely Spanish-speaking community is beneficial, and insufficient Spanish-speaking staff can lead to dysfunction. On a broader level, another way to recognize the importance of diversity and the potential for dysfunction is when a group of librarians lack the ability to engage in constructive discussion about both day-to-day and strategic initiatives. To quote Raquel Gabriel,

> What if the status quo lacks diversity in the types of employees, their viewpoints, or even their working styles? To be sure, there need to be some commonly shared values and ideas among colleagues, but there is a difference between a common culture where the majority has a shared set of assumptions and works well together to support and invigorate an institution, and a culture that remains as it is because no one wants to make an effort, or worse, because such efforts are actively or tacitly discouraged.[25]

Once again, we see the importance of balance within the culture to inculcate shared values, but there must also be respect for different perspectives. Diversity is critical and, though it presents challenges, leads to better solutions and a more adaptable organizational culture. One of the best suggestions from the literature and research is not only to be open to new viewpoints but also actively encourage constructive dissent (similar to what Toyota has done in recent years). In a library setting, this might simply entail making sure someone is questioning assumptions and decisions. Theoretically, a designated person could be assigned this role.[26]

In conclusion, there are many approaches to address specific issues that occur in a dysfunctional culture. An even more proactive way to address these for the long run is to build an adaptable culture that can learn and adjust.

ESTABLISHING A CULTURE OF LEARNING AND ADAPTIVE CHANGE

How is culture created and developed such that an organization can be most adaptive? According to Schein, this is achieved by

- creating a common language and conceptual categories
- defining group boundaries and criteria for inclusion and exclusion
- developing norms of intimacy, friendship, and love
- defining and allocating rewards and punishments
- explaining the unexplainable—ideology and religion[27]

Change is not easy, nor is establishing a culture of learning within any organization or library. Chris Argyris, a leading scholar of adaptable organizational culture, has this to say:

> Two types of learning are necessary in all organizations. The first is single-loop learning: learning that corrects errors by changing routine behavior . . . The second is double-loop learning: learning that corrects errors by examining the underlying values and policies of an organization . . . Double-loop learning is rare in most organizations.[28]

According to Argyris, most organizations are likely dysfunctional when it comes to questioning fundamental beliefs or patterns. His solution is to create a culture that can question itself without becoming defensive. Carol Wilkinson and Courtney Bruch call this "encouraging courageous conversations," which "are not the norm in every library." Other authors view this as an ability to tolerate failure, which can accompany attempts to innovate and explore new directions. For example, a study indicated that there can be great value in how individuals handle crisis or, rather, debrief in the wake of a crisis. Dee Gray and Sion Williams observe that such an approach "offers real opportunities for the workforce to rethink and re-frame learning so that innovation, change and improved performance manifest in organizational practice." As most people know from personal experience, significant change is very, very difficult and takes a great deal of time. Once again, the authors are offering solutions, not necessarily quick fixes. Library consultant Robert Moran cites a recent study that found that 90 percent of patients who had undergone coronary-artery bypass surgery failed to implement or maintain necessary lifestyle changes just two years after undergoing major surgery! He goes on to prescribe what are essentially the two most critical prerequisites for change: the ability to frame things differently and the recognition of the role that emotions play. He writes, "First, to change, one must be able to change one's frames for the new circumstance, and this takes time, often months. Second, we are not just minds. In everyday living our emotions play an equal if not greater part in behavioral change." When considering organizational culture, change can be even more complex and difficult than managing individual change. A 2015 study by Ti Yu and Chao-chen Chen identifies three critical dimensions of organizational change: "creating continuous learning opportunities, creating systems to capture and share learning, and providing strategic leadership for learning."[29]

Make no mistake. Libraries must change. As far back as 2002, Denise Troll noted:

> Libraries are struggling with what to measure and how to measure inputs and outputs in the digital environment. We currently have no standard, comparable data to assess digital library trends within or across academic libraries. Similarly, usage data from commercial vendors of electronic database resources cannot be compared easily because they measure or define the data differently.[30]

Melanie Schlosser writes that "change is needed, and it will not happen without great effort and broad participation. It is time to build a new future for libraries, brick by brick, project by project, and person by person." Furthermore, according to Schein, "The only way to build a learning culture that continues to learn is for leaders themselves to realize that there is much that they do not know and must teach others to accept that there is much that they do not know. The learning task then becomes a shared responsibility."[31]

Denise Troll's prescient 2002 article concluded that

> the choices we make today—to change or not change—will create a
> legacy for librarians and library users that defines the meaning and pur-
> pose of libraries, and structures how users will perceive and experience
> libraries in the future. What will our legacy be? What are you prepared
> to contribute to that legacy? What does your conscience say about that?[32]

The authors would argue that the library profession has grown to be at least
somewhat more adaptive since 2002, but it still grapples with the changes
wrought by how our patrons access information. Troll states that "expla-
nations of why libraries are changing require contextual information and
interpretive techniques that we currently do not have" and encourages us
to "examine our assumptions" because "a rapidly growing percentage of
the use of electronic library resources occurs outside the library." This is
only a single layer, albeit perhaps the most significant, of the multitude of
forces affecting our profession.[33]

Troll is not the only author to highlight the need for organizational
culture in libraries to engage in radical change. In a 2010 article, Krisellen
Maloney, Kristin Antelman, Kenning Arlitsch, and John Butler open with
the following statement:

> Libraries have been affected by disruptive technologies for the past decade
> or more, but they have been insulated from major changes by stable
> budgets and an academic culture that is conservative with respect to
> change. Just as disruptive technologies reshaped other industries, the
> full force of the changes brought about by Google, Amazon, Wikipedia,
> and many smaller innovators is now being felt in all types of libraries . . .
> at the same time, a generational change in attitudes towards technology
> is witnessed in library users.[34]

They summarily indicate the importance of fostering radical innovation
and change in organizational culture: "Central to achieving this goal is
fostering organizational culture that supports more risk-taking." Finally,
in their conclusion they discuss a fundamental premise upon which much
of this text is built, that "change may be expected to be a continuous state,
and those libraries treating it as such are likely to be better prepared to
respond to emerging opportunities (or threats)."[35]

CONCLUSION

Libraries can suffer from innumerable kinds of organizational culture issues that foster and embed dysfunction. If problems are specific they will need to be addressed by specific remedies. If they are more tangled, a plan that encompasses multiple solutions may be required. In the long run, an organization or library that can adapt and change positively will be more successful than those that cannot.

NOTES

1. Edgar Schein, *Organizational Culture and Leadership* (San Francisco, CA: Jossey-Bass, 2004), 225.
2. Ibid., 224.
3. Deborah Hicks, "The Construction of Librarians' Professional Identities: A Discourse Analysis," *Canadian Journal of Information and Library Sciences* 38, no. 4 (2014): 258.
4. Jason Martin, "Symbols, Sagas, Rites, and Rituals: An Overview of Organizational Culture in Libraries," *College and Research Library News* 73, no. 6 (2012): 348.
5. John Van Maanen, "People Processing: Strategies of Organizational Socialization," *Organizational Dynamics* 7, no. 1 (1978): 31–32; Vikas Anand, Blake Ashforth, and Mahendra Joshi, "Business as Usual: The Acceptance and Perpetuation of Corruption in Organizations," *Academy of Management Executive* 18, no. 2 (2004): 44.
6. Pierre Balthazard, Robert Cook, and Richard Potter, "Dysfunctional Culture, Dysfunctional Organization: Capturing the Behavioral Norms that Form Organizational Culture and Drive Performance," *Journal of Managerial Psychology* 21, no. 8 (2006): 710; Stephen Harper, "Removing Dysfunction: A Company's Culture Must Be Healthy," *Industrial Engineer* 41, no. 2 (2009): 46; Martin Dandira, "Dysfunctional Leadership: Organizational Cancer," *Business Strategy Series* 13, no. 4 (2012): 187–90.
7. Frank Sonnenberg, "Barriers to Communication," *Journal of Business Strategy* 11, no. 4 (July 1990): 56–59.
8. Barbara Kaufman, "Anatomy of Dysfunctional Working Relationships," *Business Strategy Series* 13, no. 2 (2012): 104.
9. Karen Mishra, Lois Boynton, and Aneil Mishra, "Driving Employee Engagement: The Expanded Role of Internal Communications," *International Journal of Business Communication* 51, no. 2 (April 2014).
10. Mishra, Boynton, and Mishra, "Driving Employee Engagement"; Michael Stephens, "Speak of the Devil," *Library Journal* (2016): 40.
11. Sandra L. Robinson and Rebecca J. Bennett, "A Typology of Deviant Workplace Behaviors: A Multidimensional Scaling Study," *The Academy of Management Journal* 38, no. 2 (April 1995): 55572; "Bureaucracy," in *Bloomsbury Guide to Human Thought* (London, United Kingdom: Bloomsbury, 1993).

12. Steven Applebaum, Giulio Iaconi, and Albert Matousek, "Positive and Negative Deviant Workplace Behaviors: Causes, Impacts, and Solutions," *Corporate Governance* 7, no. 5 (2007): 587.

13. David Van Fleet and Ricky Griffin, "Dysfunctional Organizational Culture: The Role of Leadership in Motivating Dysfunctional Work Behaviors," *Journal of Managerial Psychology* 21, no. 8 (2006): 705–6.

14. Don Campbell, "Angry Over the Bailouts, Angry We Won't Ever Learn," *USA Today*, November 5, 2008; Leon T. Kendall, "The Enron Saga," *Vital Speeches of the Day* 68, no. 19 (2002): 594; Barrie Litzky, Kimberly Eddleston, and Deborah Kidder, "The Good, the Bad, and the Misguided: How Managers Inadvertently Encourage Deviant Behavior," *Academy of Management Perspectives* 20, no. 1 (2006): 94; and Chris Arnold, "Former Wells Fargo Employees Describe Toxic Sales Culture, Even at HQ," *National Public Radio*, October 4, 2016.

15. Patricia Cohen, "ITT Chain of Colleges Closes Most of Its Sites," *New York Times,* (September 7, 2016): B1(L).

16. Judy Cameron, "Negative Effects of Reward on Intrinsic Motivation—A Limited Phenomenon: Comment on Deci, Koestner, and Ryan," *Review of Educational Research* 71, no. 1 (2001): 40; Rajesh Singh, "The Impact of Intrinsic and Extrinsic Motivators on Employee Engagement in Information Organizations," *Journal of Education and Library Science* 57, no. 2 (2016): 203–4.

17. Jamie Bosse, "Preventing Employee Turnover," *Journal of Financial Planning* (2011): 27; Z. Van Der Aa., J. Bloemer; J. Heeler, "Reducing Employee Turnover through Customer Contact Center Job Quality." *International Journal of Human Resource Management* 23, no. 18 (2012): 3935.

18. Dandira, "Dysfunctional Leadership,"188; "Information Silos Can Harm Workplace Culture," *Professional Safety* 61, no. 6 (June 2016): 21.

19. Stephan Liozu, "Getting Things Done," *Smart Business Pittsburgh* 20, no. 11 (April 2014): 5; Paul Keegan, "How David Allen Mastered Getting Things Done," *Business 2.0* 8, no. 6 (2007): 72–78.

20. Paul Keegan, "How David Allen Mastered Getting Things Done."

21. Richard Moniz, Jo Henry, Joe Eshleman, Lisa Moniz, and Howard Slutzky, "Stressors, Librarians, and How Mindfulness Can Help," *College and Research Libraries News* 77, no. 11 (2016): 534–35.

22. Steven H. Applebaum, Giulio Iaconi, and Albert Matousek, "Positive and Negative Deviant Workplace Behaviors," 592; Richard D. White, Jr., "The Micromanagement Disease: Symptoms, Diagnosis, and Cure," *Public Personnel Management* 39, no. 1 (2010): 74–75.

23. Edgar Rogelio Ramírez Solís, Verónica Iliàn Baños Monroy, and Margarita Orozco-Gómez, "The Inner Circle: How Politics Affects the Organizational Climate," *Journal of Organizational Culture, Communications and Conflict* 18, no. 1 (2014): 83.

24. Applebaum, Iaconi, and Matousek, "Positive and Negative Deviant Workplace Behaviors," 592; Stephen Rohan-Jones, "Taking the Politics out of the Office: Building Better Workplaces," *Incite* 33, no. 11 (November 2012): 28; Ramirez Solís, Baños Monroy, and Orozco-Gómez, "The Inner Circle," 84.

25. Raquel Gabriel, "Tying Diversity to Organizational Culture," *Law Library Journal* 102, no. 3 (2015): 511–12.

26. Hans Greimel and Mark Rechtin, "Toyota Adopts 'Devil's Advocate' in Quest to Restore Quality, Confidence." *Advertising Age* 82, no. 4 (2011): 3.

27. Schein, *Organizational Culture and Leadership*, 112.

28. Chris Argyris, "Education for Leading-Learning," *Organizational Dynamics,* 5.

29. Carrol Wilkinson and Courtney Bruch, "Building a Library Subculture to Sustain Information Literacy Practice with Second Order Change," *Communications in Information Literacy* 8, no. 1 (2014): 89; Dee Gray and Sion Williams, "From Blaming to Learning: Re-Framing Organisational Learning from Adverse Incidents," *The Learning Organization* 18, no. 6 (2011): 44; Robert Moran, "Change: More Often Than Not, We Can't," *Library Leadership and Management* 24, no. 3 (2010): 99; Ti Yu and Chao-chen Chen, "The Relationship of Learning Culture, Learning Method, and Organizational Performance in the University and College Libraries in Taiwan," *LIBRI* 65, no. 1 (2015): 10.

30. Denise Troll, "How and Why Libraries are Changing: What We Know and What We Need to Know," *Portal: Libraries and the Academy* (2002): 100.

31. Melanie Schlosser, "OSUL2013: Fostering Organizational Change Through a Grassroots Planning Process," *College and Research Libraries* 72, no. 2 (2011): 163; Schein, *Organizational Culture and Leadership*, 398.

32. Troll, "How and Why Libraries are Changing," 120.

33. Ibid.,101, 104, 114.

34. Krisellen Maloney, Kristin Antelman, Kenning Arlitsch, and John Butler, "Future Leaders' Views on Organizational Culture," *College and Research Libraries* 71, no. 4 (2010): 322.

35. Ibid., 323, 335.

3

INCIVILITY IN
THE WORK ENVIRONMENT

L evels of dysfunction in the workplace can vary from minor deviant actions with minimal, but noteworthy, impact to more aggressive behavior that causes major disruption to the organization. Incivility, which is often discussed in terms that encompass this wide range of deviant behavior, is typically a term used to describe the less-aggressive deviations. In his book *Choosing Civility: The Twenty-Five Rules of Considerate Conduct*, P.M. Forni adds some insight to the meaning behind the word: "civility . . . [is derived from] Latin *Civitas*, which means 'city,' especially in the sense of civic community. . . The city is where we enlighten our intellect and refine our social skills." Forni defines civility as action that involves "courtesy, politeness, and good manners." Thus, incivility would be the absence of such behavior.[1]

To completely define incivility, it must be connected to society. Without the defined boundaries of society and socially accepted norms, incivility cannot exist. At the 55th annual meeting of the American Sociological Association in 1960, Kai T. Erikson spoke about the roots of incivility during a presentation on the sociology of deviance:

> Deviance is considered a vagrant form of human activity, moving outside the more orderly currents of social life . . . [It] persist[s] over time, and sometimes remain intact long after the strains which originally

produced them have disappeared . . . From a sociological standpoint . . . the critical variable in the study of deviance is the social audience rather than the individual person, since it is the audience which eventually decides whether or not any given action or actions will become a visible case of deviation.[2]

Erikson makes the case that society (or the social system) is what determines civil behavior. At the time, this was a departure from existing theories that held deviant behavior was caused from unfair sanctions or some "abnormal social condition." Thus, deviance from the social norm, as defined by the overriding social body, results in incivility.[3]

The boundaries of the workplace are no different from the larger society in that workplace culture determines acceptable or unacceptable behavior. Actions that digress from the accepted organizational norm are labeled as deviant, or at a lower level, uncivil. Lynne Andersson and Christine Pearson offer an excellent definition of incivility in the workplace:

Workplace incivility is low-intensity deviant behavior with ambiguous intent to harm the target, in violation of workplace norms for mutual respect. Uncivil behaviors are characteristically rude and discourteous, displaying a lack of regard for others.[4]

Note that incivility can be an action delivered both with or without conscious intent. This is one characteristic that distinguishes incivility and minor deviant behaviors from more aggressive actions such as bullying and mobbing (which will be discussed in chapter four). Pearson and Christine Porath view individuals as important players in organizational civility. They state that individuals' "subjective interpretation of actions and how these actions make them feel" are determining factors in labeling uncivil behaviors. This pushes incivility into a more slightly subjective realm that depends on the reactions of individuals in the workplace. But overall, these individuals make up the organization and thus contribute to the accepted culture as discussed in the previous chapter. Thus, the impact of uncivil actions on the individual within the context of the work organization, coupled with the defined expected norms and behaviors, is what ultimately determines what deviant behavior is.

Incivility in the workplace can occur at any level—between peers or between supervisors and subordinates. Generally, incivility involves rude or impolite behavior. Such actions can be defined as displaying little interest in others' opinions, withholding important information, talking down to or interrupting others, disparaging or belittling others, neglecting to say please or thank you, texting or emailing or taking calls during encounters, taking others for granted, not listening, or using facial gestures or body language that reflect condescension or disinterest.[5]

The American Library Association lists additional actions which, if not practiced, could lead to incivility. These are saying hello, learning names, engaging in conversation with fellow workers, letting coworkers talk without interruption, respecting coworker's time, and being inclusive. Additionally, staff should be cognizant of when information can be conveyed, either in person or electronically, to the group or should be delivered in a more private one-on-one setting.[6]

Top Ten Uncivil Behaviors by Supervisors

1. Interrupts people
2. Is judgmental of those who are different
3. Pays little attention to or shows little interest in other's opinions
4. Takes the best and leaves the worst tasks for others
5. Fails to pass along necessary information
6. Neglects saying please or thank you
7. Talks down to people
8. Takes too much credit for things
9. Swears
10. Puts others down[7]

Elements of civility are touched on in a code of ethics for librarians found in over sixty countries with principles based on the guidelines put forth by the International Federation of Library Associations and Institutions. IFLA points to ethical behavior and treating coworkers fairly and respectfully. Civility is also approached in the Code of Ethics of the American Library Association, which advises treating "co-workers and other colleagues with respect, fairness, and good faith, and advocates conditions of employment that safeguard the rights and welfare of all employees of our institutions." Although not detailed and specific, these codes of ethics do touch on the importance of a civil and positive work environment in library organizations.[8]

PREVALENCE OF INCIVILITY

Incivility is on the rise. At the time of this writing, the most recent 2016 Weber Shandwick Civility in America poll revealed that 70 percent of Americans believe civility is at a crisis level. (This percentage was 5 percent higher than the 2014 poll and 3 percent higher than a 2014 Emily Post Institute survey.) In their studies of seventeen varying industries, Christine Porath and Emir Erez also indicate that incivility is on the rise. In 1998 only 25 percent of US workers were treated rudely once a week. This number rose to 50 percent in 2005 and just over half the workers in 2011. A Civility in America study points to rising problems in the workforce. Workers in uncivil organizational environments jumped from 28 percent of the workforce in 2011 to 35 percent in 2014. Incivility is prevalent in the library workforces as well. In a survey by the authors of over 4,100 librarians and library staff from all library types, 91 percent experience incivility at work. Nearly 47 percent must deal with it weekly; the percentage grows to 73 percent when staff who encounter it on a monthly basis are included.[9]

Worker Incivility Experienced by Library Type

- Public: 93.52 percent
- College/University: 89.14 percent
- Special: 85 percent
- School: 84.80 percent
- Other: 83.33 percent

Although much of the research on incivility is based in the United States, studies from many countries illustrate that it is a global problem. For example, a 2011 study of 180 Singapore workers from twenty different organizations found that 91 percent experienced incivility within the past five years, of which 22.2 percent experienced it "often." A study of restaurant workers in India found coworkers acted uncivilly at least once a week 32.86 percent of the time and 67.84 percent of workers experienced rudeness at least once a year. Another example comes from Sweden, where a study of 3,001 workers across a variety of professions found 73 percent of workers were victims of coworker incivility and 52 percent were targets of supervisor incivility. As these studies indicate, incivility in the workplace, regardless of cultural differences, is found across the world.[10]

Incivility studies also reveal generational differences. With four generations in the workforce, this adds an interesting element to library organizations. Millennials are the generation most likely to be uncivil to others—41 percent of respondents to the Civility in America poll and 56 percent of those surveyed by a Weber Shandwick poll admit to such behavior. The frequency of these uncivil actions declines as generations age, which supports other theories indicating older workers are more civil than their younger counterparts. Similarly, millennials experience incivility at work more than older coworkers. As many as 44 percent of millennials have encountered rude treatment at an organization, as compared to 40 percent of Gen-Xers, 34 percent of Baby Boomers, and 22 percent of the Silent Generation. Whereas millennials are both instigators and victims of incivility among the generations, they also lead the groups in reporting and defending mistreatment. For libraries where roughly 28 percent of librarians and library assistants fall in the millennial generation, it is significant that incivility is effecting nearly half of this body of workers, especially when considering implementing civility training or emotional intelligence training to counter such dysfunctional actions. Additionally, millennials (27 percent) are more likely to quit a job than older coworkers if incivility is a part of the work environment. This could potentially contribute to higher turnover of younger workers and negatively impact library operations because of increased replacement costs, new employee training, and a lack of continuity of staff. Because younger generations are more strongly impacted by workplace incivility, the prevalence of incivility in library organizations is increasing across all age demographics, but especially with millennial workers.[11]

Generation Breakdown

Generation Z	1996–2010
Millennial (Generation Y)	1980–1995
Generation X	1965–1979
Baby Boomers	1946–1964
Silent Generation	1925–1945

EFFECTS OF INCIVILITY

As rising incivility becomes an issue in library organizations, the question becomes, what are the effects of incivility? Acts of incivility can cause many problems for workers, which in turn impacts organizations. Uncivil actions can cause mental, physical, and work-related problems. Many effects negatively impact individuals' health, adding to not just personal hardship, but organizational impact from lost time on the job and reduced work performance.

Employees who must deal with an uncivil work environment may encounter mental and emotional issues. Withdrawal, diminishing self-esteem, depression, resentment, and anger are typical reactions of workers treated uncivilly. Incivility also negatively impacts workers' "motivation, commitment, and organizational citizenship behaviors." There is an increasing dissatisfaction with work, and as a result many individuals working in this type of environment slip into any number of counterproductive work behaviors (CWB). (CWB is discussed in more detail in the following chapter.) Often the uncivil environment triggers workers' worries—not only about incidents that have already occurred but of what may happen next. Edward Hallowell, psychiatrist, professor, and author, describes worry as a "special form of fear" triggering changes in the cerebral cortex that create feelings of vulnerability and powerlessness. In fact, up to 80 percent of workers who are targeted with incivility worry about these incidents. Incivility ratchets up stress levels. This in turn could lead to increased pessimism, cynicism, irritability, and oversensitivity to criticism. Overall, incivility has a major impact on mental and emotional health.[12]

Individuals may experience physical effects from incivility. Although a single incident may not have a lasting effect on an individual, incivility over time does. Individuals can experience elevated levels of glucocorticoids which contribute to a weaker immune system as well as obesity, cardiovascular disease, cancer, diabetes, and ulcers, among other problems. Merely witnessing an event or replaying it mentally triggers this physical reaction. Thus, library workers operating in uncivil surroundings may suffer significant, long-term physical ailments.[13]

In addition to mental and physical effects, incivility impacts the ability to function in the workplace. Victims of incivility often contribute less to the work environment. They may become disengaged and have diminished cognitive function as well as reduced creativity. Studies of different industries conducted by Pearson and Porath support this idea. They found uncivil work environments results in employees who have 26 percent lower energy, 30 percent lower motivation, 30 percent less vitality, 36 percent less satisfaction, and 44 percent less commitment. Based on these results, it is no surprise that drops in worker performance were discovered. Porath and Erez found that incivility caused cognitive performance on a word puzzle to drop 33 percent, brainstorming to decrease 30 percent, and creative thinking to decrease by 39 percent. With such sharp declines due to uncivil action, the negative impact to long-term productivity could be significant. In addition to performance declines, those who act uncivilly are less likely to be sought out for advice and or to be perceived as leaders in the workplace. Thus, any positive gains from sharing ideas and experience among staff are lost. Finally, incivility impacts the work team when the targeted individual uses avoidance or even revenge toward the offender. This again points to the breakdown of the working unit or team; because team concepts are an often-utilized strategy that libraries use to promote their agendas, this could be disastrous.[14]

Although much of the research to date about the effects of incivility is not library-specific, a great deal can be learned from these studies. The effects of incivility are no different in library work structures than in other work organizations. With incivility having such significant impact on the mental and physical functionality of the worker, its impact cannot be ignored. Such dysfunctional actions, over time, impact the health of both library workers and the library system itself.

CAUSES OF INCIVILITY

Incivility is on the rise, and much of the shift in behavior can be attributed to society as a whole. The culture has changed and what is acceptable today was viewed differently fifty years ago. In his book *Choosing Civility: The Twenty-Five Rules of Considerate Conduct,* Forni points to a society that is self-absorbed and living "in an image of idolatry of the self." He goes on to say that in our "frenzy for achievement, we often disregard the norms of civility." Who has not seen someone in the workforce do whatever it takes to climb the ladder? This quest for achievement can cast civility aside. Additionally, individuals today are less connected to their communities and are more independent. Along with this independence comes a belief there is no need to act civilly. There is no need for help and assistance, so why be nice?[15]

One of the most frequently cited reasons for incivility in the workplace is employee workload. Employees are just too busy to stop and be polite or take a moment to listen mindfully to their coworkers. They feel like they have too much to do. In a survey of seventeen varying industries in the United States, over half of the workers believed their uncivil actions were due to workload and 40 percent attributed uncivil behavior to having "no time to be nice." In a study of librarians from all types of libraries, 38 percent indicate workload was their top stressor and an additional 9 percent of librarians noted instructional overload. Thus, library workers are also under pressure to execute work duties. Stress caused by workload leaves individuals less patient and tolerant and more prone to rude actions. Often due to the constraints of tight budgets, libraries are asked to do more, achieve better statistics, and help more people every year—with limited, if any, additional staff. However, this contributes to the overworked and overwhelmed library workforce.[16]

The shift in the workplace from individual work to more team approaches since the 1990s may also contribute to incivility. Because of this shift, workers are more interconnected than ever before. Paralleling this movement, there has been an increase in "negative interpersonal social exchanges." Thus, as workers collaborate more closely, incivility has increased. In library environments, team approaches are commonplace because units collaborate on projects, programming, instruction, and other activities. This makes libraries prime environments for rude behavior with its frequent social interactions of workers.[17]

Finally, the mobility of today's workers may play a role in the rise of incivility. No longer are employees bound to their work organization for life. The average worker stays at a job for 4.4 years and the number is even lower for the millennials (less than three years). Moving on is the new norm. There is no loyalty to employers—employees want to work on their own terms. There is less motivation to maintain warm and polite relationships when workers plan to stay only a short time. Additionally, more workers are employed on a part-time basis and can easily move on to the next part-time job if incivility issues arise. In libraries, part-time workers are a large part of the workforce with 33 percent of librarians and 70 percent of library assistants working part time. Thus, library environments may be prone to incivility because their workforce is more transient.[18]

Overall, incivility is linked to the changing society and changing workplace. The increases in job demands due to limited staffing increases are one source of anxiety that leads to uncivil behaviors. The increased interconnectedness that results from using teams also challenges civil behavior. (Chapter nine discusses team composition and the challenges that approach faces in libraries today.) Finally, libraries, as with workplaces in general, have become organizations with part-time, transient workers with no strong motivation to maintain civil behavior. It is easier to simply move on.

SOLUTIONS FOR INCIVILITY

Throughout this book solutions are offered at various points to help combat dysfunction in the workplace. There is never one perfect answer to solve complex problems. This holds true for incivility as well. However, some success is found through utilization of human resources, training, feedback, and providing a positive and nurturing work environment.

Incivility can be stopped right at the door by hiring the right person. (The importance of screening job candidates is also treated in chapter four.) Although background checks and references are critical, so too is the candidate's attitude. Mark Murphy, author and CEO of Leadership IQ, found that of 20,000 new hires tracked, 46 percent failed, the causes for which were attributed to "lack of coachability, low levels of emotional intelligence, motivation, and temperament." Murphy notes that each organization has its own "unique" attitude. Exactly what fits into the organization and culture must be determined by management with assistance of human resource staff. Whether a prospective candidate holds these unique values should be determined through the interview process. If attitude becomes a part of the screening process during the interview phase, library organizations may be more likely to find employees who match their culture and value systems. In turn, these employees will integrate easily and bond with existing workers in a civil manner.[19]

Civility training helps to limit incivility in the workplace. One example of such intervention is called Civility, Respect and Engagement in the Workplace (CREW). This six-month training program involving meetings and workgroups was developed by the US Department of Veterans Affairs and has been successfully implemented in over 1,200 VA workgroups. For example, in a study of 2,000 Canadian health-care providers, CREW reduced incivility, decreased distress, increased job satisfaction, and improved organizational commitment. CREW addresses cooperation, conflict resolution, coworker support, diversity acceptance, and psychological safety. Additionally, administration and human resources can conduct smaller-scale training sessions that define civil and uncivil behavior, give examples of occurrences in the workplace, and provide strategies for staff to interact in a positive way.[20]

The use of 360-degree feedback has been successful in libraries, which gives workers insight from all those who surround them (higher-, equivalent-, and lower-ranking individuals) and increases self-awareness of behavior and job performance. This feedback requires observing and recording up to forty-six attributes that are broken down into the categories of "flexibility or adaptability, customer service, systems thinking, interpersonal effectiveness, creative thinking, organizational stewardship, personal mastery, and technical knowledge and skills." This method is successful for combating all levels of incivility, including bullying and mobbing (discussed in chapter four).[21]

Encouraging mindfulness reduces incivility. These concepts are presented in detail in an earlier work by the authors, *The Mindful Librarian: Connecting Mindfulness to the Practice of Librarianship*. Meditation has been shown to change the brain composition and increase the areas of the brain that help to control emotions and increase empathy, which are critical to maintaining civil actions. Mindful listening enhances communication and positive social interaction among employees. Thus, offering opportunities for library employees to meditate and take a time-out from the stress of the day is a great contributor towards creating a civil work atmosphere.[22]

Finally, providing a positive work environment reduces uncivil behaviors. In *Shine: Using Brain Science to Get the Best from Your People*, Edward Hallowell encourages building a work environment "high on trust and low on fear." Managers should be empathetic, provide positive feedback, and model civil behavior. Studies show that negative employee feedback causes individuals to avoid future interaction, whereas positive feedback keeps them connected and open to new ideas. Researcher Christine Porath emphasizes "thriving" as an antidote to incivility. Since replaying memories can trigger strong emotions, she suggests moving on from uncivil incidents quickly to prevent "insecurity, lower self-esteem, . . . and a heightened sense of helplessness" developing. Instead, focus on areas of development and learning (not necessarily related to work) to thrive cognitively and lift confidence, mood, and resilience.[23]

Tips for Modeling Civil Behavior

1. Think about the impact of words and actions.
2. Practice intentional listening and be open in communications.
3. Be inclusive and embrace diversity.
4. Appreciate differing opinions.
5. Move towards positive solutions when conflict arises.

6. Take time to review facts before reacting.
7. Limit gossip and negativity.
8. Look at the broader views as perspectives.
9. Support open communication.
10. Be respectful in all communications.[24]

Hiring for attitude as well as skills, and incorporating civility training into the work environment helps reduce the potential for incivility. Cultivating more mindful leaders and staff through meditation opportunities, and creating a positive work environment, will contribute to a harmonious workgroup.

CONCLUSION

The rude and inconsiderate behaviors that characterize the lower levels of incivility cannot be ignored. These behaviors have an impact on the individual worker's mental, physical, and emotional health. In addition, they contribute to reduced productivity and problems within the library organization. A breakdown of communication, teams, and sharing among employees leads to all kinds of dysfunction. With incivility on the rise, especially among the younger generations, library administrators and others working in library services must recognize the impact of incivility and act through improved hiring techniques and staff training. If ignored, incivility leads to poor performance, staff turnover, and the potential for more destructive actions such as counterproductive work behaviors, bullying, and mobbing (which will be discussed in the next chapter). In contrast, widespread civility and collegiality can form the groundwork for a vibrant and innovative workplace.

NOTES

1. P. M. Forni, *Choosing Civility: The Twenty-Five Rules of Considerate Conduct* (New York, NY: St. Martin's Press, 2002), 2, 9.
2. Kai T. Erikson, "Notes on the Sociology of Deviance," *Social Problems* 9, no. 30, 307.
3. Ibid.
4. Lynne M. Andersson and Christine M. Pearson, "Tit for Tat? The Spiraling Effect of Incivility in the Workplace," *Academy of Management Review* 24, no. 3 (1999).
5. JoAnn Grif Alspach, "The Toxic Wake of Rudeness: Why It Matters," *Critical Care Nurse* 38, no. 5 (2016): 10–11.

6. "Civility and Diversity: ci•vil•i•ty n 1 archaic : training in the humanities 2 courtesy, politeness; a polite act or expression," American Library Association, www.ala.org/ advocacy/diversity/workplace/civility.

7. Christine Porath, "No Time to Be Nice at Work," *The New York Times,* June 19, 2015. www.nytimes.com/2015/06/21/opinion/sunday/is-your-boss-mean.html?_r=3.

8. Committee on Freedom of Access to Information and Freedom of Expression, "IFLA Code of Ethics for Librarians and other Information Workers," *International Federation of Library Associations and Institutions,* revised August 2012, www.ifla.org/news/ ifla-code-of-ethics-for-librarians-and-other-information-workers-full-version; "Code of Ethics of the American Library Association," American Library Association, revised January 22, 2008, www.ala.org/advocacy/sites/ala.org.advocacy/files/content/ proethics/codeofethics/Code%20of%20Ethics%20of%20the%20American%20Library %20Association.pdf.

9. "Civility in America 2016: US Facing a Civility Crisis Affecting Public Discourse and Political Action," Weber Shandwick, https://www.webershandwick.com/news/article/ civility-in-america-2016-us-facing-a-civility-crisis; "Top 5 Civility Actions Every Employee Should Put Forward," *The Emily Post Institute,* http://emilypost.com/advice/ download-top-five-civility-actions-every-employee-should-put-forward/; Christine Porath and Amir Erez, "How Rudeness Takes Its Toll," *The Psychologist* 24, no. 7 (2011): 508; "Civility in America 2013," Weber Shandwick, 11, www.webershand wick.com/uploads/news/files/Civility_in_America_2013_Exec_Summary.pdf; "Civility in America 2014," Weber Shandwick, www.webershandwick.com/uploads/ news/files/civility-in-america-2014.pdf.

10. Sandy Lim and Alexia Lee, "Work and Nonwork Outcomes of Workplace Incivility: Does Family Support Help?," *Journal of Occupational Health Psychology* 15, no. 1 (2011): 102; Naman Sharma, "Effect of Workplace Incivility on Job Satisfaction and Turnover Intentions in India," *South Asian Journal of Global Business Research* 5, no. 2 (2016): 241; Eva Torkelson, Kristoffer Holm, Martin Backstrom, "Workplace Incivility in a Swedish Context," *Nordic Journal of Working Life Studies* 6, no. 2 (2016):12.

11. "Civility in America 2014," 6, 8, 11, www.webershandwick.com/uploads/news/files/ civility-in-america-2014.pdf; "Diversity Counts 2012 Table," American Library Association, www.ala.org/offices/sites/ala.org.offices/files/content/diversity/ diversitycounts/diversitycountstables2012.pdf.

12. P. M. Forni, *The Civility Solution: What to Do When People are Rude* (New York, NY: St. Martin's Press, 2008), 13; Benjamin M. Walsh, Vicki J. Magley, David W. Reeves, Kimberly A. Davies-Schrills, Matthew D. Marmet, and Jessica A. Gallus, "Assessing Workgroup Norms for Civility: The Development of the Civility Norms Questionnaire-Brief," *Journal of Business Psychology* 27 (2012): 408; Edward M. Hallowell, "Fighting Life's 'What Ifs,'" *Psychology Today,* November 1, 1997; Christine Porath

and Christine Pearson, "The Price of Incivility," *Harvard Business Review,* January/February 2013. https://hbr.org/2013/01/the-price-of-incivility; Christine Pearson and Christine Porath, *The Cost of Bad Behavior* (New York, NY: Penguin Group, 2009), 73.

13. Porath, "No Time to Be Nice at Work."
14. Alspach, "The Toxic Wake of Rudeness," 11; "Civility and Diversity: ci•vil•i•ty" n 1 & 2, American Library Association, www.ala.org/advocacy/diversity/workplace/civility; Pearson and Porath, *The Cost of Bad Behavior,* 60; Porath and Erez, "How Rudeness Takes Its Toll"; Christine Porath, "The Effects of Civility on Advice, Leadership, and Performance," *Journal of Applied Psychology* 100, no. 5 (2015):1536; Pearson and Porath, *The Cost of Bad Behavior,* 120.
15. Forni, *Choosing Civility,* 68, 174; Pearson and Porath, *The Cost of Bad Behavior,* 12.
16. Porath, "No Time to Be Nice at Work"; Richard Moniz, Jo Henry, Joe Eshleman, Lisa Moniz, and Howard Slutzky, "Stressors and Librarians: How Mindfulness Can Help," *College and Research Libraries* 77, no. 11 (2016): 535; Forni, *Choosing Civility,* 175.
17. Christine L. Porath, Alexandra Gerbasi, and Sebastian L. Schorch, "The Effects of Civility on Advice, Leadership, and Performance," *Journal of Applied Psychology* 100, no. 5 (2015): 1527.
18. Jeanne Meister, "The Future of Work: Job Hopping Is the 'New Normal' for Millennials," *Forbes,* www.forbes.com/sites/jeannemeister/2012/08/14/job-hopping-is-the-new-normal-for-millennials-three-ways-to-prevent-a-human-resource-nightmare/#5b45e09c5508; Pearson and Porath, *The Cost of Bad Behavior,* 45; Jennifer Dorning, "Library Workers: Facts and Figures," *Department for Professional Employees Research Department,* http://ala-apa.org/files/2012/03/Library-Workers-2011.pdf.
19. Dan Shawbel, "Hire for Attitude," *Forbes,* www.forbes.com/sites/danschawbel/2012/01/23/89-of-new-hires-fail-because-of-their-attitude/#5a04f1d16742; Mark Murphy, *Hiring for Attitude: A Revolutionary Approach to Recruiting and Staff Performers with both Tremendous and Superb Attitudes* (New York, NY: McGraw Hill, 2012.), 1.
20. "Civility, Respect, and Engagement in the Workplace (CREW)," *US Department of Veterans Affairs,* www.va.gov/ncod/crew.asp; Rebecca A. Clay, "That's Just Rude," *Monitor on Psychology* 44, no. 10 (2013): 34; William Hernandez, Amy Luthanen, Dee Ramsel, and Katerine Osatuke, "The Mediating Relationship of Self-Awareness on Supervisor Burnout and Workgroup Civility and Psychological Safety: A Multilevel Path Analysis," *Burnout Research* 2 (2015): 41.
21. Hernandez, et al., 40.
22. Richard Moniz, Jo Henry, Joe Eshleman, Howard Slutzky, and Lisa Moniz, *The Mindful Librarian: Connecting the Practice of Mindfulness to Librarianship* (Waltham, MA: Chandos Publishing, 2016), 179.

23. Juliet Harrison, "Interview with Edward M. Hallowell, MD, Author of *Shine: Using Brain Science to Get the Best from Your People*," *Human Resource Management International Digest* 19, no. 4 (2011): 44; Richard E. Boyatizis, "Leadership and Management Development from Neuroscience," *Academy of Management Learning and Education,* 13, no. 2, (June 2014): 301; Christine Porath, "An Antidote to Incivility," *Harvard Business Review,* https://hbr.org/2016/04/an-antidote-to-incivility.

24. Barbara Richmond, "10 Actions You Can Focus on to Influence Culture of Respect, Civility in Your Workplace," *Legacy Business Cultures,* http://legacycultures.com/10-actions-you-can-focus-on-to-influence-culture-of-respect-civility-in-your-workplace/.

4

TOXIC BEHAVIORS OF STAFF

Whereas incivility in the workplace (as discussed in chapter three) can have a significant negative impact on an organization, the toxic behaviors of staff cause an even higher degree of disruption in the workplace. Social psychologist, author, and authority on workplace bullying Gary Namie states that "on a 10-point continuum of organizational disruption" from "incivility, bullying, and physical violence," incivilities range from 1 to 3 and bullying behaviors range 4 to 9. (A score of 10 is "reserved for battery and homicide.") Toxic behaviors can range from bullying and mobbing to other dysfunctional actions that can be classified as counterproductive types of behaviors.[1]

Studies and discussion about worker satisfaction and aggressive behaviors have been around since the early 1900s. Edward Alwsworth's classic *Social Psychology,* published in 1919, addresses the "mob mind" and Robert Hoppock's *Job Satisfaction,* a summary of thirty-five early twentieth-century worker satisfaction studies, was published in 1935. In the 1980s, Swedish psychologist Dr. Heinz Leymann studied aggressive work groups that ganged up on fellow workers and labeled the phenomenon as "mobbing," Following Leymann's research, the push towards labeling and studying more toxic worker behaviors evolved. The concept of "workplace bullying" (a one-on-one aggression) was introduced in the United States by Gary Namie and Ruth Namie in 1998. The first library-related article on toxic behaviors was written in 2007 by Thomas Hecker, who addressed mobbing in the library workplace. Although there has been some progress examining toxic employees in the library workplace, research is still somewhat limited. Library research that has been conducted to date falls in line with results from other organizational studies and much can be learned and applied from reviewing the topic from all types of work groups.[2]

BULLYING AND MOBBING

The term "workplace bullying" was first used by Andrea Adams, a journalist who drew attention to a bank in England whose manager was abusive to employees. Subsequently, Adams did a BBC radio program on the topic and in 1992 published the first book on bullying, *Bullying at Work: How to Confront and Overcome It*. Largely due to her work, bullying became the focus of continued study in Europe and later in the United States, with attention brought by *Bully Proof Yourself at Work! Personal Strategies to Stop the Hurt* by Gary Namie, Ruth Namie, and Mark Hughs. (The Namies continue their involvement through the Workplace Bullying Institute, of which Gary Namie is director.) Overall, attention to bullying in libraries has had limited exposure in print. After Hecker's 2007 publication, librarian Bonnie Osif drew attention to bullying and libraries in her 2010 article that reviewed literature on bullying. Only one article reviewed in the piece, however, focused on the library setting. Of more significance is a 2016 publication by Shin Freedman and Dawn Vreven, who conducted a study of bullying in academic libraries in the United States. Freedman and Vreven acknowledge there is a "lack of recent research on bullying in the library." Additionally, in 2016 the existence of bullying in the library was supported by the results of a study by Hak Joon Kim, Carole Anne Gear, and Arlene Bielefield. In 2017, a study by the authors identified the existence of bullying in the library workplace. Although there has not been extensive library-specific exploration, there is evidence that bullying occurs in these settings just as in other workplaces and organizations.[3]

One definition of bullying comes from Andrea Adams. In a 1994 speech (given one year before her death), she shared the following:

> Workplace bullying constitutes offensive behaviour through vindictive, cruel, malicious or humiliating attempts to undermine an individual or groups of employees. And these persistently negative attacks on their personal and professional performance are typically unpredictable,

irrational and often unfair. This abuse of power or position can cause such chronic stress and anxiety that the employees gradually lose belief in themselves, suffering physical ill-health and mental distress as a result.[4]

Bullying is a type of mistreatment by one individual of another that is repeated over time.

The characteristics of bullying include both verbal and nonverbal actions such as "dismissive body language, . . . eye rolling, turning of the back, and making dismissive sounds." A 2012 study by CareerBuilder of workers in the United States found that targets are acted upon by bullies in the following ways[5]:

- **42%** Falsely accused of mistakes
- **39%** Ignored
- **36%** Used different standards/policies . . . than other [workers]
- **33%** Constantly criticized
- **31%** Someone [failed to] perform certain duties, which negatively impacted [target's] work
- **28%** Yelled at by [the] boss in front of coworkers
- **24%** Belittling comments . . . made about [target's] work during meetings
- **26%** Gossiped about
- **19%** [Coworker] stole credit for . . . work
- **18%** Purposely excluded from projects or meetings
- **15%** Picked on for personal attributes

In their study of academic libraries, Freedman and Vreven found that withholding information was the leading bullying technique, followed by "being ignored or excluded" and having "opinions or views ignored." Bullies sometimes invade or snoop in the spaces and materials belonging to their coworkers. As these characteristics indicate, workplace bullying is most often non-physical. A 2014 study indicated a physical encounter happens in only 4 percent of the cases. Gary Namie characterizes it as a "nearly invisible . . . psychological violence." Indeed, these characteristics of bullying, for the most part, are occurring in more subtle ways in library environments.[6]

Several studies have shown that bullying is prevalent among workers in a variety of work environments, including libraries. In 2009 a European study across all types of organizations showed bullying impacted 41 percent of all workers. The Workplace Bullying Institute's most recent (2014) study shows 27 percent of US workers have current or past bullying experiences and 21 percent of workers witness it. Bullying also occurs in the academic workplace. A 2010 United Kingdom study of over 600 higher-education professionals found that 38 percent of all respondents had been bullied in the previous six months and 47 percent had been in the past five years. In the United States, a 2012 study of four-year colleges and universities revealed that a total of 62 percent of faculty and staff indicated they had been bullied or witnessed bullying within eighteen months of the study. A 2015 study specific to academic libraries in the United States supports past findings that 40 percent of academic librarians have experienced bullying and 53 percent had witnessed it. Staff in libraries throughout the United States experience bullying. A 2016 study of 571 library workers in six northeastern states reported that 46 percent of workers had been bullied. As indicated by a large 2017 study conducted by the authors, 40 percent of librarians and library staff in the United States have been bullied. These statistics leave no doubt that bullying exists in our work environments—including libraries.[7]

Workplace Bullying Institute United States National Survey Results

Past and Present Bullied Workers
- 2014—27 percent
- 2010—35 percent
- 2007—37 percent

Witnesses to Bullied Workers
- 2014—21 percent
- 2010—15 percent
- 2007—12 percent[8]

In addition to in-person, one-on-one bullying, there is also the phenomenon known as cyberbullying. Although more widely known for its use by teens and in social media, cyberbullying cannot be ignored in the library workplace. Cyberbullying is "bullying carried out through means related to the Internet," which could involve texting, email, or social media sites. This type of communication can result in subtle bullying through humor, gossip, or other negative exchanges. The common bullying technique of excluding someone can occur when an individual is purposely left out of email exchanges or is not sent announcements. The ability to communicate electronically with employees all hours of the day can be abused. A 2012 study in England showed 14 to 20 percent of workers had been cyberbullied. An Australian study found that 10.7 percent of workers had been bullied electronically. Numerous Australian studies found cyberbullying more prevalent and intense among public workers (a group to which library staff belong). The authors' study of US library staff indicated nearly 15 percent are cyberbullied, with college and university library workers experiencing the greatest amount. Although not as pervasive as in-person bullying, cyberbullying still contributes to the toxic bullying environment.[9]

Bullying is described as taking place over an extended period, which is supported by many studies. A 2003 European study found the mean duration was eighteen months, and an Irish study indicated bullying in the workplace lasted more than three years. Studies by the Workplace Bullying Institute indicate the average length of bullying in the United States is twenty-two months. At that point, 61 percent of targets leave their jobs either by quitting, being forced out, or being fired, and 13 percent are transferred. Similar findings are found in the academic realm. A 2015 study of four-year university staff found bullying lasted two or more years 53 percent of the time. These and other studies support the fact that bullying is sustained over extended time periods. It continues, often for years, hurting both victims and organizations.[10]

Although bullying can happen to or be practiced by anyone, trends can be identified. Bully perpetrators are most often men who typically hold higher rank. In the United States, men are bullies 69 percent of the time as compared to 31 percent of females. A 2014 Workplace Bullying Institute study shows that those of higher rank are bullies 56 percent of the time, and coworkers bully 33 percent of the time. The authors' study on mindfulness indicated 14 percent of librarians saw their coworkers as their greatest work stressor. In colleges and universities, tenured faculty, directors, and deans rank highest as perpetrators. A 2016 study by Kim, Gear, and Bielefield discovered that males form the majority of bullies in supervisory positions, but females dominate in bullying coworkers. The authors' 2017 survey indicated a nearly equal amount of male and female bullies in supervisory positions. Although supervisors rank number one among all libraries as instigators, accounting for 30 percent, bullying among peers occurs 20 percent of the time and is more often triggered by females. Unfortunately, bullies target some of the best and most well-meaning employees in an organization. Most targets escape by moving on or transferring from the department, but the bullies remain to repeat their toxic behavior with other workers.[11]

The personality traits and motivations of bullies are not completely clear. There are a variety of reasons why they instigate such behaviors. Some bullies believe they have a right to power while others are driven by ego or narcissism. Other bullies have low self-esteem, are self-absorbed, or even vindictive. There are no clear lines to define a bully, who comes in various forms. Unfortunately, such toxic employees rarely change their behavior and most often continue until they are removed from the work organization.[12]

In the library workplace, females and minorities are the most frequent targets of a bully's wrath. The Workplace Bullying Institute found that females were targets 60 percent of the time. Additionally, Hispanics were the most bullied ethnicity in the workplace, followed by African-Americans, Asians, and Caucasians. This finding also holds true for libraries. A 2015 study of academic libraries showed Asian and African-American librarians at higher risk for being targeted. The study also showed a higher degree of bullying to the four- to seven-year period of employment (possibly related to tenure) of librarians. The authors' 2017 survey of US libraries points to increased bullying of Native Americans, followed by African Americans and Hispanic or Latino workers. Females (41 percent) ranked ahead of men as bully targets (32 percent).[13]

Mobbing, although a slightly different phenomenon, is often described as a type of bullying. The roots of research on the mobbing concept began in the 1960s. Konrad Lorenz (the 1973 Nobel Prize winner in Physiology or Medicine) identified this behavior in animals. His work was the impetus for studies of the interaction of aggressive children in the 1970s by Peter-Paul Heinemann, a Swedish physician. Subsequently, Heinz Leymann, a Swedish doctor of pedagogical psychology, began his research in 1982 on workplace aggression in German factories. As mentioned, Leymann used the term "mobbing" to describe what he found in the workplace, for the first time giving a name to this type of work behavior. Once identified, the understanding and awareness of mobbing behaviors spread throughout Europe in the early 1980s. The term did not reach the United States until 1999, via the book *Mobbing: Emotional Abuse in the American Workplace*, by Noa Zanolli Davenport, Ruth Kistler Schwartz, and Gail Pursell Elliott. Kenneth Westhues's *Workplace Mobbing in Academe: Reports from Twenty Universities* (2004) later brought attention to mobbing in the academic realm. This book was followed by *Winning, Losing, Moving On: How Professionals Deal with Workplace Harassment and Mobbing* (2005).[14]

The action of mobbing is fundamentally different from bullying. Mobbing involves a group of people who target an individual, rather than the one-on-one targeting that is characteristic of bullying. Leymann defines it as follows:

> Psychical terror or mobbing in the working life means hostile and unethical communication which is directed in a systematic way by one or a number of persons mainly toward one individual. These actions take

place often (almost every day) and over a long period (at least six months) and because of this frequency and duration, result in considerable psychic, psychosomatic and social misery.[15]

Like bullying, mobbing has an impact on the mental and physical condition of the target and continues over an extended length of time, typically until the target leaves the workplace environment.

Thomas Hecker's 2007 article "Workplace Mobbing: A Discussion for Librarians" addressed this phenomenon in the library setting. Hecker wrote, "workplace mobbing occurs in libraries, but it is usually unrecognized and unchecked." In 2009, Susan Motin brought the topic of bullying and mobbing to the ACRL 14th National Conference. In 2010, Reba Leiding's article "Mobbing in the Library Workplace" approached the topic once again, noting that "the concept of mobbing is not well-recognized in the United States." More recently, Freedman and Vreven's 2016 study addresses the mobbing component as part of their research on workplace incivility and bullying happening in academic libraries. The importance of library organizations and administrations understanding this concept is underscored by research by both Heinz Leymann and Kenneth Westhues, which indicate mobbing is twice as likely to occur in organizations where "goals may be ambiguous, critical thinking is encouraged, and workers have relative autonomy." These are all typical characteristics of the library work setting and are found in school, public, academic, and special libraries. A study by the authors supports the idea that mobbing is taking place in US libraries. Of the 3,837 library workers responding to the survey, nearly 17 percent have experienced mobbing, with the highest frequency in special and academic libraries.[16]

The act of mobbing occurs in stages. Typically, an initial, unresolved incident is a trigger point. From this one issue, the target is isolated by fellow workers in a variety of ways, which creates a hostile work environment as mobbing shifts to stage two. Although Leymann's studies identified forty-five mobbing methods, a few of the more common ones are listed below.

- Target is given the silent treatment (excluded from discussions).
- Target is talked about rather than to, in his or her presence.
- Target's opinions are ignored in meetings.
- Target's work is subject to sudden critique.
- Target is assigned minimal tasks and/or a heavy workload.[17]

Additionally, the target's reputation is maligned and sometimes the individual is subject to threats and/or violence. Many of these actions are similar or identical to bullying. However, what is significantly different is the group dynamic. As mobbing continues, the target's support group is peeled away as potential work allies side against him. These other coworkers align because of "feelings of safety and inclusion" in a sort of ancestral groupthink method of survival. Coworkers who otherwise would lend support to the target fear staying apart from the group as they witness mobbing incidents and wonder if they could be the next mob victim. As the targeted worker becomes more vulnerable, "stress, anxiety, and suffering become highly elevated." Stripped of any support from coworkers and feeling the brunt of continual assaults and ostracism, the target exists in an endlessly cruel work environment. The next stage of mobbing involves the target filing an official complaint with management or administration. Unfortunately, as is the case with bullying, mobbing has historically been ignored by these leaders, and often the target is blamed for the actions of the mob. The final stage occurs when the traumatized target leaves the group by transferring departments, taking a new position, or quitting work altogether. According to Leymann, this entire process lasts an average of fifteen months, eight months less than the work life of a bullied target. As with bullying, in the worst-case scenario a mobbed victim takes his or her life.[18]

Typically, targets of mobbing are different from other members of the group or do not share perceived group characteristics. In some way, the targeted individual typically stands out from the accepted cultural norm. This uniqueness may be related to any number of characteristics, including nationality, race, sex, religion, beliefs, or other defining characteristics. For example, a librarian belonging to a minority group who works in a group of people of a different ethnicity, or the sole male library worker in an all-female department or branch, is more likely to be the target of mobbing. In fact, a more balanced male-female working ratio has been shown to reduce mobbing. Leymann's studies also found disabled workers are mobbed at five times the rate of others without disabilities. As these examples illustrate, the mob victim has some belief or characteristic that is different from the norm.[19]

In addition to individuals differing from the cultural norm, there are other reasons for mobbing. These may include "psychological pathology, jealousy, greed, or desperation" as employees jockey for resources, promotions, or power. As with bullying, inflated self-worth could be a characteristic of an instigator. Although these are some characteristics of a worker more prone to mobbing, the studies do not point specifically to any one type of worker personality that initiates the mob behavior.[20]

The impact of both bullying and mobbing on the individual can affect mental and physical health. Studies have shown that targets can suffer "social isolation and maladjustment, psychosomatic illnesses, depressions, compulsions, helplessness, anger, anxiety and despair" among other symptoms. Even post-traumatic stress disorder occurs in bullied individuals, and targets continue to have a higher-than-average occurrence of psychiatric problems several years after the bullying event. Physical problems caused from the prolonged stress of bullying include "cardiovascular disease, cancer, diabetes, ulcers, . . . [and] obesity" among other illnesses. A study of 571 librarians in the northeastern United States indicated that 58.7 percent of bullied workers suffered health issues including stress, anxiety, depression, headaches, and sleep problems.[21]

As the aggressive actions of bullying and mobbing impact the worker and the work environment, employee morale and productivity plummet These behaviors have a significant financial impact on the organization from lost productivity and employee turnover. A research team from Australia's Griffith University estimated the cost at $6 to $13 billion in 2013. A 2013 report of US organizations puts the figure at $355 billion. In the United States, the cost of time wasted dealing with bullies ranges from $2,805 to $12,630 per year based on worker salary. Additionally, in a 2015 higher education study, Leah P. Hollis found that 62 percent of staff were impacted by bullying, and that financial losses that typically amount to 150 percent of an employee's salary are incurred in hiring a replacement. With a mean higher-education salary of $67,000, the turnover cost is $100,500 per employee. Hours lost to bully avoidance could run as high as $6,870 per person annually, with total bullying costs ranging from 4.7 million to just over 8 million dollars depending on the size of the college or university. With median US librarian pay in 2015 at $56,880, this would suggest an $85,320 cost to replace a librarian who leaves a library system due to bullying. Should resolution of bullying or mobbing involve a lawsuit, the costs of handling the situation would go even higher. The Workplace Bullying Institute estimates that such expenses could range from $30,000 to $60,000 to resolve the situation out of court and more if the case goes to trial. Unchecked bullying and mobbing behaviors in an organization result in real and significant financial losses.[22]

Despite the fact that aggressive behaviors like bullying and mobbing occur in all types of organizations including libraries, managers, administration, and human resource departments are reluctant to act. The 2014 Workplace Bullying Institute survey found that 72 percent of employers fail to address this, with a wide range of responses ranging from denying the behavior to encouraging it, and in only 12 percent of the instances is action taken to eliminate it. A 2012 CareerBuilder survey found that of those who reported the issue to human resources (only about half of those bullied), action was taken only 43 percent of the time. Freedman and Vreven also noted a difference in perception from library administrators and librarians in academic libraries. Administrators were aware of bullying actions of staff but refused to act to avoid confrontation. Steven Bell, Temple University's associate university professor for research and instructional services, reports that many library leaders are aware these occur but choose to ignore them instead of fixing the problem. Upper library management typically refuses to address bullying and mobbing that occurs among staff.[23]

Advice for those individuals being bullied in the workplace comes from Judith E. Glaser, CEO of consulting and coaching company Benchmark Communications, who suggests using a variety of strategies including "ignoring, confronting, documenting, reporting, and stay[ing] positive." While this is good advice, it is challenging for targeted workers to navigate their work environments every day. If bullying actions are linked to social media, blocking and unfriending are possible solutions. In 2010, 45 percent of Americans have taken this course of action to reduce their exposure to incivility. For those who are at the center of bullying and mobbing actions, daily work is a struggle with emotional, psychological, and physical ramifications.[24]

A better solution than leaving the individual to handle a hostile work environment is for the library manager to intervene. These aggressive actions can be decreased or even stopped if library managers take action. First, managers must be aware of what is going on in their ranks by spending some time walking around the library and interacting with employees. Second, managers must not be afraid to take measures to neutralize bullying (which, however, will require the support of the entire library organization). Library managers must be fair and treat all employees equally. Fairness of managers has been linked to positive employee behavior. As with bullying, mobbing behavior can be countered by the action of a manager early on because mobbing starts with a single, unresolved incident. Resolution of the triggering episode by a supervisor could prevent the escalation of this toxic behavior. Once a mobbing incident has escalated it may take the entire organization's actions to counter the behavior of the mob group.[25]

Ultimately, combating and preventing mobbing (as well as bullying) must involve the entire library organization. Although managerial action can help negate the actions of a bully or diffuse a mobbing issue in an isolated department or branch, it is the library organization as a whole that must carry the message to the entire workforce. This is the best solution to these dysfunctional worker behaviors. The highest levels of library administration must first become aware of what is happening among the staff and not merely ignore or dismiss the climate employees are working in. The library administration should create inclusive mission statements, defined job descriptions, clear lines of authority, and practice good internal communication. These actions help prevent bullying and mobbing. Additionally, the organization should foster a code of ethics that defines the behavior expected from personnel and make regular attempts to educate both current and incoming staff about uncivil mobbing behaviors and ethical expectations. Library organizations can impact bullying and mobbing behaviors by training employees in about emotional intelligence (EI), as discussed in chapter one. High EI has been shown to moderate bullying behaviors. Additional training in interpersonal skills, conflict resolution, and stress management, all of which are concepts addressed in this book, are other avenues these organizations can use. Finally, library administrators need to incorporate an anti-bullying policy within a code of work ethics. The policy should clearly define unacceptable behavior as well as enforcement and intervention methods. Examples of bullying policies can be found at the Bullitt County (KY) Public Library (www.bcplib.org/PDF/Policies/Anti-bullying.pdf) and the Oregon State University Library (http://eoa.oregonstate.edu/bullying-policy). Kenneth Westhues provides excellent guidelines for an anti-bullying policy on his website (www.kwesthues.com/dignitypolicies01.htm).[26]

Anti-bullying Policy Components

- Purpose of bullying policy
- Policy statement(s)
- Definition of bullying (types and examples)
- Procedural guidelines (reporting policy, retaliation policy)
- Responsibilities of organization, managers, and staff
- Consequences of behavior (discipline, training, and prevention)

By acknowledging its need to act, library administration will build awareness of staff interactions and should subsequently respond with clear policies, a code of ethics, and emotional intelligence training to foster a positive and safe work environment.

When addressing bullying and mobbing, library administrators should involve their human resource departments to minimize the chance of hiring toxic employees. Initially, potential hires should be thoroughly screened. Using self-assessment instruments during the hiring process may help weed out poor candidates. Newly hired candidates should be first informed about and then observed for positive behaviors in the beginning stages of employment. Human resource departments and library administrators must work together to take regular opportunities to educate all staff on bullying and mobbing to build awareness of the potential problem and explain how employees can report such occurrences. By defining bullying and mobbing, training staff, and building awareness, these behaviors can be minimized or even thwarted before they occur.[27]

Fortunately, in many parts of the world, human resource departments are supported by legislation that addresses bullying and mobbing. European countries began addressing workplace bullying through legislation in the early 1990s after Leymann's initial work on mobbing came to light. Australia's Fair Work Act adopted a specific section on bullying in 2014. Since 2004, Canada has addressed workplace conduct in a series of laws. Although the United States lags behind other countries, anti-bullying legislation is slowly catching up. Currently, thirty-two state legislatures have introduced the Healthy Workplace Bill, which directly addresses bullying in the workplace. For those working in the United States, the growing push to put anti-bullying policy into law will lend additional support to library organizations and human resource departments when dealing with these difficult issues.[28]

PASSIVE-AGGRESSIVE

Another type of toxic behavior is exhibited by the passive-aggressive employee. The term "passive-aggressive" was first used in 1945 by the United States War Department to describe soldiers' reactions to military stress, which showed "patterns of obstructive and resistant behavior with aggressive outbursts" in reaction to military demands. More recently it has been defined as a combination of traits that reflect "superficial compliance that masks opposition and rebellion against authority." The passive-aggressive employee puts on a positive facade but actually undermines the cohesiveness of both the work unit and the organization.[29]

Although passive-aggressive individuals believe they are misunderstood, others view their behavior as negative, irritating, and unpredictable. Their ever-changing behavior and frequent blaming or criticizing of other employees and their work adds a difficult dynamic to any workplace, libraries included. Passive-aggressive workers may even tamper with the work of others, procrastinate on their own duties, or conduct other undermining actions toward employees and the organization. These types of workers put on positive attitudes for supervisors and coworkers, but then undercut them with their words and actions. Passive-aggressive individuals can use email to spread their views and negative attitude. Passive-aggressive demeanor is a form of aggressive and toxic behavior that, if not checked, can spread to other employees who view it as a method to survive or get ahead. A passive-aggressive employee can destroy the culture and "self-esteem of individuals working there." This behavior is not exclusive to lower-level workers; managers can fall into passive-aggressive actions such as giving vague guidelines, critiquing minor and ignoring major issues, undermining staff behind their backs, remaining remote or distant towards employees, or limiting employee training, among others. These actions are typically triggered by a perception that the organization does not truly care or support them.[30]

Examples of Passive-aggressive Library Workers

- A smiling library attendant agrees to shelve a cart of books before closing, but really does not want to do it. As a result, books are quickly put onto the shelves in improper order.
- A librarian enthusiastically accepts a new project to create instructional online tutorials, but in truth disagrees with the concept. As a result, deadlines to create and insert the tutorials into an online learning system at the start of the semester are intentionally missed.
- A circulation worker happily agrees to take an extra desk shift, but resents being asked. As a result, he ignores the chat-reference requests which pop up on the computer during his time at the desk.
- A librarian eagerly agrees to serve on a team, but is unhappy about the additional work. As a result, she is often late to or absent from team meetings.

Examples of Passive-aggressive Library Managers

- A library manager gives vague instructions, such as how to set up a book display, and then criticizes the employee work once done.
- A library manager is unhappy with an employee's work, but complains to other coworkers and never addresses the employee directly about the problem.

- A library manager comes to work as scheduled, but typically remains in his office all day and rarely interacts with employees or gives feedback on performance.
- A manager criticizes staff for minor actions, such as not adding paper to the copier, but refuses to address a larger staff concern about pending layoffs.

Some suggestions for handling passive-aggressive library employees include addressing their perceived minor issues, limiting the length and period of complaints, stopping any emotional outbursts, and explaining the negative consequences of their actions. For example, if a library assistant shelves books incorrectly at closing because of unwillingness to take on the task, a supervisor could try explaining how difficult it will be to find materials and how much additional time will need to be spent shelf-reading to locate the lost books. Administrators can offer leadership training and provide additional support to help the passive-aggressive manager.[31]

Workers must initiate productive exchanges with managers to ask for specific details on projects and for feedback on their work. However, despite these interventions, this personality type typically will not change. Ultimately, library administrators must decide whether to tolerate the passive-aggressive behavior or to let the employee go.

COUNTERPRODUCTIVE BEHAVIORS

Counterproductive behaviors in the workplace can take different forms and impact production, property, culture, and coworkers. Counterproductive behavior is defined as action that "intends to inflict harm on a person or organization." These actions differ from much of the incivility discussed in the previous chapter because they are motivated by malicious intent. In 2005, Spector and Fox identified forty-five different counterproductive behaviors in their Counterproductive Work Behavior Checklist (CWB-C). Although this chapter reviews some of the counterproductive behaviors library workers exhibit, it is impossible to address all of them here.[32]

What causes these malicious counterproductive behaviors in the workplace? Psychotherapist Richard Billow believes that inherently "individuals require trustworthy emotional and mental interaction with other human beings" and if this need is not met they "resist, rebel, and refuse." Therefore, the library must provide a safe environment and encourage positive interaction of its workers. Otherwise workers may respond with damaging behavior. Although they do not rank as high as bullying on the Namies's

1–10 workplace disruption scale, these dysfunctional behaviors can still significantly impact library workers and the organization.[33]

Many common counterproductive worker behaviors can be easily identified. First, there is the employee who blames others for her own mistakes. As previously mentioned, this could be a characteristic of a passive-aggressive personality, but it also could be that the employee is looking for a scapegoat. For example, if a library worker failed to reserve a meeting room, she could blame it on someone else and say that she thought it was the other person's responsibility.[34]

Second on the list of counterproductive staff is the chronic complainer. This person is in a dysfunctional mental zone that results in negative thoughts, words, and actions. Imagine library workers who constantly groan about what they must do and never fail to relay how unhappy they are to come to work each day.

A third counterproductive behavior is avoidance. These individuals do their jobs but stay clear of issues and often avoid interpersonal contact. The avoidant boss typically is lost concerning the direction she wants to take and does not provide constructive feedback to employees.[35]

The fourth dysfunctional symptom is withdrawal. Often overlooked because withdrawn employees do not create visible problems, managers should recognize that this too is dysfunctional behavior. A withdrawn employee may be more apt to be tardy, absent, or file grievances. For example, a quiet library worker does his assigned tasks but never interacts with other employees or volunteers for additional projects. The employee withdraws from the organization both physically and emotionally and no longer engages in positive and productive ways.[36]

The fifth behavior is worker resistance. This is often related to change, which is the new norm in libraries. It is defined as an "unconscious process . . . that block[s] . . . conscious processing." Imagine the library worker who resists the use of a newly implemented scheduling software program and continues to handwrite event schedules on paper.[37]

The sixth counterproductive behavior is refusal. Unlike resistance, refusal is a conscious and "willful nonparticipation in discovering or learning." Another word to characterize this behavior is stubbornness. For instance, a librarian who refuses to attend an outreach event is exhibiting refusal behavior.[38]

The seventh and final dysfunctional behavior to which library workers can resort to is a slow-down or stalling-type behavior. Research has shown that withdrawing, followed by intentional stalling, are the two of the top counterproductive behaviors of teaching faculty. In the library, workers may intentionally postpone planning programs or fail to complete instructional presentations as ways of refusing to do these assignments. These common counterproductive behaviors are found in many libraries, and they should be recognized and addressed by the managerial staff as dysfunctional behavior.[39]

There are several causes for these counterproductive behaviors. Leymann theorized the nonconformity occurs when an individual "does not believe a behavior to be true or proper." This is related to perceptions of workers and how they view their work environment. As mentioned before, fairness is a component of a civil workplace. Studies indicate that if perceptions are unfavorable, counterproductive behavior is likely to occur. Employees who perceive favoritism or inequality in work-related decisions deem the environment unfair and are susceptible to counterproductive actions. For example, based on equity theory, an inequitable raise distribution at year's end could be perceived as unfair by many of the library staff. The inability to cope with work-related stress has been shown as a source for dysfunctional behavior. Workers who feel stressed tend to act out in the work environment. Working in a negative environment also plays a role in counterproductive work behavior because it raises stress levels, which in turn lead to dysfunctional actions. This negative environment could be triggered by aggressive behaviors such as bullying or mobbing, some of the lesser counterproductive attributes that manifest in daily life in a library, or job-related issues like job security, workload, or other perceived pressures. As mentioned in chapter three, in a 2016 study by the authors found that librarians feel pressure from a variety of sources, with workloads and coworkers causing 60 percent of their workplace stress. Finally, boredom and inadequate stimulation in the work environment have also been shown to lead to counterproductive behaviors.[40]

Interestingly, older workers, higher-educated individuals, and those with higher integrity are less inclined to engage in counterproductive work behaviors. For staff who do engage in such behavior, there are some available strategies. As with bullying and mobbing, increasing emotional intelligence has been shown to help offset other counterproductive work behavior. Library organizations and their managers must be consistent and fair in their dealings with library staff. If this is done, staff is less inclined to act out in dysfunctional ways. It is important to offer employees opportunities for stress reduction. The authors' 2016 book *The Mindful Librarian: Connecting the Practice of Mindfulness to Librarianship* makes an extensive case for the use of mindfulness and meditation to reduce stress and enhance collaboration in the library workplace. Taking time out during the workday to focus on breathing, taking a walk, or meditating are simple measures to reduce daily stress. Training that focuses on techniques to manage time and develop coping strategies are helpful responses to counterproductive behaviors.[41]

Counterproductive work behaviors can be countered by conversation. Catherine B. Soehner and Ann Darling have described how to handle these exchanges in their book *Effective Difficult Conversations: A Step-By-Step Guide*. Among their tips, they suggest conversations involve focusing on facts, soliciting viewpoints, active listening, being engaged in the exchange, and exploring viable options for resolution. Another approach is offered by author Kathleen Kelley Reardon, who suggests training employees to combat what she terms "unwanted repetitive episodes" (URPs) in conversations. Reardon explains that URPs are unproductive communication patterns that occur between two individuals. For example, two library employees fall into a disagreement about how to execute a library policy, and both argue their own stances, thus causing frustration and leading nowhere. Instead of falling into such useless, repetitive communication patterns, Reardon suggests these conversation comebacks tips:[42]

- Reframe
- Rephrase
- Rejoin
- Restate
- Request
- Rebalance
- Reorganize
- Rebuke
- Retaliate[43]

These types of responses change the course of the conversation and break the unproductive back and forth exchanges.

CONCLUSION

All dysfunctional actions discussed—bullying, mobbing, and passive-aggressive or counterproductive behaviors—are detrimental to the organization. Although each is a unique method, the outcomes are similar. The positive and productive culture of the library workplace is ruined. The toxic behaviors distract from the mission of the library, lower productivity, and are costly to handle. Often employees are harmed emotionally, psychologically, and physically. The employee loses awareness of the library's mission while trying to survive the daily work environment. To combat this dysfunctional behavior, library leaders must first become aware that the dysfunction exists. Then library organizations must step up and act. Policies on bullying, mobbing, and a safe workplace environment should be created and put into place. Library administration should partner with human resources to avoid hiring toxic workers and to introduce training that addresses dysfunctional behaviors for current employees. Unless the library executive team rallies to make the workplace a positive and safe place, both employees and managers have limited ability to offset a toxic workplace. For both managers and staff, additional training in emotional intelligence, coping and conversation skills, and conflict resolution will also help combat a toxic work environment. Without this support, dysfunction will spread, harm, and eventually destroy the library work environment.

NOTES

1. Gary Namie, "Workplace Bullying: Escalated Incivility," *Ivey Business Journal,* (November/December 2003): 1.

2. Edward Alsworth Ross, *Social Psychology: An Outline and Sourcebook,* (New York, NY: The MacMillan Company, 1908); Jeffrey M. Cucina and Nathan Bowling, "Robert Hoppock: Early Job Satisfaction and Vocational Guidance Pioneer," *The Industrial-Organizational Psychologist* (October 2015); Namie, "Workplace Bullying: Escalated Incivility," 1; Thomas E. Hecker, "Workplace Mobbing: A Discussion for Librarians," *The Journal of Academic Librarianship* 33, no. 4 (July 2007).

3. Tim Field, "Andrea Adams Trust," June 2001, www.bullyonline.org/old/successun limited/archive/AAT.htm; Shin Freedman and Dawn Vreven, "Workplace Incivility and Bullying in the Library: Perception or Reality?," *College and Research Libraries* 77, no. 6 (November 2016): 731; Hak Joon Kim, Carole Anne Gear, and Arlene Bielefield, "Bullying in the Library Workplace," *Library Leadership and Management,* in press.

4. Andy Ellis, "Andrea Adams, British Pioneer: Bio and Text of 1994 Speech," *Workplace Bullying Institute,* 2015, http://workplacebullying.org/multi/pdf/adams.pdf.

5. Susan Hubbs Motin, "Bullying or Mobbing: Is it Happening in Your Academic Library?" *ACRL 14th National Conference Proceedings,* Chicago: Association for College and Research Libraries, 2009, 292 and Jennifer Grasz, "CareerBuilder Study Finds More Workers Feeling Bullied in the Workplace," August 29, 2012, www.careerbuilder .com/share/aboutus/pressreleasesdetail.aspx?sd=8%2F29%2F2012&id=pr713&ed=12 %2F31%2F2012.

6. Freedman and Vreven, "Workplace Incivility," 286; "Does Bullying Provide Job Security? You'll Be Infuriated by the Answer," *VitalSmarts,* 2016, https://www.vitalsmarts .com/press/2014/06/does-bullying-provide-job-security-youll-be-infuriated-by-the -answer; Namie, "Workplace Bullying: Escalated Incivility," 2.

7. Staale Einarsen, Helge Hoel, and Guy Notelaers, "Measuring Exposure to Bullying and Harassment at Work: Validity, Factor Structure, and Psychometric Properties of the Negative Acts Questionnaire-Revised," *Work and Stress* 23, no. 1 (January–March

2009): 35; Gary Namie, "2014 WBI US Workplace Bullying Survey," www.workplace bullying.org/wbiresearch/wbi-2014-us-survey/; "Bullying in Further and Higher Education," *University and College Union Report,* 2010, 2; Leah P. Hollis, "Bully University? The Cost of Workplace Bullying and Employee Disengagement in American Higher Education," *SAGE Open,* June 15, 2015, http://sgo.sagepub.com/content/5/2/ 2158244015589997; Freedman and Vreven, "Workplace Incivility," 743–44; Hak Joon Kim, Carole Anne Gear, and Arlene Bielefield, "Bullying in the Library Workplace," *Library Leadership and Management,* anticipated 2017: 5.

8. Gary Namie, "2014 WBI Workplace Bullying Survey," www.workplacebullying.org/ wbiresearch/wbi-2014-us-survey/; Namie, "Results of the 2010 WBI US Workplace Bullying Survey," www.workplacebullying.org/wbiresearch/2010-wbi-national -survey/; Namie, "Results of the 2007 WBI US Workplace Bullying Survey," www.workplacebullying.org/wbiresearch/wbi-2007/.

9. Tommaso Beretolotti and Lorenzo Magnani, "A Philosophical and Evolutionary Approach to Cyber-Bullying: Social Networks and the Disruption of Sub-Moralities," *Ethics Info Technology* 15 (2013): 285; Paul Mannion, "Hidden Cyberbullying is as Common as Conventional Counterpart in the Workplace," *The University of Sheffield News,* November 5, 2012, https://www.shef.ac.uk/news/nr/cyberbullying-festival -social-sciences-christine-sprigg-carolyn-axtell-sam-farley-1.222243. https://www.shef .ac.uk/news/nr/cyberbullying-festival-social-sciences-christine-sprigg-carolyn-axtell -sam-farley-1.222243; Carmel Privitera and Marilyn Anne Campbell, "Cyberbullying, the New Face of Workplace Bullying?," *CyberPsychology and Behavior* 12, no. 4 (July 2009): 395; Felicity Lawrence, "Prevalence and Consequences of Negative Workplace Cyber Communication in the Australian Public Sector," PhD dissertation, Office of Education Research Faculty of Education Queensland University of Technology, 2015, http://eprints.qut.edu.au/88058/1/Felicity_Lawrence_Thesis.pdf.

10. Hollis, "Bully University"; Namie, "Workplace Bullying: Escalated Incivility," 2; Namie, "2014 WBI US Workplace Bullying Survey."

11. Namie, "2014 WBI US Workplace Bullying Survey"; Richard Moniz, Jo Henry, and Joe Eshleman, "Stressors, Librarians, and How Mindfulness Can Help," *College and Research Library News* 77 (2016), no. 11: 535; Hollis, "Bully University"; Kim, Gear, and Bielefield, "Bullying in the Library Workplace," 6.

12. Susan Hubbs Motin, "Bullying or Mobbing: Is it Happening in Your Academic Library?" *ACRL 14th National Conference Proceedings,* Chicago: Association for College and Research Libraries, 2009: 294; Bonnie A. Osif, "Workplace Bullying," 207, *Library Leadership and Management* 24, no. 4 (2010): 207.

13. Gary Namie, Daniel Christensen, and David Phillips, "2014 WBI US Workplace Bullying Survey," 2014, http://workplacebullying.org/multi/pdf/WBI-2014-US-Survey.pdf and Freedman and Vreven, "Workplace Incivility," 640–41.

14. Kenneth Westhues, "Origins of the Study of Workplace Mobbing," 2016, www.kwest hues.com/mobbing.htm; Motin, "Bullying or Mobbing"; Heinz Leymann, "Mobbing and Psychological Terror at Workplaces," *Violence and Victims* 5, no. 2 (1990): 120.

15. Heinz Leymann, "Mobbing and Psychological Terror at Workplaces."

16. Thomas E. Hecker, "Workplace Mobbing: A Discussion for Librarians," *The Journal of Academic Librarianship* 33, no. 4 (July 2011): 439; Reba Leiding, "Mobbing in the Library Workplace," *College and Research Library News,* July/August 2010: 364–65; Freedman and Vreven, "Workplace Incivility."

17. Hecker, "Workplace Mobbing: A Discussion."

18. Hecker, "Workplace Mobbing," 44043, 441; Leymann, "Mobbing and Psychological Terror at Workplaces," 121–22.

19. Hecker, "Workplace Mobbing, 442."

20. Leiding, "Mobbing in the Library Workplace," 365.

21. Stale Einarsen, Helge Hoele, Dieter Zapf, and Cary Cooper, *Bullying and Emotional Abuse in the Workplace: International Perspectives in Research and Practice* (London: Taylor and Francis, 2003), 127, 129–32; Christine Porath, "No Time to be Nice at Work," *New York Times Sunday Review,* June 19, 2014, www.nytimes.com/ 2015/06/21/opinion/sunday/is-your-boss-mean.html?_r=3; Kim, Gear, and Biele-field, "Bullying in the Library Workplace," 8.

22. Michael Crumpton, "The Costs of Having a Bully in the Library," *The Bottom Line: Managing Library Finances* 27, no. 1 (2014): 18; Hollis, "Bully University"; Occupa-tional Outlook Handbook, "Librarians," www.bls.gov/ooh/education-training-and -library/librarians.htm; "Estimating the Cost of Bullying," Workplace Bullying Insti-tute, 2015, www.workplacebullying.org/individuals/solutions/costs/.

23. Namie, "2014 WBI US Workplace Bullying Survey," 12; Jennifer Grasz, "CareerBuild-er Study Finds More Workers Feeling Bullied in the Workplace" August 29, 2012, www.careerbuilder.com/share/aboutus/pressreleasesdetail.aspx?sd=8%2F29%2F201 2&id=pr713&ed=12%2F31%2F2012; Freeman and Vreven, "Workplace Incivility," 18; Steven Bell, "Toxic Leaders, Toxic Workers: Learning to Cope," *Library Journal,* June 24, 2015, http://lj.libraryjournal.com/2015/06/opinion/leading-from-the-library/tox-ic-leaders-toxic-workers-learning-to-cope-leading-from-the-library/#.

24. Crumpton, "Costs of Having a Bully in the Library," 20; "39% of American Public Tuning Out of Social Networks Due to Incivility, According to New Weber Shandwick Survey," *PR Newswire,* June 23, 2010. www.prnewswire.com/news-releases/39-of -american-public-tuning-out-of-social-networks-due-to-incivility-according-to-new -weber-shandwick-survey-96971629.html.

25. Wendi J. Everton, Jeffrey A. Jolton, and Paul M. Mastrangelo, "Be Nice and Fair or Else: Understanding Reasons for Employees' Deviant Behaviors," *Journal of Manage-ment Development* 26, no. 2 (2007):118.

26. Leiding, "Mobbing in the Library Workplace," 366; Zainab Bibi, Jahanvash Karim, and Siraj ud Din, "Workplace Incivility and Counterproductive Work Behavior: Moderating Role of Emotional Intelligence," *Pakistan Journal of Psychological Research* 28, no. 2 (2013): 330; Sara Branch and Jane Murray, "Building Relationships and Resilience in the Workplace: Construction of a Workplace Bullying Training Program," paper presented at the *Australia and New Zealand Academy of Management 22nd ANZAM Conference 2008: Managing in the Pacific Century,* The University of Auckland, Auckland, New Zealand, 9.

27. Baird Brightman, "How to Overcome the Six Most Toxic Employee Behaviors," *Leadership Now,* December 12, 2013, www.fastcompany.com/3023318/leadership-now/how-to-overcome-the-6-most-toxic-employee-behaviors.

28. Andrew Ball, "The New Workplace Bullying Laws: What They Mean for You," *HC Online,* 29 July 2013, www.hcamag.com/opinion/the-new-workplace-bullying-laws-what-they-mean-for-you-177608.aspx and "Healthy Workplace Bill: What About Outside the United States?," *Workplace Bullying Institute,* 2016, http://healthyworkplacebill.org/problem/.

29. Joseph T. McCann, "Passive-Aggressive Personality Disorder: A Review," *Journal of Personality Disorders* 2, no. 2 (June 1988): 170, doi:http://dx.doi.org/10.1521/pedi.1988.2.2.170 and Laurence Miller, *From Difficult to Disturbed: Understanding and Managing Dysfunctional Employees* (AMACOM, Division of American Management Association: New York NY, 2008).

30. McCann. "Passive-Aggressive Personality Disorder"; Miller, *From Difficult to Disturbed;* Amy Rees Anderson, "Passive-Aggressive Behavior Will Destroy a Company's Culture," *Forbes,* March 6, 2013, www.forbes.com/sites/amyanderson/2013/03/06/passive-aggressive-behavior-will-destroy-a-companys-culture/#13391e8f369a; Stephanie Schings, "Do Nothing Bosses," *Society for Industrial and Organizational Psychology,* 2016, www.siop.org/Media/News/nothing_bosses.aspx.

31. McCann, "Passive-Aggressive Personality Disorder."

32. Lisa Penney and Paul Spector, "Job Stress, Incivility, and Counterproductive Work Behavior (CWB)," *Journal of Organizational Behavior* 26, no. 7 (2005): 779 and Paul E. Spector and Suzy Fox, *Counterproductive Work Behavior: Investigation of Actors and Targets* (Washington, DC: APA Books, 2005).

33. Richard M. Billow, "The Three R's of Group: Resistance, Rebellion, and Refusal," *International Journal of Group Psychotherapy* 56, no. 3 (July 2006): 261.

34. Elise F. Topper, "Stress in the Library Workplace," *New Library World* 108, no. 11/12 (2007): 563.

35. Miller, *From Difficult to Disturbed,* 14–15.

36. Everton, Jolton, and Mastrangelo, "Be Nice and Fair or Else," 120.

37. Richard M. Billow, "On Refusal," *International Journal of Group Psychotherapy* 45, no. 4 (2007): 419–20.

38. Ibid., 420.

39. Bibi, Karim, and ud Din, "Workplace Incivility and Counterproductive Work Behavior," 328.

40. Hecker, "Workplace Mobbing: A Discussion for Librarians," 442; Joanna Czarnota-Bojarska, "Counterproductive Work Behavior and Job Satisfaction: A Surprisingly Rocky Relationship," *Journal of Management and Organizations* 21, no. 4 (2015): 461; Nathan A. Bowling and Kevin J. Eschleman, "Employee Personality as a Moderator of the Relationships between Work Stressors and Counterproductive Work Behavior," *Journal of Occupational Health Psychology* 15, no. 1 (2011): 100; Richard Moniz, Jo Henry, Joe Eshleman, Lisa Moniz, and Howard Slutzky, "Stressors, Librarians, and How Mindfulness Can Help," *College and Research Libraries News* 77, no. 11 (2016): 535; Czarnota-Bojarska, "Counterproductive Work Behavior and Job Satisfaction," 461.

41. Czarnota-Bojarska, "Counterproductive Work Behavior and Job Satisfaction," 461; Bibi, Karim, and ud-Din, "Workplace Incivility and Counterproductive Work Behavior," 325; Richard Moniz, Joe Eshleman, Jo Henry, Howard Slutzky, and Lisa Moniz, *The Mindful Librarian: Connecting the Practice of Mindfulness to Librarianship* (Waltham, MA: Chandos Publishing, 2016).

42. Catherine B. Soehner and Ann Darling, *Effective Difficult Conversations: A Step-by-Step Guide* (Chicago, IL: ALA Editions, 2017), 33–56; Kathleen Kelley Reardon, *Comebacks at Work: Using Conversation to Master Confrontation* (New York, NY: Harper Collins, 2010): 54.

43. Reardon, *Comebacks at Work,* 88–89.

5

ORGANIZATIONAL DEVIANCE AND WORKPLACE POLITICS

I n 1995, Sandra Robinson and Rebecca Bennett combined previous findings with their own research in hopes of creating a "bridge . . . between unrelated bodies of research . . . and organizational and interpersonal deviances" that would lead to theories of workplace deviance. They defined four organizational deviations—political, personal, production, and property. Although more recent research has gone well beyond this initial work, these aspects of dysfunction are still applicable today. Chapter four dealt with the more aggressive interpersonal dynamics and counter-productive work behaviors that impact production. In addition to these two areas of dysfunction, there are also property and political work deviations. Property deviation includes theft, sabotage, and vandalism, and political deviation includes behaviors such as gossip, favoritism, and betrayal, among others. Much of what Robinson and Bennett classified as deviation in these two areas is now generally considered organizational deviance.[1]

In addition to organizational deviance, workplace politics often add to the dysfunction of organizations. Politics can come in many forms. This chapter will focus on the impact of gossip, rankism, unconscious bias (as it relates to the work environment), and lobbying in the workplace and how such behaviors impact library organizations.

ORGANIZATIONAL DEVIANCE

The term "organizational deviances" (or "workplace deviances") refers to the actions of an employee who intends to harm the organization itself rather than hurting an individual worker. This type of deviance is defined as a "mismatch of employees' behavior with the expectations and rules of the organization." Although there are a number of these dysfunctional actions, this writing will focus on cyberloafing, fraud, theft, and sabotage. [2]

Six Managerial Triggers of Deviant Behaviors

1. The compensation/reward structure
2. Social pressures to conform
3. Negative and untrusting attitudes
4. Ambiguity about job performance
5. Unfair treatment
6. Violating employee trust[3]

Cyberloafing is a form of organizational deviance. The term "cyberloafing" originated in a 1995 *New York Daily News* article but gained wider notoriety with a 2002 publication in the *Journal of Organizational Behavior* by Kim Geok Vivian Lim, professor at the National University of Singapore, on cyberloafing and organizational justice. Cyberloafing, also called cyberslacking, refers to workers using the Internet for tasks unrelated to their jobs. This behavior can take place on a work computer or any type of personal electronic device. Monica Whitty and Adrian Carr define it as "the overuse of the Internet in the workplace for purposes other than work." Such actions can be divided into personal downloading (music, videos), personal information research (news, hobbies, sports), personal e-commerce (online shopping, business transactions), or personal communication (dating, emailing friends, travel plans). These examples of workplace deviance are common—a recent study of US companies revealed 60 to 80 percent of workers engaged in these behaviors. Another study of workers across different types of jobs indicates a variety of cyberloafing behavior exists in up to 90 percent of employees. A study by the authors indicates 18 percent of library workers regularly cyberloaf; the top three activities are news, social media, and personal communications. Regarding cell phone use, the Civility in America 2013 study found that 34 percent of the population believes it contributes to incivility, and this number jumps to 87 percent when individuals use their cell phones while talking to another. There is some evidence that cyberloafing may have a positive impact, especially for males, because briefly browsing the Internet acts as a "mind break." However, excessive cyberloafing, non-work email communications, and unethical use of the Internet (e.g., visiting gambling or pornographic sites) have a negative impact on productivity and cannot be ignored by organizations, including libraries.[4]

Cyberloafing actions can be linked to specific causes in the workplace as well as employee personalities. As mentioned in prior chapters, employee perception of fairness is directly linked to dysfunctional actions, including cyberloafing. When an employee perceives his treatment to be unfair, "feelings of displeasure [and] rage are more likely to seek retaliation against the organization." In cyberloafing, studies point to workload, both too low and too high, in addition to "irreconcilable demands in the workplace" and dealing with role conflicts between duties and policy or personal beliefs as causes for such behavior. For example, a circulation worker who has finished routine duties for the day may turn to cyberloafing rather than take on new library tasks or projects. Regarding personality, less agreeable, less conscientious, and more extraverted individuals tend to engage in cyberloafing.[5]

Although employee time on the Internet cannot be eliminated, library organizations should not ignore cyberloafing. Internet usage policies should be created covering acceptable use of company property in addition to sanctions for abuse of the policy. Policies for use of personal electronic devices should also be in place. Additionally, use of deterrents such as Internet filters or website blocking could be considered in some situations. A recent study of the manufacturing, banking, and educational fields by Joseph Ugrin and J. Michael Pearson indicated the threat of being fired reduced many cyberloafing activities (except for viewing pornography), and both non-work emails and social media usage was reduced with a combination of the threat of dismissal with an Internet usage detection system. Finally, because work balance is needed to minimize cyberslacking, library managers should be aware of employee workloads and assign just enough work but not too much.[6]

Employee Cell Phone Policy (Newark Public Library)

Phone Calls

I. Telephones are provided for business purposes.

II. Personal calls should be placed during break times.

III. Incoming personal calls should be avoided unless there is an immediate family concern, and should be kept as short as possible (3 minutes or less).

IV. Personal calls are to be taken away from the public's view.

V. Use of personal cell phone devices must be kept to a minimum.

VI. These devices should not be used when working behind the desk, dealing with a patron and only when necessary.

VII. Use of cell phones for texting is also not appropriate while stationed at a public desk.[7]

Another form of organizational deviance involves fraud and/or theft. In the retail sector, theft has been on the increase the past decade: in 2015 one in thirty-eight employees stole from their employers, with an average of $772 per incident. Library employees also engage in theft and embezzlement in their places of employment. New, uncataloged materials, less-used reference books, DVDs, CDs, office supplies, and furniture are among items taken by staff. Some 1,000 rare and valuable works from the Lambeth Palace Library in London were found at the home of a former employer after his death in 2013. At the National Library of Ireland, a library employee took approximately 250 books worth over 80,000 IEP or $110,580 US dollars. Embezzlement is another problem for libraries. For example, in 2012 a Saugus (MA) Public Library employee pleaded guilty to taking over $800,000. In 2015, an executive assistant at New City Library, New York, was indicted on charges of stealing nearly $124,000. Theft of cash can take place on a smaller scale. A Westerville (OH) Public Library worker who had been employed for thirty-two years embezzled $20,000 from 2011 to 2014 simply by taking $20 to $40 each day.[8]

As with other deviant behaviors, actions involving fraud and theft are linked to the work environment and personality. Poor working conditions, unfair treatment, compensation issues, and violating employee trust can trigger these types of retaliatory behaviors. Personality traits of "low conscientiousness, low emotional stability, low agreeableness, cynicism, and external locus of control" are also linked to such actions. Regardless of the motive, once this type of crime occurs, library administration must act quickly.[9]

Because the possibility of employees engaging in theft increases when there is motive and opportunity, preventive action is the library organization's best weapon. First, policies should be in place to cover such serious acts and communicated to all library staff. These policies should address both the ethical expectations for library workers as well as the consequences of crossing the line into criminal actions. Surveillance equipment is another option for monitoring employees to reduce theft. However, if staff members believe they are being watched and feel that the organization does not trust them, these workers may respond with "distrust [and] low levels of satisfaction" in their relationships with management. Encouraging online payments for fines or lost books, rather than cash, is another method to reduce opportunities for theft. Finally, measures as simple as tightening inventory controls and eliminating excessive inventory stock will also reduce theft.[10]

Embezzlement can be reduced with preemptive actions. Although we will not explore financial security and accounting methods in depth, a few means of prevention are worth noting

1. Separate the duties of individuals who handle funds and record finances.[11]
2. Document all financial information and transactions and conduct independent reviews or audits on a regular basis. Wide-scale reviews can be done on a large scale by using an external agency or CPA, or on a smaller scale by, for example, a supervisor checking on staff.[12]
3. Require all employees who have opportunities to embezzle funds to be bonded. This gives the library an opportunity to recover stolen funds if needed.[13]
4. Carefully secure all financial records, as well as cash, checkbooks, and signature stamps.[14]
5. Conduct thorough background checks of those hired to handle finances or inventories.[15]

Guidelines for handling and transporting cash, reviewing bank statements, tracking blank checks, submitting expense reports, handling mileage reimbursement, and use of company credit cards should be clearly written, conveyed, and implemented. Some libraries (e.g., special or public libraries) may do their own accounting, whereas academic or school libraries may go through a larger organizational accounting department. Regardless of the organizational structure, good accounting practices and guidelines for handling money should be a part of every library system.

Library Embezzlement Methods

1. Failing to deposit collected fines and fees
2. Forging signatures on checks
3. Writing checks to oneself
4. Taking kickbacks from vendors
5. Double-billing for expenses
6. Falsifying reimbursable expenses
7. Re-endorsing payment checks made out to library
8. Submitting fraudulent payment vouchers
9. Diverting cash to personal accounts or pockets[16]

A third type of organizational deviance is sabotage. Sabotage by workers evolved in the late 1700s and early 1800s as an attempt by workers to improve wages, working conditions, and overall treatment. There are many theories about the evolution of the word "sabotage," but it became accepted in vocabulary around this historical period and can be found in an 1808 French dictionary. A committee of the confederal congress held in Tolouse, France, in 1897 officially recognized sabotage as a method of worker retaliation. It passed the following resolution[17]:

> Resolved, That whenever there arises between employers and workers a conflict due, either to the employers' exactions or to the workers' initiative, and a strike does not produce results satisfactory to the workers, the workers shall use boycott or sabotage or both according to the rules laid down in this report.[18]

Sabotage is rooted in anger and is an intentional act to harm the organization via actions ranging from minor deviances to major acts. Today, sabotage "involves damaging or destroying an organization's or colleague's equipment, workspace, or data." It can involve maligning reputations (of individuals and the organization), as well as production delays or disruptions. Additionally, sabotage could include destruction of property (buildings, furnishings, computers, or data) that severely hampers library operations or results in significant property losses. Whatever its form, sabotage impacts outcomes, procedures, and interpersonal interactions within the organization.[19]

Sabotage results from an individual's reaction to the work environment. Studies suggest "powerlessness, frustration, facilitation of work, boredom/fun, and injustice" as possible causes for such deviant actions.

Although empowering employees helps quickly resolve numerous issues that occur in daily work and will help to maintain a positive work environment, employees who feel tied to mandatory work behaviors regardless of circumstance may be inclined to rebel with an act of sabotage. This is especially true if the worker has experienced several frustrating events and reaches a point of having had enough. As mentioned in chapter two's discussion of workplace culture, often deeply embedded routines cause employee frustration in an ever-changing library environment. Imagine if a staff member suggests implementing roving reference to assist students reluctant to ask for help, only to be told never to leave the reference desk because that is the way the library had always operated. The library staff might feel rebuked and frustrated and decide to leave the desk anyway to provide assistance on the floor. This violation of organizational rules or protocols is a form of sabotage. Acts of sabotage are also used to break up the boredom of daily routines, but they are most often used in response to perceived unfair treatment. Imagine a librarian being told to stay late to administer an information literacy session to a night class. If this extra work is not balanced by additional time off or rotated among all librarians, an injustice may be perceived. This librarian may decide to start taking extra-long lunches or leave early one afternoon without clearing it with a supervisor in an attempt to offset the perceived injustice. This too is an act of sabotage. These examples of sabotage are simply deviances from the standards of the work environment and are harmful, and minor.[20]

Sabotage can take a more destructive route. More serious acts typically are motivated by a combination of a distributive injustice (unfair allocation) and a procedural or interactional injustice. For example, a library worker passed over for a promotion by a supervisor who has shown favoritism for another colleague could retaliate by erasing valuable computer files, releasing a computer virus, or destroying library equipment. At this level, sabotage has a significant impact on the library operation. Whether a minor deviation of work procedures or a more serious act, the employee's need to retaliate or restore equity in the library work environment play a critical role.[21]

Rewarding employees for proper behavior with incentives, positive feedback, and by acknowledging their efforts goes a long way in combating sabotage. Because sabotage is rooted in the perceived fairness of the work environment, every effort to achieve equal distribution of work, pay, and rewards is essential. Tied to this equality are defined individual and group goals, which should be objectively reviewed on a regular basis. Library organizations must actively listen to employees who may voice concerns about procedures or methods and be willing to review ideas for change and movement in new directions. Finally, empowering the employee to act within defined parameters of reasonable policy will also encourage a positive, engaged, and effective work environment that minimizes deviant acts of sabotage.

Organizational deviances occur on a scale ranging from minor to major. Issues with cyberslacking may negatively impact production but cause less impact than other actions such as theft, embezzlement, or sabotage. Proactive prevention through regulations, controls, and ethics is the best method to combat these types or dysfunctional behaviors. Treating library workers fairly and engaging employees in the success of the organization via feedback and involvement also play roles in minimizing these negative behaviors.

GOSSIP

Gossip is rooted in the Old English word *godsibb,* which means *god-parent.* It refers to females who would talk among themselves at the birth of a baby. Gossip will always be present in work organizations, libraries included. It is defined as information shared with others, which includes some "common interests" about an individual who is not present during the information exchange. The focus of gossip is on people, not events, things, or objects. Gossip differs from rumor. Rumor is typically an announcement or informa-tion colored by personal opinion, whereas gossip implies a type of intimacy achieved through the act of sharing information among individuals.[22]

Reasons for Gossip

1. Sharing information	4. Group bonding
2. Entertainment	5. Status enhancement[23]
3. Pleasurable experience	

Gossip can have both a negative and positive effect in the workplace. On the positive side, numerous studies indicate gossip can be useful in main-taining the normal behavior and expectations of an organization. In fact, a 2010 study found as gossip increases "norm violations decrease" and "norm conforming behavior [increase]." It can be used as a form of storytelling and can illustrate an employee's positive behavior. For instance, positive gossip about a librarian who exhibited exemplary teamwork and contributions who was then promoted to a management position could be useful to others in the library organization by serving as a model. Gossip also can strengthen the group. Because it is an intimate act, those who participate in the gossip exchange experience a type of bonding. A "deeper level of trust" results (especially for negative gossip) among those individuals who have shared a gossip experience. A 2014 study of public, academic, and special libraries in Nigeria indicated that although 63 percent of library directors felt gossip negatively impacted productivity, positive benefits were attained via learning about issues, solving problems, and decision-making. Library gossip can be used as a means of communication. In *Library Management 101: A Practical Guide,* Lisa Hussey observes that gossip can be used as a form of informal, networked exchange in interpersonal communications.[24]

Although all gossip is not bad, it has negative consequences. Gossip can be false in three ways—flagrant, trait, and exaggerated. First, gossip can spread false information about an individual. Even if this form of maligning does not reach the level of bullying, as discussed in the previous chapter, it can be damaging. Flagrant gossip is a statement about someone that is simply false. Second, gossip can surround a trait or characteristic about an individual that he does not possess. Finally, gossip can simply be a gross exaggeration of a characteristic or action. Gossip can be negative when engaged in for pleasure or entertainment while on the job. Not only does this potentially isolate the targeted employee, it is a waste of valuable work time. Often, gossipers are viewed by supervisors in a negative light because of the implication of malicious intent, and as a result they may be characterized as low performers. Gossip also can be used by individuals as a power move or act of control because it can be a way of manipulating or enhancing the perceived value of an individual among the group members. Finally, although gossip may strengthen the group in some ways due to its intimate nature, it also fractures the group because it excludes the targeted worker. Even worse, the gossip may be stereotyping in nature, which does even further harm to the cohesiveness of the group, department, and organization.[25]

It is impossible to eliminate gossip from the library workplace. However, some actions can be taken to limit it. On an individual level, gossip stops if the group it is shared with "refuses to respond" and therefore denies "it of social support." On a management level, an open-door policy that encourages employees to talk about issues they may have with coworkers can also reduce gossiping. Because gossip, especially when negative in nature, can ostracize, malign, and harm employees and lead to unhappy staff and increased turnover, library organizations must be involved in the solution. Library administrations could partner with the human resources department to develop awareness training for staff on the potentially negative impact gossip can have on workplace productivity and its coworkers. However, library organizations should use caution with official gossip policies as court rulings have found gossip policies unlawful at the time of this writing under section 7 of the National Labor Relations Act.[26]

RANKISM

Issues of rank in the workplace are nothing new. The term "rankism" describes a concept first introduced by Robert Fuller in his 2003 book *Somebodies and Nobodies: Overcoming the Abuse of Rank*. In another publication, Fuller defines it as "abuse or discrimination based on a difference of rank." He continues, "When somebodies use the power of their position in one setting to exercise power in another, that's rankism. When somebodies use the power of their position to put a permanent hold on their power, that, too, is rankism."[27]

Rankism is a dysfunctional behavior where a leader belittles, berates, insults, or abuses employees of lower organizational status. At its most benign, rankism is uncivil behavior and at its worst can lead to discrimination, bullying, or abuse. Although aspects of these behaviors are discussed in other chapters, rankism is treated here because it plays a role in office politics in many organizations, including libraries.

Like all organizations, libraries have hierarchies, and along with this type of structure comes employee rank. For many who achieve a position of power, the tendency towards "unequal treatment or degradation" of those with lower status may be possible. This causes stress, frustration, and tension in the workplace, and employees are more likely to react with retaliation or other deviant behaviors such as sabotage. Imagine the library manager who gives directives on every aspect of her department to ensure it is done her way and then belittles workers who have not done their work exactly as directed. Hostility and resentment would soon surface. Rankism also appears in academic library environments, because higher levels of education have been shown to contribute to individuals' feelings of superiority over those less degreed. Someone who holds a position of power can also be involved in sexual assault. A blog post in *The Librarian in Black* describes several sexual harassment incidents involving a library supervisor and other library-associated individuals who hold rank and power. Library organizations are not immune to any consequences of rankism and power.[28]

There are several steps library organizations can take to combat rankism. First, higher administration and managers should all be made aware of the importance of listening and being open to the suggestions and ideas of lesser-ranked employees. Open lines of communication are linked to reduced tension in the workplace, so this type of cooperation is critical for librarians in academic settings when dealing with faculty. Another method is to allow employees the opportunity to rise in rank temporarily, for example, while working on a given project or serving on a team. This concept is in line with attributes of a more mindful organization that assigns the most skilled or experienced individual to lead a project rather than merely assigning the project leader by rank. Additionally, library organizations can lay out a written plan of advancement for library employees that eliminates favoritism and encourages self-development. Avenues for advancement should be available. For the many academic libraries with tenure systems, this will be a challenging task that nonetheless must be addressed if rankism is to be eliminated. Regarding sexual harassment, libraries should have a workplace violence policy in place. (An example of the Freeport Memorial Library workplace violence policy is found at http://freeportlibrary.info/about-the-library/mission-and-vision-statements/99-policies/286-workplaceviolence.) Finally, rewarding staff engagement and participation is also important in building a work environment that promotes engagement rather than rankism.[29]

BIAS

Much has been written about all forms of bias. To some degree it is found in the interactions of staff in all work environments. This book offers a brief review of unconscious bias and its subset, cognitive bias, as it relates to the library workplace.

There are over 150 types of unconscious bias, which can be defined as a mental process "by which the brain uses associations that are so ingrained" that they cannot control or be aware of them. Individuals are unaware of the influence of unconscious bias. The brain tags and stores information in different locations. Much bias is processed in the amygdala (fight or flight area) but stereotyping is linked to the temporal and frontal lobes. Social stereotyping is associated with the left temporal lobe. Thus, bias is hardwired into how information is classified in the brain. Because of these tag and storage methods of bias associations, it is difficult to change.[30]

Unconscious bias impacts the workplace in several ways. Consultant and psychotherapist Suzanne Price identifies five types of unconscious bias that impact the work environment.

First, people have an affinity bias that causes them to be drawn to, and even hire, individuals like themselves. For libraries, this is an important issue because it impacts the hiring process. In a work organization that strives to be diverse and welcoming to all, this type of bias can result in the opposite effect. In the United States, library staff already reflect a significantly lower percentage of ethnic diversity when compared to the workforce as a whole. Therefore, bias in the hiring process must be addressed.[31]

Diversity in the Workforce[32]

	Librarians 2015	US Workforce 2014	US Workforce Projected 2050
African American	8.50%	12.64%	15.00%
Hispanic/Latino	4.80%	15.30%	30.00%
Asian	2.80%	6.06%	9.60%

Second, a clear view of individual actions is distorted due to the halo effect. The halo effect is an unconscious bias that causes individuals to see only good things in people that they like. This unconscious bias could negatively impact daily interactions but also impact accurate and fair employee evaluations.[33]

Third, perception bias involves stereotyping or assumptions that are associated with a particular group of people. Librarians and library staff interact with a variety of groups. This includes other departments or divisions of the library and academic or administrative divisions, but it also could include people. Perception bias could be found in those who are different through culture, religion, race, handicap, or another characteristic.[34]

Fourth, confirmation bias involves individuals who seek to confirm some preexisting belief "about their own social identity group." This could impact library work conducted by teams or groups, which is a large part of library function. An individual with confirmation bias will be less open to opinions that differ from their own.[35]

Finally, people gravitate towards a groupthink view to be accepted by others. (This concept is also found in mobbing behavior where those around a targeted individual come together in their mob and practice a kind of groupthink.). Again, the library as an organization does not benefit from diverse thinking because there is a belief that thinking differently is not acceptable and will make an individual appear different from the group. This appearance of difference makes the individual more likely to be a target of bullying or mobbing if those dysfunctions exist in the library workplace. All these types of unconscious bias affect the library organization's culture, worker interaction, recruitment and hiring, and promotions or appraisals.

A subset of unconscious bias is cognitive bias. Cognitive bias deals with an individual's perception of information when it is influenced by personal experiences and beliefs as well as their environment. Cognitive bias impacts reality versus perception. Here the focus of cognitive bias will be on the manager-employee relationship. M. Valle Santos and M. Teresa Garcia define three types of cognitive bias in managers: simplification bias, affective influence bias, and interaction bias. These forms of cognitive bias relate to the simplification of a complex stimulus, the personal beliefs of the managers, and a combination of the two.[36]

First, managers may be biased in decision-making because they base their choices on more recent events instead of reflecting on occurrences over a longer timeframe. Research indicates that there is more distortion in managerial perception of past occurrences than present ones and this is termed the "recency effect." In the library, this plays a role in a manager's perception of an employee. For example, if the annual evaluation period is approaching, a staff member may make a conscious effort to be on time to work and show a positive and productive effort in his duties. However, at the beginning of the year, this same employee may have been consistently late and failed to execute duties as expected. When a manager evaluates the employee only on the most recent events, it reflects the cognitive bias of the recency effect. Another area of influence is the primacy effect, or first impression, which is on the opposite end of the spectrum from the recency effect. Managers experiencing the primacy effect are more likely to gravitate to new information that confirms already established beliefs. For example, if a library manager forms an initial impression that a new hire tends to cut corners, and even if the employee improves with time, the manager may look for instances of work behavior to confirm their initial determination. Managers' personal beliefs, such as subconscious stereotyping, also influence their actions with staff. As indicated in unconscious bias, stereotyping can impact all aspects of the manager-worker relationship. A library manager's perspective can be influenced by staff who advertise their contributions or perform tasks the manager deems important. Although this employee may not excel in all areas, or perhaps performs poorly in others, the manager only sees the highlights and perceives a good worker. This kind of evaluation reflects cognitive bias. Finally, studies indicate that managers oversimplify situations that are abstract or more distant from their daily work environments. For example, a library manager's evaluation of the overall impact of staff instruction towards the larger library goals of increasing graduation rates may result in the conclusion that the library positively contributes to student success. However, because of cognitive bias, the manager fails to respond with a more in-depth response, such as conducting an analysis showing the impact of information literacy instruction on student grades, and if it makes a difference.[37]

Unconscious bias is difficult to change, but organizations are beginning to address this dysfunction. In 2014, roughly 20 percent of large organizations addressed unconscious bias in their employee training, which is an increase from only 5 percent in 2009. Companies such as Google, BAE Systems Inc., Excel, Genentech, T. Rowe Price, and Roche Diagnostics all engage in unconscious-bias training. Libraries, too, can consider including unconscious bias as a part of their training for employees. Additionally, self-awareness training and 360-degree feedback from peers help to identify unconscious bias, as does the use of diversified teams that bring employees together to work on projects or achieve goals. This is also true for hiring teams. Staff evaluations and promotions should be based on objective goals and achievements such as SMART goals, and rating scales should be clearly defined. A study of the resumes of current employees to evaluate their education and experience can be done. Finally, as when combatting other dysfunctional behaviors, a code of ethics and defined expectations of professional etiquette created with support from the human resources department will also combat unconscious bias.[38]

LOBBYING

In the arena of office politics there are those individuals who manipulate through internal lobbying. The Cambridge Business English Dictionary defines lobbying as "the activity of trying to persuade someone in authority." In the workplace, this persuasion is used to influence other workers or superiors. A lobbyist in a library organization is no different than those at other companies; all use manipulation to push through personal ideas, agendas, and strategies. This can occur from anywhere in the company—laterally, bottom up, or top down. Top-down lobbying often involves minimal dialogue and undisclosed agendas, which can be classified as a type of vertical bullying. Although these lobbying actions may indeed bring new concepts to the organization, their method of delivery may have a negative impact on the library work environment.[39]

First, lobbying can have a negative impact when lobbyists are so caught up with their ideas or plans that they fail to look backward at historical information that may influence a concept, or forward to the overall impact a plan may have on the library as a whole. Second, such actions to push through a personal agenda may include some behind-the-scenes negotiation or meetings. This excludes others in the organization who may perceive the move as deceptive and self-serving, and deprives the process of potentially valuable input from other library staff. Third, lobbyists are inclined to surround themselves with similar people. While this makes it easier to launch new ideas, it limits perspective. Fourth, lobbyists may talk about ideas in grand fashion, but fall short when it comes to execution. This could potentially leave the library in a tenuous position, especially if deadlines or budgets are linked to the concept.[40]

There are several ways to avoid falling into the lobbyist trap. First, open and inclusive communication should always invite participants to introduce new concepts or ideas. Allow employees to have input and be a part of a concept's creation as well as its execution. Ideas could be solicited using surveys, teams, or focus groups, and so on. Keep in mind the overarching goals of the library organization and stay within that focus. Some ideas may be wonderful but not actually fulfill the library's goals.

CONCLUSION

Although organizational deviance and politics in the workplace can never be completely eliminated, reducing such behavior should be a goal of every library organization. Organizational deviances that affect production and organizational operation, such as fraud, theft, and sabotage, must be addressed. If not, such "violation[s] . . . will jeopardize the welfare of the organization." This is obvious with serious deviances, but less visible in production deviance (e.g., cyberloafing) or social deviance (e.g., gossip). Additional problems can evolve from rankism as well as unconscious bias in the library workplace. Finally, using lobbying to achieve political goals can contribute to dysfunction when personal agendas unfold in closed-door discussions. Each type of deviance requires a unique response to check it. However, libraries ultimately must address these types of dysfunction with a balance of policies and control accompanied by a leadership style that includes input from the library staff.[41]

NOTES

1. Sandra L. Robinson and Rebecca J. Bennett, "A Typology of Deviant Workplace Behaviors: A Multidimensional Scaling Study," *The Academy of Management Journal* 38, no. 2 (April 1995): 559–61.

2. Ali Aksu, "Organizational Deviance and Multi-Factor Leadership," *Education Research and Reviews* 11, no. 8 (2016): 589.

3. Barrie E. Litzky, Kimberly A. Eddleston, and Deborah L. Kidder, "The Good, the Bad, and the Misguided: How Managers Inadvertently Encourage Deviant Behaviors," *Academy of Management Perspectives* 20, no. 1 (February 2006): 100.

4. Gholamrez Jandaghi, Seyed Mehdi Alvani, Hassan Zarci Matin, and Samira Fakheri Kozekanan, "Cyberloafing Management in Organizations," *Iranian Journal of Management Studies* 8, no. 3 (July 2015): 336; Monica T. Whitty and Adrian N. Carr, "New Rules in the Workplace: Applying Object-Relations Theory to Explain Problem Internet and Email Behaviour in the Workplace," *Computers in Human Behavior* 22, no.2 (March 2006): 237; T. Ramayah, "Personal Web Usage and Work Inefficiency," *Business Strategy Series* 11, no. 5 (2010): 295–301. doi:http://dx.doi.org/10.1108/17515631011080704, http://nclive.org/cgi-bin/nclsm?url=http://search.proquest.com/docview/750216512?accountid=13217; Kansas State University Newsroom, "Policy, Enforcement May Stop Employees from Wasting Time Online at Work," *Newswise*, January 2013, www.newswise.com/articles/view/598668/?sc=dwhr&xy=5040021; Viven K. G. Lim, "The IT Way of Loafing on the Job: Cyberloafing, Neutralizing and Organizational Justice," *Journal of Organizational Behavior* 23, no. 5 (August 2002): 676; "Civility in America 2013," Weber Shandwick, www.webershandwick.com/uploads/news/files/Civility_in_America_2013_Exec_Summary.pdf; K. G. Viven Lim and Don J. Chen, "Cyberloafing at the Workplace: Gain or Drain on Work?," *Behaviour and Information Technology* 23, no. 5 (November 2009): 676.

5. Jandaghi et al., "Cyberloafing Management in Organizations," 340–42.

6. Joseph C. Ugrin and J. Michael Pearson, "The Effects of Sanctions and Stigmas on Cyberloafing," *Computers in Human Behavior* 29, no. 3 (May 2013): 817.

7. "Personnel Policy," *Newark Public Library*, www.newarklibrary.org/policies/personnel-policy.

8. "Annual Theft Survey," Jack L. Hayes International, Inc., http://hayesinternational.com/news/annual-retail-theft-survey; Glen E. Holt, "Theft by Library Staff," The Bottom Line: Managing Library Finances 20, no. 2 (2007): 87–88; Martin Vennard, "The Curious Tale of Stolen Books," BBC News Magazine, 2013, www.bbc.com/news/magazine-22249700/; "National Library Employee Held Over €80k Book Theft," *News Irish News,* 2013, www.independent.ie/irish-news/national-library-employee-held-over-80k-book-theft-29775615.html; "Saugus Library Employee Pleads Guilty to Stealing Over $800K," *CBS Boston,* 2012, http://boston.cbslocal.com/2012/09/28/saugus-library-employee-pleads-guilty-to-stealing-over-800k/; Alex Taylor and

Steve Lieberman, "Former New City Library Employee Accused of Stealing Nearly $124,000," *The Journal News,* December 10, 2015, www.lohud.com/story/news/crime/2015/12/10/new-city-library-embezzlement/77034092/; Lori Kurtzman, "Westerville Library Worker Accused of Stealing $20,000," *The Columbus Dispatch,* October 23, 2014, www.dispatch.com/content/stories/local/2014/10/23/Westerville-library-theft.html.

9. Litzky, Eddleston, and Kidder, "The Good, the Bad, and the Misguided," 93.

10. Ibid., 88, 98–99.

11. Nancy Hurst, "The Book Stops Here: Should Library Boards Be Held Accountable for Embezzlement?," *Public Libraries* 52, no. 5 (2013): 39.

12. Ibid.

13. Ibid.

14. Ibid.

15. Elisa F. Topper, "Working Knowledge: Safeguarding Against Employee Fraud," *American Libraries* 36, no. 7 (2005): 86.

16. Hurst, "The Book Stops Here," 39.

17. Brian Martin, *Nonviolence verses Capitalism* (London: War Resisters International, 2001) and Andre Tridon, *The New Unionism* (New York, NY: B.W. Huebrsh, 1913).

18. Andre Tridon, *The New Unionism* (New York, NY: B.W. Huebrsh, 1913).

19. Muhammad Nadeem Anwar, Muhammad Sarwar, Riffat-un_nisa Awan, and Muhammad Irfan Arif, "Gender Differences in Workplace Deviant Behavior of University Teachers and Modification Techniques," *International Education Studies* 4, no. 1 (2011): 195 and Maureen Ambrose and Marshall Schminke, "Sabotage in the Workplace: The Role of Organizational Injustice," *Organizational Behavior and Human Decision Processes* 89, no. 1 (2002): 948–50.

20. Ambrose and Schminke, "Sabotage in the Workplace," 948; Judie McLean Parks and Deborah L. Kidder, "'Till Death Do Us Part . . . ': Changing Work Relationships in the 1990s," in *Trends in Organizational Behavior (Vol. 1),* ed. C. L. Cooper and D. M. Rousseau (London, United Kingdom: Wiley and Sons, 1994).

21. Jerald Greenberg and Bradley J. Alge, "Aggressive Reactions to Workplace Injustice," in *Dysfunctional Behavior in Organizations, Part A: Violent and Deviant Behavior,* ed. R. W. Griffin, A. O'Leary-Kelly and J. M. Collins (London: JAI Press, 1998); Maureen Ambrose and Marshall Schminke, "Sabotage in the Workplace: The Role of Organizational Injustice," *Organizational Behavior and Human Decision Processes* 89, no. 1 (2002): 959.

22. Travis J. Grosser, Virginie Lopez Kidwell, and Giuseppe (Joe) Labianca, "A Social Network Analysis of Positive and Negative Gossip in Organizational Life," *Group and Organization Management* 3, no. 2 (February 2010): 177–212 and Sandy Valmores Chua and Kristine June de la Cerne Uy, "The Psychological Anatomy of Gossip," *American Journal of Management* 14, no. 3 (2014): 65.

23. Chua and Uy, "The Psychological Anatomy of Gossip," 65–66.

24. Brian Robinson, "Character, Caricature, and Gossip," *The Monist* 99, no. 2 (April 2016): 201; Grosser, Kidwell, and Labianca, "A Social Network Analysis of Positive and Negative Gossip," 4- 5; Richard Olorunsola, "Gossip and Library Management: An Examination of the Perceptions of Library Managers," in *Advances in Librarianship, Volume 38,* ed. Anne Woodsworth and W. David Penniman, (Bingley, United Kingdom: Emerald Group Publishing Limited, 2014); Lisa K. Hussey, "Organizational Communication," in *Library Management 101 a Practical Guide,* ed. Diane L. Velasquez (Chicago, IL: ALA Editions, 2013).

25. Brian Robinson, "Character, Caricature, and Gossip," *The Monist* 99, no. 2 (April 2016): 204 and Grosser et al., "A Social Network Analysis of Positive and Negative Gossip," 9.

26. Chua and Uy, "The Psychological Anatomy of Gossip," 68; Alan M. Kaplan, "Employment Benefit and Labor Updates: No-Gossip Policy Violates Federal Law," *MasudaFunai,* 2014.

27. Robert W. Fuller, "A New Look at Hierarchy," *Leader to Leader,* no. 21 (Summer 2001): 7 and Robert W. Fuller, *Somebodies and Nobodies: Overcoming the Abuse of Rank* (Gabriola Island, US: New Society Publishers, 2004).

28. Helen L. MacLennan, "Incivility by Degree: The Influence of Educational Attainment on Workplace Civility," *Journal of Conflict Management* 5, no. 1 (2015): 36; Bela Florenthal and Yulia Tolstikov-Mast, "Organizational Culture: Comparing Faculty and Staff Perceptions," *Journal of Higher Education Theory and Practice* 12, no. 6 (2012): 83; Sarah Houghton, "Laundry and Skeletons: The Reality of Sexual Assault and Harassment," *The Librarian in Black* [blog], October 3, 2014, http://librarianinblack .net/librarianinblack/laundry-and-skeletons-the-reality-of-sexual-assault-and-harass ment/.

29. Florenthal and Tolstikov-Mast, "Organizational Culture: Comparing Faculty and Staff Perceptions," 83; Karl E. Weick and Kathleen M. Sutcliffe, "Mindfulness and the Quality of Organizational Attention," *Organization Science* 17, no. 4 (2006): 519; Fuller, "A New Look at Hierarchy," 11; Florenthal and Tolstikov-Mast, "Organizational Culture," 84.

30. Suzanne Price, "Think Slow: How Unconscious Bias Effects the Workplace," *BCCJ Accumen* (April 2014): 37; Horace McCormick, "The Real Effects of Unconscious Bias in the Workplace," *UNC Executive Development* (2015): 5.

31. Suzanne Price, "Think Slow: How Unconscious Bias Effects the Workplace," *BCCJ Accumen,* (April 2014): 37.

32. Jennifer Doring, "Library Worker: Facts and Figures," Department for Professional Employees, http://dpeaflcio.org/programs-publications/issue-fact-sheets/library -workers-facts-figures/; "Labor Force Characteristics by Race and Ethnicity, 2014," US Bureau of Labor Statistics. November 2015, https://www.bls.gov/opub/reports/

race-and-ethnicity/archive/labor-force-characteristics-by-race-and-ethnicity-2014.pdf: 2; "The Growing Diversity of the US Workforce," *Medscape,* February 12, 2017, www.medscape.com/viewarticle/717040.

33. Price, "Think Slow," 37.

34. Ibid.

35. Ibid.

36. M. Valle Santos and M. Teresa Garcia, "Managers' Opinions: Reality or Fiction," *Management Decision* 44, no. 6 (2006): 755–56.

37. Valle Santos and Garcia, 755–756 and Armen E. Allahverdyan and Aram Galstyan, "Opinion Dynamics with Confirmation Bias," *PLOS one* 9, no. 7 (2014): 8.

38. Joan Lubbin, "Bringing Hidden Biases into the Light; Big Businesses Teach Staffers How 'Unconscious Bias' Impacts Decisions," *Wall Street Journal Online,* January 9, 2014, http://nclive.org/cgibin/.nclsm?url=http://search.proquest.com/docview/1476212282?accountid=13217; Horace McCormick, "The Real Effects of Unconscious Bias in the Workplace," *UNC Executive Development* (2015): 5; Sarajit Poddar, "Biases in Performance Management: How to Overcome Them?" *LinkedIn* [blog], January 19, 2015, https://www.linkedin.com/pulse/biases-performance -management-how-can-overcome-sarajit-poddar-hrmp; Beverly J. Glover, "The Role of HR in Managing Workplace Bias," [PowerPoint Slides], *Oklahoma City Human Resources Society,* 2016, https://www.ochrs.org/sites/ochrs/uploads/images/ meetings/OCHRS_HR_Role_in_Managing_Workplace_Bias.pdf.

39. "Lobbying," Cambridge Business English Dictionary, 2016, http://dictionary .cambridge.org/us/dictionary/english/lobbying and Fritz Ngale Ilongo, "Workplace Bullying as Psychological Violence in Institutions of Higher Learning," PhD dissertation, 2013, University of the Free State Bloemfontein, South Africa.

40. Paula Storm, Robert Kelly, and Susann deVries, "Office Politics," *Library Journal* 133, no. 18 (2008): 34.

41. Aksu, "Organizational Deviance and Multi-Factor Leadership," 590.

6

POOR COMMUNICATION IN THE WORKPLACE

E ffective communication is vital to the success of a library or organization. It is through communication that library objectives
are conveyed and workers help achieve these overarching goals
through interactions with each other as well as with library users.
In addition to reaching goals, good communication increases employee cer-
tainty, satisfaction, and perceived performance. Because communication is
such an essential element of library operations, when barriers arise or the
lines of communication break down, it can result in workplace dysfunction.[1]

Communication is a "process of transmitting information and common
understanding from one person to another." As far back as 1949, information flow was addressed by Claude Elwood Shannon and Warren Weaver's
linear model of communication. This model was based on the use of a hardwired telephone (Shannon and Weaver worked for Bell Laboratories) and
flowed from a person or source through a transmitter and channel until it
reached the receiver (another telephone) and finally the receiving party. A
unique part of this model is that it considers how the transmission process
can cause communication problems, which is called "noise."[2]

Communication theory evolved to illustrate information flow with a
gatekeeper inserted into the communication process (the Intermediary
Model), which introduced the possibility of modifying or controlling the
information conveyed before it reached the receiver. In 1954 a feedback loop

was the next theory to evolve (Schramm's Interactive Model). This concept suggested that communication did not stop when the message was received, but continued when the receiver communicated back, creating a loop in the process. The concept of a sender and receiver taking turns with encoding, sending, receiving, and decoding messages was featured in the Transactional Model, which emerged in the 1970s. These two theories expounded on the repetitive process of encoding and decoding information. This alone can lead to miscommunication in the coding process, but the Transactional Model also treats the influence of physical, physiological, and psychological distractions. This model was then a foundation for the more complex Ecological Model developed by Davis Foulger in 2004. Foulger termed senders and receivers as creators and consumers whose roles continually switched depending on the cycle of communication. Additionally, Foulger noted that communication evolves into a creative and social process through the use of language, robust media options, and messages that can be influenced (or distorted) by selective attention, perception, language, and other social considerations. As these theories hint, the process of communication is not simple and can be subject to inaccuracies.[3]

Workplace communication in organizations, including libraries, can be distorted by a variety of factors. As mentioned in chapter two, silos impact communication in the library because they cause information to stagnate. Additionally, the channels information flows through can impact how effectively messages are shared. Other factors such as apprehension, introversion, passive listening, lack of empathy, or dismissive responses may block communication. In turn, these barriers result in a negative impact on leadership and the library work environment.

COMMUNICATION CHANNELS

In organizations, including libraries, communication can flow in a variety of ways. This includes top down, bottom up, horizontally, and cross laterally (a combination of team members representing multiple levels in the organization). Although a combination of these four information flows are best to avoid information silos, each method presents its own challenges. The downward flow of information runs the risk of becoming distorted as it flows from one level in the organizational chain to the next. For example, an initiative to eliminate a reference section is passed down to several branches. Some branches interfile the books but retain their designation as reference material, whereas other branches remove the designation and allow the materials to be checked out. Somewhere in the downward flow of new policy information, the particulars of how to handle the elimination of reference were distorted. There is a possibility such information may stop flowing at some point. For instance, a manager may fail to pass along information to her workers, in which case reference materials would never be interfiled into the collection. The reverse movement—the upward flow of information—may result in distorted information or fail to reach the top, especially if it is bad news. Often upward information is not reported if an employee fears negative consequences, has a poor relationship with the direct manager, or the manager fails to act. In the reference example, workers may notice newer editions of reference items arrive labeled to circulate while older reference materials still marked as in-house use sit on the shelf. Although they notice the problem, workers fail to report the issue because, based on historical patterns of behavior, they believe their manager will do nothing about it. Horizontal communication may also fall short if not all information is shared or there is competition between individuals or departments. Such lateral communication may bypass managers, nullifying any input and conflict resolution skills. In the reference example, the cataloging and circulation departments may be disputing who has responsibility to implement the new reference policy; because of the departmental disagreement, clear communication to other library workers breaks down. Finally, while a cross-lateral combination of team members may suggest positive communication flow, unless their efforts and discoveries are shared outside of their group, critical information may only be shared among select members.[4]

The larger communications channels can provide challenges, and so too can issues surrounding senders and receivers. Senders of information have the challenge of creating content and choosing a medium. Is the content accurate and correct? Is it expressed in a manner that will be understood by the receiver? Is it conveyed through the best-understood medium—be it in person, by email, through a shared online document, video conferencing, or some other means? How information is constructed and sent affects whether it is understood. Senders must choose the medium used to send the information. In turn, receivers have the challenge of decoding the message correctly. This message interpretation can be skewed by factors such as culture, language, gender, age, or even personal experiences. For example, would new employees understand changes communicated with a library policy or software program if they were still learning the original parameters? Receivers could fail to decipher messages carefully due to time constraints, information overload, or other work distractions.

How closely are emails read when the inbox contains thirty messages (or more) by noon? Can someone's full attention truly be given to a new policy change document attached to an email while preparing to teach an information literacy class in an hour? A recent study indicated that 38 percent of librarians felt overloaded with work, so time is also an influencing factor in decoding communications. Additionally, communication can be derailed by individuals advising, patronizing, preaching, or interrupting. Message content and intent is important. Thus, communication breakdown can occur numerous ways in the basic elements of coding and encoding messages.[5]

Positive information flow can be developed by encouraging sharing and open communication in the library organization. A continued movement towards developing positive relationships between supervisors and staff will also facilitate a positive information exchange. The authors of *Difficult Conversations: How to Discuss What Matters Most* encourage individuals to identify "feelings, key identity issues, and possible distortions or gaps" in interpreting and receiving information. Reframing verbal messages so they can be clearly understood and confirming that they were heard can also be useful. If the information is important, consider repeating it in multiple formats, such as verbalizing it in addition to sharing it electronically. Because of information overload, minimizing unnecessary communications might also be considered. For example, to combat information overload, in 2017 France introduced a law that banned after-work emails in companies of fifty or more workers. Adequate time for employees to process information and changes should be allowed. Although there is no single solution to solve communication flow problems, these are some options to consider.[6]

COMMUNICATION BLOCKS

As already established, there are any number of factors that could block communication in library work environments. In addition to the limitations of flow and communication channels, barriers to communication can be rooted in the psychology of individual employees. Although this book does not delve into personality disorders or other mental and emotional problems, it will touch on a few common communication blocks. These include communication apprehension, introverted personalities, passive listening, lack of empathy, and dismissive communication.

The term "communication apprehension" was originally coined in the late 1970s by communications professor, author, and researcher James McCroskey. He defined it as "an individual's level of fear or anxiety associated with either real or anticipated communication with another person or persons." It is an anxiety-based unwillingness to engage in communication. Roughly 15 to 20 percent of individuals experience such anxiety on a regular basis. Reasons for this are based in either context or personality. Context communication apprehension refers to setting. McCroskey divides these arenas into "group discussions, interpersonal conversations, formal meetings, and public speaking" engagements. Research indicates that introverts show high anxiety levels in all four of these forms of speaking. Many librarians teach classes or give conference presentations and as a result have become more comfortable in these settings. However, others, both librarians and paraprofessionals, may be more anxious about speaking in formal settings. If these individuals suffer from high communication anxiety, they are also less likely to engage in conversations on a smaller scale, such as team or individual discussions. If that happens, the flow of communication and ideas is inhibited. In a 2017 survey of librarians and library staff, social skills ranked last of five emotionally intelligent attributes, which supports the idea that communication challenges in social settings are indeed a problem for many library employees. The employee's personality or individual traits can cause communication apprehension. Studies indicate the level of communication anxiety is influenced by an individual's shyness and willingness to communicate. Differing from introversion (which is discussed later in the chapter), shyness is a behavior based in a fear of social disapproval. Shy individuals are quiet and reserved, prefer working alone, and are not perceived as leaders. For those in managerial positions, communication apprehension can lead them to make decisions without input from others in the organization. Because libraries often emphasize group work and team decision-making, communication apprehension can greatly inhibit an employee's participation. Additionally, such anxiety limits what information library workers may convey to their immediate supervisor about problems, operations, or issues. As a result, both the employee and the library organization suffer.[7]

Reduction of communication anxiety can be achieved with targeted intervention. Most common is a "systematic desensitization," where an individual is put into a relaxed state and then the anxiety stimuli is paired mentally with this calm state rather than an anxious one. Cognitive therapies focus on replacing anxiety-provoking thoughts with rational ones. For example, an anxious communicator may replace "my opinions will not be wanted" with more positive thoughts such as "all opinions are wanted." Communication skills training are one suggested solution for employees who need this assistance, because it will help individuals with speaking in front of others by lowering anxiety and boosting confidence. Finally, an alternative communication form (such as electronic media) may be used as it is not intimidating to the anxious communicator.[8]

When speaking in uncomfortable environments, introverted personalities for whom setting determines anxiety can impact communication in other ways. This is significant because many library staff members are introverted. The landmark 1994 ACRL study by Mary Jane Scherdin found 63 percent of staff introverted. However, a more recent international study of over 2,000 academic librarians found numbers somewhat reduced. Introverted and unadaptive library workers were most prevalent in cataloging (23.7 percent) and school librarianship (20 percent), although all academic library employees showed some evidence of these traits. Introverts take time to consider information and decipher it before responding. Because of that, they are "slower to make decisions, often exhausted by social situations, and prefer working alone." Unlike extroverts who may dominate a meeting by openly expressing their opinions, introverts may want to hold back and think more about the topic before commenting. Introverts may be reluctant to join teams that make group decisions because their tendency is to revert to the solace of their offices. Although studies show that all library staff do not fall into this category, many do, which complicates communication. Introverted leaders face challenges; although they are viewed positively by introverted workers, they tend to conduct fewer meetings and communicate through electronic media instead of face-to-face discussions. This minimizes their effectiveness as inclusive and mindful library leaders.[9]

In addition to working on confidence when speaking, there are other tools for introverted library workers. First, library workers should become aware of their preferred communication methods and determine if these slant towards more introverted or extroverted tendencies. As stated in the first chapter, it starts with the self. Next, introverted individuals can improve conversational skills and comfort levels by talking with others at networking events. Some find communication confidence in speaking groups such as Toastmasters or other public-speaking groups. Writing down important points prior to meetings may help remind the individual of what to say when engaged in group discussions. Finally, scheduling regular meetings with staff promotes conversation and personal interaction.[10]

Passive or mindless listening can also contribute to the breakdown in communication. This type of listening involves hearing words but missing the message being conveyed. A 1950 article by writer William H. Whyte in *Fortune* magazine expresses what this type of communication is like. He wrote, "The great enemy of communication, we find, is the illusion of it.

We have talked enough; but we have not listened. And by not listening we have failed to concede the immense complexity of our society—and thus the great gaps between ourselves and those with whom we seek understanding." Through the process of a message being encoded, delivered, and received, the listener must decipher elements including words, context, tone, and nonverbal expressions. This information exchange may also be influenced by distractions, time limitations, or other external factors. Passive or mindless listeners fall short in their awareness of this process and the elements of the information exchange. As a result, the clear communication that is desired by both parties fails.[11]

The importance of good listening skills cannot be emphasized enough. To assist patrons, librarians must listen closely to what they say. Additionally, their interpersonal communications with other staff and stakeholders, of which listening is a component, are essential to achieve library success. The authors' book *The Mindful Librarian: Connecting the Practice of Mindfulness to Librarianship* discusses in depth the practice of mindful listening and communication. Merideth Schwartz's article "Top Skills for Library Professionals: Careers 2016" lists communication skills—including active listening—as one of eleven critical attributes for the future.[12]

There are some tips to improve listening. Active listeners should be engaged and completely focused on the speaker's words, gestures, and tone to clearly decipher the intended message. Listeners who exchange information with speakers who have non-native accents must be alert to context, identify topics, and focus on meaning rather than individual sounds to improve this type of communication exchange. Asking questions or repeating points back to the sender to clarify are helpful for active engagement and information processing. Finally, responding in a respectful but honest way when encoding the return message will facilitate a continued positive information exchange.[13]

Active Listening Tips

---

1. Always look at the speaker.
2. Concentrate on the ideas being proposed.
3. Avoid framing your response . . . while he or she is still talking.
4. Listen to what you are saying.
5. Do not speak until the other person has stopped.[14]

Lack of empathy in communication exchanges can contribute to dysfunction. Empathy is a component of a competent communicator—an individual who is actively engaged and cognizant of the impact the exchange is having on the receiver. Communication researcher Chao Chen contends that an empathetic information exchange contains four parts. These are an understanding of the situation and emotions by the sender, recognizing the emotions experienced by the receiver, connecting the sender to the emotions being experienced by the receiver, and the sender expressing concern for the receiver's emotional state. Thus, a positive communication exchange involves empathy so an appropriate response is chosen. Conversely, a lack of empathy will lead to a poor communication exchange and may result in secondary acts of dysfunction or create ill-will.[15]

Personal Communication Exchange Lacking Empathy

Manager: Why aren't these items added to the catalog record yet?

Circulation staff: I am waiting to be trained on the software.

Manager: You've been here three months now. I thought John was training you.

Circulation staff: I have asked John several times to show me but he always responds he is too busy. It has been frustrating.

Manager: Then you should have come to me instead of just sitting around doing nothing all this time.

Lack of empathy is also a component of digital communications. Because the use of electronic communication is asynchronous, individuals are removed from dealing with the immediate reaction to the message. As a result, the potential empathy involved in the exchange is lost. Additionally, as will be discussed in chapter eight, the absence of verbal and nonverbal cues may not only contribute to a misunderstanding of the message being conveyed, but also limit the empathy involved in the exchange. Christopher Terry and Jeff Cain, both professors at the University of Kentucky College of Pharmacy, point out that the psychological disconnection between individuals experienced through electronic communication reduces empathy. They state, "the subconscious psychological factors associated with the online disinhibition effect negatively impact the likelihood that empathy will be expressed in digital environments." Because libraries increasingly rely constantly on evolving digital communications, this disconnection from a "real person" when communicating by such means may increase negative emotions.[16]

Empathy training has been shown to have a positive effect on employees. Gary Hosey, founder of the United Kingdom's Emotional Intelligence Company, provides some insight to these training components. The first step is improving basic "listening and learning behaviours" to understand what is being communicated. This is followed by using questions to expand and deepen conversations, which leads to empathy and appreciative listening. Currently, 20 percent of US employers utilize this training. This type of exchange is similar to a reference exchange where a librarian must determine the needs of a patron. However, empathic listening involves understanding the emotions attached to the communication and relating to how the patron may feel. Studies indicate this type of training does improve the level of understanding for in-person communication exchanges. Early indications point to a possible positive impact on electronic communications as well, but this awaits further research and exploration.[17]

Finally, dismissiveness can be a contributor to poor communication in the library organization. Imagine a librarian at a team meeting to discuss strategies to increase student usage of electronic resources. Perhaps the librarian came into the meeting with an idea for a weekly outreach to the student community center, but when the idea was presented the group leader listened impatiently, sat with her arms crossed at the table, and sighed with relief when the staff member stopped talking before she criticized the idea. This type of dismissive response shuts down the immediate discussion but also discourages future ideas from being suggested. One of the leading language theorist and philosophers, John Langshaw Austin, noted that words can change how individuals behave by being judgmental, influential, declaring intent, expressing feeling, or clarifying. A few dismissive words can immediately shut down communications. Corey Halaychik's *Lessons in Library Leadership: A Primer for Library Managers and Unit Leaders* explains how the use of nonverbal gestures such as "crossed arms, clenched fists, pointed fingers, invading personal space, and fiddling with objects" can indicate a closed-off or aggressive demeanor. These nonverbal actions also minimalize the communication exchange.[18]

To avoid such dismissive communication, active listening and receptiveness to all ideas is needed. The importance of active listening cannot be overstated. For some, active and open listening skills and awareness of body language may be acquired through communication training. Another attribute, respect, is also required. Respect for others in the communication flow not only facilitates a positive exchange but avoids embarrassing incidents or negatively impacting the self-esteem of coworkers.[19]

Thirteen Active Listening Skills

1. Restating/paraphrasing
2. Summarizing facts
3. Brief promptings
4. Reflecting on words expressed
5. Giving feedback
6. Labeling emotions for objectivity
7. Probing/questioning
8. Validating issue/problem/feelings
9. Effectively pausing
10. Utilizing silence
11. Using "I" in statements
12. Redirecting negative emotions
13. Discussing consequences of action/inaction[20]

IMPACTS OF COMMUNICATION

Poor communication has a negative impact on the library and its workers. First, it is linked to lower employee engagement. It also reduces authenticity and credibility, important attributes in library leadership. Finally, poor communication increases distrust and fear in the workplace.

The concept of employee engagement has been the focus of many studies since 1990, when William A. Kahn targeted three components—physical, cognitive, and emotional—which are involved in an individual's work engagement. Although other researchers have different views of the original employee engagement concept, most researchers still involve the original three areas that were the focus of Kahn's research. An engaged employee is more productive and connected to the organization. However, this positive fit can be derailed by poor communication. Communication has been linked to enhanced employee engagement. Two-way communication where the employee has a participative voice is positively correlated to engagement. Conversely, poor communication leads to disengagement. A 2012 Dale Carnegie study of 1,500 employees found that 61 percent of employees who were satisfied with their ability to have input into their organization were also found to be fully engaged. For library organizations, this means good, internal communication is necessary to promote employee's interest, contributions, and dedication.[21]

Authenticity is also linked to communication. This aligns with authentic leadership, which has been shown to be vital for establishing trust and confidence in followers. To maintain authenticity, library leaders must support what they say with their actions. Research indicates "a supervisor's consistency between words and actions increases employees' trust and dependence." Another component of authentic communication comes in the translation of conversations from employees through managers to higher levels in the organizations. This translation can break down if the communication is distorted, either unintentionally or intentionally. It is deemed authentic if it is "grounded through negotiations, and is not underlain by intrigue, manipulation or violence." Typically, library organizational structures are built so that organizational levels are headed by supervisors. There may be a supervisor of an area (e.g., head of adult programming or head of an information literacy team) or higher-level administrators such as managers or directors of divisions, branches, or the entire library organization. At every level, these supervisors are considered spokespersons for those under them. If they fail to correctly convey the voices of those they represent, inauthenticity results. If this occurs, managers lose credibility, and the respect and trust of employees who become unsatisfied, disengaged, and more likely to leave the organization.[22]

Communication plays a role in creating distrust, even fear, among employees or even between a worker and the library organization. Relationship-based distrust, as the previous chapters have expounded, is based in conflicts, insults, and gossip leading from low to highly toxic deviant behaviors. It also is defined "as negative expectations of the intentions or behavior of another," and in the work setting relates to executing work tasks poorly or maliciously. A failure to follow through creates distrust. As explained in chapter two's discussion of culture, distrust grows out of the lack of communication in the organization. Fear is a reflection of distrust as well as a barrier to communication and a reflection of distrust. When employees are fearful, it can affect their level of communication. Numerous studies have shown that fear leads to withholding information in a wide range of areas. Conversely, sharing information contributes positively to the organization's operation and increases innovation. Fear can be rooted in any number of causes, including fear of confrontation, reprisal, inadequacy, retaliation, and loss of job among others.[23]

To reduce fear, trust must be established in the library workplace. Communications must be open, participative, and relationship-based. For library leaders, "openness, honesty, and transparency" are important components to build and retain trust.[24] (Chapters nine and ten will discuss trust.)

Relational Communication Strategies

A. Frequent and two-way communication
B. Indirectness and informal modes
C. High in quality, accurate, complete, adequate, timely, credible
D. Participative with the open sharing of tacit and explicit knowledge
E. Shared meaning base
F. Open organizational and interorganizational communication climate
G. Frequent face-to-face interactions
H. Affiliative interpersonal relationship
I. Loose interorganizational teams
J. Electronic virtual communities and open information repositories
K. Interorganizational communities of practice[25]

CONCLUSION

The act of communication can be impacted by many variables. The library workplace, like many others, is typically a hierarchical organization. Communication challenges in the structure come from too little horizontal sharing, distorted messages flowing up and down, and blocked flow at any one of the structural levels. Library staff play a role in communication problems because of problems such as communication apprehension and introversion, which limit communication exchanges; passive listening; and dismissive communication. Additionally, a lack of empathy during message transactions reflects not only insufficient concern for how the messenger feels but also reveals a disconnection in the communication process. The collective result of these communication issues leads to real problems for libraries—lower employee engagement, reduced authenticity of leaders, decreased credibility of the message sender, and an increased distrust and fear among employees. Libraries should acknowledge the importance of promoting positive and open communication at all levels to successfully navigate their objectives and promote a positive employee workforce.

NOTES

1. Heidi Bartoo and Patricia M. Sias, "When Enough is Too Much: Communication Apprehension and Employee Information Experiences," *Communication Quarterly* 52, no. 1 (Winter 2004): 15.

2. Akua Ahyia Adu-Oppong and Emmanuel Agyin-Birikorang, "Communication in the Workplace: Guidelines for Improving Effectiveness," *Global Journal of Commerce and Management Perspective* 3, no. 5 (2014): 208; "Models of Communication," *International Association of Communication Activists*, www.iacact.com/?q=models; David Foulger, "Models of Communication Process," http://davis.foulger.info/research/unifiedModelOfCommunication.htm.

3. Foulger, "Models of Communication Process"; Sneha Mishra, "Transactional Model of Communication," *Businesstopia*, www.businesstopia.net/communication/transactional-model-communication.

4. Charles R. McConnell, "Making Upward Communication Work for Your Employees: Channels, Barriers, and the Open Door (Part 1 of 3)," *The Health Care Supervisor* (Gaithersburg, MD) 4, no. 4 (July 1986): 75; "Advantages and Disadvantages of Horizontal Communication," *The Business Communication*, https://thebusinesscommunication.com/advantages-and-disadvantages-of-horizontal-communication/http://open.lib.umn.edu/exploringbusiness/chapter/8-5-communication-channels/.

5. Richard Moniz, Jo Henry, Joe Eshleman, Lisa Moniz, and Howard Slutzky, "Stressors and Librarians: How Mindfulness Can Help," *College and Research Libraries* 77, no. 11 (2016): 535; John M. Grohol, "Become a Better Listener: Active Listening," Psych Central, https://psychcentral.com/lib/become-a-better-listener-active-listening/.

6. Douglas Stone, Bruce Patton, and Sheila Heen, *Difficult Conversations: How to Discuss What Matters Most* (New York, NY: Penguin Books, 2000), 132; Jean Anderson, "How to Enjoy France's Right-to-Disconnect Law without Living in France," *Quartz Media*, updated January 3, 2017, https://qz.com/876892/france-passed-a-law-banning-work-emails-after-work-but-you-can-do-it-yourself/.

7. James C. McCroskey, "Oral Communication Apprehension: A Summary of Recent Theory and Research," *Human Communication Research* 4, no. 1 (1977): 79; James C. McCroskey, "Communication Apprehension: What Have We Learned in the Last Four Decades?," *Human Communication: A Publication of the Pacific and Asian Communication Association* 12, no. 2 (2009): 164; Travis L. Russ, "The Relationship between Theory X/Y: Assumptions and Communication Apprehension," *Leadership and Organization Development Journal* 34, no. 3 (2013): 241; Susan K. Opt and Donald A. Loffredo, "Rethinking Communication Apprehension: A Myers-Briggs Perspective," *The Journal of Psychology* 134, no. 5 (2000): 566; McCroskey, "Communication Apprehension"; Russ, "The Relationship between Theory X/Y," 241–42.

8. Hilary Taylor Holbrook, "Communication Apprehension: The Quiet Student in Your Classroom," Eric Digest (1987): 3; Lynne Kelly and James A. Keaten, "Treating Communication Anxiety: Implications of the Communibiological Paradigm," *Communication Education* 49, no. 1 (2000): 51; Bartoo and Sias, "When Enough is Too Much."

9. Jennifer A Bartlett, "New and Noteworthy: The Yin and Yang of Personality Types." *Library Leadership and Management* (2002): 1–5, http://nclive.org/cgi-bin/nclsm?url =http://search.proquest.com/docview/1030773565?accountid=13217; J. M. Williamson, A. E. Pemberton, and J. W. Lounsbry, "Personality Traits of Individuals in Different Specialties of Librarianship," *Journal of Documentation* 64, no. 2 (2008): 281; Matthew Kuofie, Dana Stephens-Craig, and Richard Dool, "An Overview Perception of Introverted Leaders," *International Journal of Global Business* 8, no. 1 (2015): 64, 101.

10. Kuofie, Craig, and Dool, "An Overview Perception of Introverted Leaders."

11. Trevor Bentley, "The Special Skills of Listening," *Management Development Review* 6, no. 6 (1993): 16; Garson O'Toole, "Exploring the Origins of Quotations: The Biggest Problem in Communication Is the Illusion That It Has Taken Place," http://quote investigator.com/2014/08/31/illusion/.

12. Meredith Schwartz, "Top Skills for Tomorrow's Librarians | Careers 2016," *Library Journal* (2016), http://lj.libraryjournal.com/2016/03/careers/top-skills-for-tomorrows -librarians-careers-2016/#_.

13. Dawn Amsberry, "Using Effective Listening Skills with International Patrons," *Reference Services Review* 37, no. 1 (2009): 14.

14. Harry R. Carter, "Going for the Gold: Learn How to Listen," *Firehouse*, August 2014: 94.

15. Chao Chen, "Empathy in Language Learning and Its Inspiration to the Development of Intercultural Communicative Competence," *Theory and Practice in Language Studies* 3, no. 12 (2013): 2268.

16. Christopher Terry and Jeff Cain, "The Emerging Issue of Digital Empathy," *American Journal of Pharmaceutical Education* 80, no. 4, article 58, (2016): 2.

17. Stephanie Sparrow, "Empathy, Empathy, They All Want Empathy," *Training and Coaching Today* (March 2007): 17; Lublin, Joann S. "Management: Companies Try New Strategy: Empathy." *Wall Street Journal*, June 22, 2016, http://nclive.org/cgi-bin/ nclsm?url=http://search.proquest.com/docview/1798615664?accountid=13217; Archana Shrivastava, "Active Empathic Listening as a Tool for Better Communication." *International Journal of Marketing and Business Communication* 3, no. 3 (2014): 14, http://nclive.org/cgi-bin/nclsm?url=http://search.proquest.com/docview/ 1733234922?accountid=13217.

18. Etsuko Oishi, "Austin's Speech Act Theory and the Speech Situation," *Esercizi Filosofici* 1, (2006):4, www2.units.it/eserfilo/art106/oishi106.pdf; Corey Halaychick, *Lessons for Library Leadership: A Primer for Library Managers and Unit Leaders* (Chandos-Elsevier, Boston, 2016): 109.

19. Halaychik, "Lessons for Library Leadership."

20. John M. Grohol, "Becoming a Better Listener: Active Listening," *PsychCentral*, https:// psychcentral.com/lib/become-a-better-listener-active-listening/.

21. Mary Welch, "The Evolution of the Employee Engagement Concept: Communication Implications," *Corporate Communications: An International Journal* 16, no. 4 (2011): 332; Minijeong Kang, Minjung Sung, "How Symmetrical Employee Communication Leads to Employee Engagement and Positive Employee Communication Behaviors: The Mediation of Employee-Organization Relationships," *Journal of Communication Management, London* 2, no. 1 (2017): 82–102; Mary Welch, "The Evolution of the Employee Engagement Concept: Communication Implications," *Corporate Communications: An International Journal* 16, no. 4 (2011): 338; Dale Carnegie Training, "Dale Carnegie Training Reports Study Findings on Employee Engagement," *Close-Up Media*, Inc., February 18, 2013.

22. Dan-Shang Want and Chia-Chun Hsieh, "The Effect of Authentic Leadership on Employee Trust and Employee Engagement," *Social Behavior and Personality* 42, no. 4 (2013): 621 and Simon Torp, "Authenticity in Management Metaconversations," *Journal of Communication Management* 14, no. 3 (2010): 207.

23. Taina Savolainen, Palmira Lopez-Fresno, and Mirjami Ikonen, "Trust-Communication Dyad in Inter-Personal Workplace Relationships—Dynamics of Trust Deterioration and Breach," *The Electronic Journal of Knowledge Management* 12, no. 4: 234–35; Jennifer J. Kish-Gephart, James R. Detert, Linda Klebe Trevino, and Amy C. Edmonson, "Silenced by Fear: The Nature, Sources, and Consequences of Fear at Work," *Research in Organizational Behavior* 29, (2009): 165, 234.

24. Savolainen, Lopez-Fresno, and Ikonen, "Trust-Communication Dyad in Inter-Personal Workplace Relationships," 239.

25. Bill Donaldson, Thomas O'Toole, and Mary Holden, "A Relational Communication Strategy for Successful Collaborative Innovation in Business-to-Business Markets," in *Strategies and Communications for Innovations*, eds. Michael Hulsmann and Nicole Pfeffermann (Berlin: London: Springer, 2011), 213.

7

CONFLICT MANAGEMENT

Conflicts are a normal part of life and the library workplace. As pointed out by Maria Dijkstra, Bianca Beersma, and Arne Evers, "Interpersonal conflict is clearly a consequence of people interacting with each other and therefore a normal experience in society and in organizational life." Speaking specifically about the workplace, Carsten De Dreu states, "Workplace conflict emerges when one party—be it an individual or group of individuals—perceives its goals, values, or opinions being thwarted by an interdependent counterpart." The past twenty to thirty years have seen a significant amount of scholarship related to conflict in the workplace in general. Other authors have pointed out that in recent decades conflict has increased "enhanced by considerable uncertainty, changes in technology, market fluctuations and the global economy." All these factors have had a significant impact in the library world, especially technology. To a much lesser degree, some literature has touched upon factors that relate specifically to libraries. Although this book addresses conflict throughout, it is necessary to break out and explore conflicts and conflict management in more detail.[1]

According to Raquel Gabriel,

> Although there is a stereotype of the library as a calm oasis, I am sure
> that every librarian would scoff at the suggestion that conflict doesn't

exist within our institutions. Whether it is with the communities we serve, our colleagues, or our supervisors, I find it hard to imagine any library—just like any other workplace—without some level of conflict that needs to be managed and addressed.[2]

Again, the topic of conflict and its management will overlap with virtually every other chapter in this book. It involves a consideration of everything from workplace communication and culture to extreme examples such as workplace bullying and violence. The intent, however, is to explore the literature to consider why conflicts arise in the library workplace; what models, theories, or instruments might be relevant for understanding it better; and determining the best approaches to take across circumstances and situations. Most individuals understand that library managers must develop their skills in conflict management. According to Jerrell Coggburn, R. Paul Battaglio, and Mark Bradbury, "managers recognize that conflict is inevitable, and that managing conflict is an essential responsibility." Seminal research on conflict has indicated that it may constitute an average of 30 percent of a given manager's job. Although this was an overall finding for many workplaces, this does not sound out of line for library managers. It might even underestimate time spent managing conflict. That said, although the focus here is on managers, this can have wider application. How do librarians interact and manage conflict with each other in lateral relationships? How do librarians manage conflict with supervisors? How are conflicts between workgroups handled? Why is it that one of the most challenging conflict management situations is that between library staff and patrons? And, most importantly, what can be done to do better at managing conflict that arises from or fosters dysfunction in the library workplace?[3]

Why should library staff care so much about conflict? Conflict in the workplace, especially when handled improperly, has led to a multitude of dysfunctional outcomes for employees and organizations, which include low job satisfaction and performance, burnout, turnover, multiple health issues, psychological strain on employees, rigidity in thinking, and poor quality of life.[4]

THEORIES AND APPROACHES

As has been discussed previously, "a critical first step in conflict management is to assess the amount, source, level and style of handling the conflict." This latter piece is crucial and relates directly to some of the foundational theories and approaches in successfully handling conflict. According to M. Afzalur Rahim, a pioneer in the scholarship of conflict management, the very first studies of conflict and conflict management focused on how much concern one party had for himself and how much concern he had for others. Although this model is simplistic, it is useful because it led to other models that included this basic duality. Another important element of conflict management is to consider whether the conflict is about a task (or process) or relational. The former can be positive while the latter tends to lead to dysfunction much more readily if not handled well.[5]

Besides the dualistic model that considers the difference between one's self and another entity in conflict management, the most frequently used framework for conflict management considers five basic strategies or styles. Discussions on these strategies have varied widely concerning when they are best used and because of personal preferences toward certain strategies.

- *Avoiding* occurs when an individual has little concern for either herself or the other involved in the conflict. On the surface, this may sound negative, but the reality is that there are some limited cases (to be discussed below) where this strategy may not be entirely inappropriate.
- *Obliging* is a circumstance where one party in a conflict has a higher concern for the other and less for herself. Therefore, she may seek a solution that meets the needs of the other while disregarding her own.
- *Dominating* is when someone has high regard for his own perspective but little for the other party. In this case, a "selfish" solution is sought.
- *Integrating* is an approach that tends to focus on problem-solving and finding common ground to meet the needs of both parties. It is generally the most recommended approach, but may not be the best solution in every situation.
- *Compromising* is an approach where a moderate amount of concern leads to a solution designed to incorporate some of the concerns from each side of a conflict.[6]

Avoiding will typically lead to bigger problems. However, in some instances this strategy is useful. If a conflict is trivial or transient in nature, avoidance keeps the incident from becoming a bigger problem than is warranted. It is important to consider the time involved to reach a collective solution. Although not generally recommended, in rare cases "confronting the other party outweighs the benefits [of avoidance]." For example, it might not be worth addressing a minor or fleeting issue with a difficult colleague or supervisor.[7]

Avoidance does, however, have negative consequences. One study that explored the effectiveness of teams highlighted another danger or dysfunction of this approach, noting that teams that used this overall strategy

> avoided difficult conversations in the interest of preserving interpersonal relationships and never really seemed to face the difficult task of integrating various interests and perspectives to create a superior team product. Thus, [participants] maintained interpersonal harmony at the cost of relatively poor task performance.[8]

Avoidance can lead to other problems. For example, individual members who internalize concerns that they can't address may suffer psychological damage. Avoidance can also lead to incivility or an explosive confrontation down the line.

Obliging is another behavior that, on its surface, has elements of dysfunction. It requires an individual to sacrifice interests that conflict with the other's. In some conflicts, the outcome for one matters significantly more than the other. In such a circumstance giving in would not necessarily be the worst option. It can also be used to support the ideas of others in a positive, but not necessarily productive, way. Obliging does limit "creative problem solving . . . [and] opportunities for joint gains."[9]

Dominating is the flip side of obliging. Dominating conflict management not only prevents opportunities for collaboration, but may also lay the foundation for reduced cooperation and conflict resolution. When continued over time, such actions may be construed as bullying behavior (discussed in chapter four). However, there may be an urgent situation where action needs to be taken and a decision needs to be made. Generally, this approach damages relationships, however, so its recommended use is extremely selective.

Integrating is worth focusing on somewhat more closely than the other approaches or strategies. Although more time-consuming, it has the greatest potential for success in most situations. According to Margaret Hopkins and Robert Yonker, "the Integrating style of handling conflict is directly associated with the ability to effectively solve complex problems." Likewise, Marilyn Fox, Kathleen Dale, and Bradley Mayer found that the work of other researchers identifies the integrative approach as most effective overall, and that "the integrating strategy was perceived as the most appropriate and effective strategy because it focuses on both the other and the self." The two key elements to this approach are that it is predicated upon respect for both parties in a conflict and is focused on problem-solving. According to

Jose Leon-Perez, Francisco Medina, Alicia Arenas, and Lourdes Mundu-ate, "Problem solving is an assertive and cooperative way of dealing with conflicts and involves an attempt to work with the other person to find a solution which fully satisfies the concerns of both parties; therefore, it helps to reduce the intensity and hostility of conflict."[10]

Compromising resembles the integrative approach, but involves more give-and-take than straightforward problem-solving. In other words, it is not so much a win-win that is sought but a partial win for both sides. There are some circumstances where this is appropriate; it generally tends to be more effective than dominating, obliging, or avoiding. For example, there may be intractable conflict when there is little trust, and a problem-solving approach won't work. In the meantime, compromise can be used to get some "wins" for each side and possibly build some trust.

Five Strategies of Conflict Management

1. Avoiding	3. Dominating	5. Compromising[11]
2. Obliging	4. Integrating	

HANDLING PERSONALITY AND CULTURAL DIFFERENCES

Personality and cultural differences can have an enormous impact on how people perceive and handle conflict. One study has highlighted how having an internal (versus external) locus of control can predispose someone to be better able to handle conflict. In the conclusion of their study about inter-nal locus of control and conflict, Dijkstra, Beersma, and Evers write, "We have demonstrated that employees who experience high levels of internal locus of control suffer less from interpersonal conflict in terms of psy-chological strain than those who experience low levels of internal locus of control." Sometimes personal issues can also be significant; these include work-personal life balance, political disposition, interpretation of laws or procedures, and overall values. A study by Dannii Y. Yeung, Helene Fung, and Darius Chan determined that age can play a significant role because older employees tend to use more passive strategies and younger employees tend to employ what they deem destructive strategies.[12]

One of the central ways that individuals can enhance their overall dis-position and even craft their own personalities is by cultivating emotional intelligence. This topic was covered in much greater detail in chapter one, but it is relevant to touch upon it again briefly. As mentioned, there are different strategies that may be applied to given situations. According to Hopkins and Yonker, who explored the connection between emotional intelligence and effective conflict management, "individuals in a conflict situation require the skills and ability to make informed judgments in order to effectively manage the conflict. Emotions are a contributing factor to an individual's conceptualization of a conflict and the decision-making capability needed to effectively manage the conflict." They add that the "repertoire of EI abilities enables a manager to respond appropriately and avoid a narrow, one-size-fits-all approach to different conflict scenarios." Research conducted by Jennifer Lawless and Aurora Trif noted that their research "supports the view that conflict management is adjusted by . . . managers to the conflict situation and the organisational aspects, rather than being relatively stable depending on their personal aspects." Thus, it is worth realizing that while personality is a factor, emotional intelligence allows for flexibility within an individual's personality that can be beneficial in managing conflict.[13]

Cultural differences can be a significant factor in managing conflicts. According to Joan Howland,

> In librarianship we have witnessed a slow, but steady, growth in the diversity of our profession with an increasing number of non-whites in upper management positions. We can be encouraged by a number of initiatives, particularly the American Library Association (ALA) Spectrum Scholarship program, which will ensure that bright, motivated individuals from diverse backgrounds are attracted to librarianship and receive the financial support to pursue the requisite graduate education.[14]

Others have written about the general differences between Western and non-Western approaches to conflict management. According to Hannah-Hanh Nguyen and Jie Yang, "Cross-cultural researchers have evidenced that the existing western-oriented conceptual framework of conflict management (based on the self-interest perspective) may be inadequate in describing eastern conflict-managing behaviors." They report that studies have shown that, compared to American workers, Chinese workers tend to shy away from direct confrontation. The implication of this research is that there may be no single best model to apply. Managers should be aware that individuals sharing similar cultural values are the most likely to cooperate within a group and developing bridges and commonalities among the group members may be necessary to avoid conflicts.[15]

Howland goes on to highlight some other key elements that contribute challenges regarding conflict management in the modern library. From her perspective, the fluctuating power dynamics that arise from the influx of a more diverse workforce coupled with rapid change in library services can be the source of conflict between newer and veteran librarians. Her solution is to take

> an approach that strategically integrates veteran power holders in an organization with new hires from diverse backgrounds through committee work, teams, and project pairings. This approach provides an avenue for individuals from different backgrounds to become better acquainted and to learn to respect one another.[16]

Another challenge Howland explores is how to manage a wide range of views and opinions. While this is a boon to our libraries, it is important to be deliberate when choosing approaches to address it. Citing Janis R. Joplin and Catherine Daus, she states:

> Synthesizing diverse opinions, finding shared ground, and reaching at least some modicum of agreement may be one of the most time-consuming, emotionally-wrenching, and energy-draining activities any of us can undertake. . . The critical exercise is to separate substance from rhetoric and to determine the essential content of the message, rather than get lost in the manner of delivery or the particular characteristics of the person expressing the opinion.[17]

A perceived lack of empathy is another challenge. This is related to the process of addressing issues of favoritism. Although this is a familiar challenge, it could grow as librarians are recruited from more diverse backgrounds. Understanding the different perspectives that employees bring to the profession is necessary to prevent impenetrable cliques or in-and-out groups from forming. Howland makes two additional points. The first concerns the need to fight tokenism and banish suspicions that an individual was hired to increase diversity. Hires should be respected because they have the qualities required to do the job. Everyone, especially management, must be sensitive to—or rather advocate for—diversity. Howland next recommends an outlook that views challenges as opportunities:

Opportunities will be realized only by those individuals who discipline themselves to be focused, astute, creative, non-judgmental, and action-oriented. By confronting challenges head on—regardless of whether these challenges are driven by miscommunication, intolerance, ignorance, insecurity, callousness, irresponsibility, or lethargy—we can utilize the knowledge gained to create strategic advantages for ourselves and those constituencies that we wish to support.[18]

Six Challenges in Managing Conflict

1. Fluctuating power
2. Managing diverse opinions
3. Increasing empathy
4. Addressing tokenism
5. Holding everyone accountable to respect diversity
6. Consider challenges to be opportunities[19]

Howland is not the only author to explore the intersection of diversity and conflict management in the library workplace. Gabriel speaks to the critical need for managers to be sensitive to diversity within the organization. One of her suggestions is that the manager or an appropriately assigned mentor reach out to new staff and ensure they do not feel isolated. She also offers the useful suggestion to consider how meetings are run to make sure everyone gets an opportunity to provide input. This can be straightforward. One of the most common approaches is to ask, "Have we heard from everyone?" and then request that those who have not shared their thoughts do so.[20]

In closing this discussion, it is worth noting that diversity is a great benefit to any library. Employing people from different backgrounds and with different views can lead to better services, solutions, and staff development. It is just important that this be handled with care, perhaps by utilizing some of the ideas shared above. This will be briefly revisited at the end of the chapter.

SITUATIONAL CONFLICT MANAGEMENT

Andrew Carton and Basima Tewfik make the case that "the strategies appropriate for managing one type of conflict may systematically backfire by using other types." Similarly, the kinds of conflict librarians may encounter occur within a variety of contexts. Conflict might exist between an employee and subordinate, between employees, between employees and customers (or patrons), and even between workgroups (both internal and external to the library).[21]

Conflict between groups or subgroups is often overlooked. According to Carton and Tewfik, "subgroups can become isolated from one another, causing differences among them to become so extreme that teams struggle to converge on solutions. Teams can reduce this risk by employing boundary spanners—members who keep lines of communication open between subgroups." In libraries, this could relate to units within a library or external units. For example, academic libraries might find themselves in conflict with another division of the institution. There are some interesting solutions that can be applied. For instance, at Johnson & Wales University in Charlotte, North Carolina, the library staff has met with other workgroups on campus such as the Center for Academic Support to build mutual understanding and to determine shared goals. Similarly, liaison roles may extend beyond academic departments and into other key workgroup areas on a college or university campus (e.g., counseling services, tutoring services, and career development). There are many ways that student services overlap. If these overlaps are seen as shared, as opposed to part of isolated silos, campus services will be much more effective overall. Again, liaisons play a key role in connecting these otherwise separate and conflicting work groups and can be referred to as "boundary spanners."[22]

Conflicts between manager and employee or between individual staff members are most typically the focus of research. These two potential arenas for conflict permeate this book. One of the worst or most taxing situations, however, has been shown to be the relationship with customers or patrons. According to a study conducted by Michael Sliter, Shuang Yueh Pui, Katherine Sliter, and Steve Jex, "the results generally supported the assertion that customer IC is a stronger predictor of negative employee outcomes than coworker IC." One theory behind this idea is that there is even less control over relationships with customers than with colleagues and this leads to more emotional labor or stress.[23]

Before moving on, it is worth mentioning a study about positive conflict and how it can benefit interpersonal work communication. Generally, we think of anger as negative, but it can have an interesting positive impact in some circumstances. A study by Lisa Stickney and Deanna Geddes explored what happened when employees vented their anger to other colleagues. Surprisingly, they determined that this could, in some cases, lead to positive change. It did so by forming a bond of sorts between the person who vented and a prospective ally who was then able to advocate in a positive manner for change. They found "that observer anger advocacy is related to perceptions of *positive* [emphasis added] change at both interpersonal and organizational levels. Interpersonally, advocates report an improved relationship with their angry colleague, and organizationally, they report positive changes regarding the situation that triggered the anger episode."[24]

HEALTHY VERSUS NON-HEALTHY CONFLICT MANAGEMENT

According to Coggburn, Battaglio, and Bradbury, "When organizations practice constructive conflict management, employees should be able to express their opinions in a climate of openness, even if that means disagreeing with management. This should lead to greater job satisfaction and ensure a fuller airing of alternatives, better decisions, and better performance." In fact, one of the most dysfunctional approaches to conflict is to minimize it too much. They continue, "Managerial practices resulting in too little conflict may shape and reflect an organization hypersensitive to discord, dissent and innovation."[25] As noted by Craig Runde, the director of the Center for Conflict Dynamics at Eckerd College,

> When conflict is managed well, it can lead to improvements in creativity and innovation, higher-quality decision-making, and improved implementation. The creativity and innovation come from more robust discussions where one idea leads to another, and the process begets new and better solutions. These same discussions can allow for more rigorous vetting of the ideas, which leads to better decisions.[26]

Runde goes on to discuss the importance of training for employees in this regard (a point we will come back to at the end of this chapter).

Although there are many sources of unhealthy management of conflict and dysfunction, a stifling bureaucracy is a critical concern when attempting to create more positive or functional intent. Shweta and Srirang Jha offer this warning, "Bureaucracies and departmentalization have often been linked to stifling basic human instincts of independence and self-actualization, thus causing hostilities and negative emotions." Again, one key factor is whether conflict is task-related. According to Carton and Tewfik, many studies indicate that "moderate amounts of task conflict improve performance when the other forms of conflict are dormant." Such meditated conflict can lead to a much deeper understanding of issues that would not have come about any other way. According to Olu Ojo and Abolade Dupe Adesubomi, "better ideas are produced, people were forced to search for new approvals, longstanding problems . . . were dealt with, people were forced to clarify their view, the tension stimulated interest and creativity, and people had a chance to test their capacities."[27]

KEY CONFLICT MANAGEMENT SKILLS

- Act as a role model, especially when it comes to demonstrating the skill of cooperation. All librarians need to do more of this. Changing how conflict is handled begins with one person at a time.[28]
- Foster and encourage group unity and shared purpose in the library workplace. Obviously, management plays a significant role, but any library staff member can contribute to this. Focus on common bonds among staff when managing conflict. In other words, highlight shared or overlapping goals on a regular basis.
- Move towards a more internal locus. Although evidence indicates that having an internal or external locus of control may be a relatively stable aspect of personality, and that internal locus results in increased resilience and leads to more effective resolutions. This could be promoted by consciously recognizing the aspect of work over which you have the greatest control.[29]
- Increase the amount of coaching or training available to managers. According to Tahir Saeed Shazia, Almas Anis-ul-Haq, and GSK Niazi, "Organizations should train leaders to ensure that their primary focus is on people management. This means reducing anxiety and anger among employees, promoting optimism and confidence, developing people's skills, helping them manage conflict, building trust within and across teams and ensuring alignment around achieving the best possible organizational aims and objectives." Brubaker et al. suggest that "coaches can conduct in-depth rehearsals of anticipated discussions that the party is concerned about and help them more fully

explore the conflict and its impact." They further suggest that organizations move "from intervention to prevention" through ongoing training in conflict management.[30]

- Establishing egalitarian norms while reinforcing understanding for hierarchical differences can benefit in managing and preventing conflict. In some situations, rotating responsibilities when appropriate can be helpful.[31]

- Recognize emotions and how they are impacting the conflict management process. Enforce a cool-down period if necessary. Not every conflict needs to be solved on the spot.[32]

- Implement mindful practices, as discussed by the authors of this book and others. In the words of Craig Runde "mindfulness approaches have been shown to change brain function in a way that allows negative emotions to recede and a more positive mood to reemerge. With it comes an emotional balance that allows people to be able to engage the conflict more effectively." This could involve not just mindfulness meditation and similar practices but also "writing in a journal, frequently assessing strengths and weaknesses, and actively seeking directed feedback from others." Authors Sean Valentine, Lynn Godkin, and Philip Varca state that "mindfulness is also known to augment individuals' information processing in a manner that prompts increased self-control and subsequent positive behavior."[33]

- Remain flexible and open and encourage others to do so. Runde offers this excellent advice: "Managing conflict involves both talking and listening to others. Of the two functions, listening is often the more important and, for most people, more difficult."[34]

- Be proactive, especially as a library manager. Do not let conflict fester, especially relational conflicts. A study of conflict management in libraries by Vijayakumar Mallappa and Manoj Kumar K.S. states that in libraries "the administrative authorities should try to detect the conflict among the library staff in [its] initial stage itself, otherwise it will lead to distraction."[35]

- Appoint a devil's advocate to foster discussion about areas of potential conflict, for example, when participants rely heavily on assumptions. Mary Krautter, head of reference and instructional services at the University of North Carolina at Greensboro, writes, "The devil's advocate can be a potentially valuable factor in promoting an atmosphere of openness and creative problem solving without increasing unproductive conflict."[36]

CONCLUSION

Everyone deals with conflict. It must be addressed. It may be that its nature matters less than how well individuals can center and prepare themselves to respond appropriately. As highlighted throughout this book, librarians are in the midst of radical change. This adds to our need to approach conflict management from a positive and non-dysfunctional manner. According to Ojo and Adesubomi,

> Changes . . . are always with us but [they are] not always welcome. Resistance to change is natural and it arises because of habit once established, fear of the unknown, conformity to customary expected ways of behaviour, and misunderstanding the implications of change and individual differences. [37]

Librarians need to model change, keep their minds open, and constructively approach conflict management.

NOTES

1. Maria Dijkstra, Bianca Beersma, and Arne Evers, "Reducing Conflict-Related Employee Strain: The Benefits of an Internal Locus of Control and a Problem-Solving Conflict Management Strategy," *Work and Stress* 25, no. 2 (April 2011): 167; Carsten K.W. De Dreu, "The Virtue and Vice of Workplace Conflict: Food for (Pessimistic) Thought," *Journal of Organizational Behavior* 29, no. 1 (January 2008); Marilyn L. Fox, Kathleen Dale, and Bradley Mayer, "Conflict Management Style, Transformational Leadership and Follower's Attitudes: A Test of Direct Effects and the Mediating Role of Transformational Leadership," *Leadership and Organizational Management Journal* no. 4 (December 2013): 10.

2. Raquel J. Gabriel, "Managing Conflict," *Law Library Journal* 103, no. 4 (Fall 2011): 686.

3. Jerrell D. Coggburn, R. Paul Battaglio, and Mark D. Bradbury, "Employee Job Satisfaction and Organizational Performance: The Role of Conflict Management," *International Journal of Organization Theory and Behavior* 17, no. 4 (Winter 2014): 503; Andrew M. Carton and Basima A. Tewfik, "Perspective—A New Look at Conflict Management in Work Groups," *Organization Science* 27, no. 5 (September 2016): 1125.

4. Dijkstra, Beersma, and Evers, "Reducing Conflict-Related Employee Strain."; Fox, Dale, and Mayer, "Conflict Management Style," 11; De Dreu, "The Virtue and Vice of Workplace Conflict," 13.

5. Valentina Bruk-Lee, "Conflict Management," in *Encyclopedia of Industrial and Organizational Psychology* (Thousand Oaks, CA: Sage Publications, 2007) and M. Afzalur Rahim, "A Measure of Styles of Handling Interpersonal Conflict," *Academy of Management Journal* 26, no. 2 (June 1983): 368.

6. Jennifer Lawless and Aurora Trif, "Managing Interpersonal Conflicts at Work by Line Managers," *Irish Journal of Management* 35, no. 1 (April 2016): 76.

7. Ibid.

8. Kristin J. Behfar, Randall Peterson, Elizabeth Mannix, and William M. K. Trochim, "The Critical Role of Conflict Resolution in Teams: A Close Look at the Links between Conflict Type, Conflict Management Strategies, and Team Outcomes," *Journal of Applied Psychology* 93, no. 1 (January 2008): 184.

9. Raymond A. Friedman, Simon T. Tidd, Steven C. Currall, and James C. Tsai, "What Goes Around Comes Around: The Impact of Personal Conflict Style on Work Conflict and Stress," *The International Journal of Conflict Management* 11, no. 1(200): 39.

10. Margaret M. Hopkins and Robert D. Yonker, "Managing Conflict with Emotional Intelligence: Abilities that Make a Difference," *Journal of Management Development* 34, no. 2 (2015): 226–244; Fox, Dale, and Mayer, "Conflict Management Style," 13; Jose M. Leon-Perez, Francisco J. Medina, Alicia Arenas, and Lourdes Munduate, "The Relationship between Interpersonal Conflict and Workplace Bullying," *Journal of Managerial Psychology* 30, no. 3 (2015): 258.

11. Bruk-Lee, "Conflict Management."

12. Dijkstra, Beersma, and Evers, "Reducing Conflict-Related Employee Strain," 177; Coggburn, Battaglio, and Bradbury, "Employee Job Satisfaction and Organizational Performance," 500; Dannii Y. Yeung, Helene H. Fung, and Darius Chan, "Managing Conflict at Work: Comparison between Younger and Older Managerial Employees," *International Journal of Conflict Management* 26, no. 3 (2015): 357.

13. Hopkins and Yonker, "Managing Conflict with Emotional Intelligence," 237; Lawless and Trif, "Managing Interpersonal Conflicts," 85.

14. Joan S. Howland, "Challenges of Working in a Multicultural Environment," *Journal of Library Administration* 33, no. 1–2 (2001): 107.

15. Hannah-Hanh D. Nguyen and Jie Yang, "Chinese Employees' Interpersonal Conflict Management Strategies," *International Journal of Conflict Management* 23, no. 4 (2012): 384; Smaranda Boros, Nicoleta Meslec, Petru L. Curseu, and Wilco Emons, "Struggles for Cooperation: Conflict Resolution Strategies in Multicultural Groups," *Journal of Managerial Psychology* 24, no. 5 (2010): 551.

16. Howland, "Challenges of Working in a Multicultural Environment," 109–11.

17. Ibid., 112.

18. Ibid., 114–18.

19. Ibid., 109–18.

20. Gabriel, "Managing Conflict," *L* 688–89.

21. Carton and Tewfik, "Perspective—A New Look at Conflict Management," 1125.

22. Ibid.

23. Michael T. Sliter, Shuang Yueh Pui, Katherine A. Sliter, and Steve M. Jex. "The Differential Effects of Interpersonal Conflict from Customers and Coworkers: Trait Anger as a Moderator," *Journal of Occupational Health Psychology* 16, no. 4 (2011): 433.

24. Lisa T. Stickney and Deanna Geddes, "More Than Just 'Blowing off Steam': The Roles of Anger and Advocacy in Promoting Positive Outcomes at Work," *Negotiation and Conflict Management Research* 9, no. 2 (2016): 150.

25. Coggburn, Battaglio, and Bradbury, "Employee Job Satisfaction and Organizational Performance," 503–505.

26. Craig E. Runde, "Conflict Competence in the Workplace," *Employment Relations Today* 40, no. 4 (December 15, 2013): 26.

27. Shweta Jha and Srirang Jha, "Antecedents of Interpersonal Conflicts at Workplace," *Journal of Management and Public Policy* 1, no. 2 (2010): 75; Carton and Tewfik, "Perspective—A New Look at Conflict Management," 1127; Olu Ojo and Abolade Dupe Adesubomi, "Impact of Conflict Management on Employees' Performance in Public Organisation in Nigeria," *Studies In Business and Economics* 9, no. 1 (2014): 128.

28. Fox, Dale, and Mayer, "Conflict Management Style, Transformational Leadership and Follower's Attitudes," 26.

29. Fox, Dale, and Mayer, "Conflict Management Style," 13; Carton and Tewfik, "Perspective—A New Look at Conflict Management," 129; Dykstra, Beersma, and Evers, "Reducing Conflict-Related Employee Strain," 178–79.

30. Craig E. Runde, "Conflict Competence in the Workplace"; Hopkins and Yonker, "Managing Conflict with Emotional Intelligence," 240; Neil H. Katz and Linda T. Flynn, "Understanding Conflict Management Systems and Strategies in the Workplace: A Pilot Study," *Conflict Resolution Quarterly* 30, no. 4 (Summer 2013): 405; Tahir Saeed Shazia, Almas M. Anis-ul-Haq, and GSK Niazi, "Leadership Styles: Relationship with Conflict Management Styles," *International Journal of Conflict Management* 25, no. 3 (2014): 214–23; David Brubaker, Cinnie Noble, Richard Fincher, Susan Kee Young Park, and Sharon Press, "Conflict Resolution in the Workplace: What Will the Future Bring?," *Conflict Resolution Quarterly* 31, no. 4 (Summer 2014): 363, 381.

31. Carton and Tewfik, "Perspective—A New Look at Conflict Management," 1130, 1133.

32. Runde, "Conflict Competence in the Workplace," 28.

33. Runde, "Conflict Competence in the Workplace," 28; Hopkins and Yonker, "Managing Conflict with Emotional Intelligence," 240; Sean Valentine, Lynn Godkin, and Philip Varca, "Role Conflict, Mindfulness, and Organizational Ethics in an Education-Based Healthcare Institution," *Journal of Business Ethics* 94, no. 3 (July 2010): 463.

34. Craig E. Runde, "Conflict Competence in the Workplace," 28.

35. Vijayakumar Mallappa and Manoj Kumar KS, "Conflict Management in Management Library Professionals," *DESIDOC Journal of Library and Information Technology* 35, no. 3 (May 2015): 200–05.

36. Mary Krautter, "Advocating for the Devil: Transforming Conflict in Libraries," (2013): 9.

37. Ojo and Adesubomi, "Impact of Conflict Management on Employees' Performance," 127.

8

INEFFECTIVE COLLABORATION

An early example of library collaboration is the emergence of subject bibliographers in the 1940s. These special librarians advised faculty members about scholarly materials and were the precursors of the modern academic liaison. In the 1960s the emergence of computer technology initiated another form of librarian collaboration as librarians embraced emerging computer technology. Their collaborations led to the formation of ALA's Information Science and Automation Division (now the Library and Information Technology Association) in 1966. Internally, libraries began to structure their own organizations into operating units, which was a step towards a collaborative environment. Interdependent work units included circulation and reference staff as well as employees who handled the increasingly complex fiscal and operational aspects of the library. This type of work group division paralleled other work organizations from the 1940s to the 1970s. By 1991, the concept of utilizing work teams in the library was just taking hold and, as Francie Davis noted at the 10th Annual ACRL Conference, a "few academic libraries [had] adopted team management as their standard." However, by the end of the twentieth century, libraries and other work organizations saw problem-solving take place through groups and work teams. As the twenty-first century unfolds, collaboration as a method of operation continues to flourish in all types of libraries in a variety of ways.[1]

When collaboration is innovative and purposeful, it can be a positive force that brings together individual talents to further a common goal. Although most studies still point to the negative impact of ineffective collaboration, a few recent insights indicate that even ineffective collaboration can have a positive impact when dissenting voices keep ideas in play and stimulate group discussion. However, too much ineffective collaboration can be disruptive to a team's work and derail chances for positive results. Several deterrents prevent cohesive group work. As illustrated in chapter two, one barrier could be the prevailing attitude of the organizational environment itself, which can reduce opportunities for collaboration. A poor workplace design can also limit the collaborative efforts of team members. Other barriers include lack of trust, distance between group members, stress levels, and attitudes. Whether or not meetings are planned and run in an effective manner can impact collaboration. Finally, the psychological and emotional aspects of an individual's resistance to change influences the degree to which they collaborate.[2]

BARRIERS

Workplace collaboration is a social undertaking and is therefore vulnerable to breakdown in a variety of ways. School media specialist Dawn Frazier identifies the causes of insufficient time, inadequate technological support, and the failure of librarians to understand faculty and student needs and connect library resources to meet these needs. Although much improved, the hierarchical attitudes of faculty often prevail, typically because of the emphasis on degrees and tenure status in academic settings. These attitudes challenge the efforts of librarians and faculty to collaborate. Staff diversity, as well as the number of a library's different branches and divisions, can impact efforts to collaborate in both academic and public libraries. Along with these challenges, there are various other factors that limit collaborative efforts. These are rooted in the organization itself or the individual psyches of library workers.[3]

If a culture of collaboration is not encouraged by the library organization, it is difficult to bond successful work groups. An entire chapter of this book is dedicated to the exploration of how to best utilize teams. Collaboration is a component of a successful team. If collaboration is not used correctly, a team is no more than a group of people getting together. In addition to creating effective teams, it is important that organizations' leaders model good collaborative behavior. Research conducted by Lynda Gratton, professor of management practice at the London Business School, indicates that of one hundred factors studied, leadership role modeling is the most important in creating a culture of collaboration. If employees see management working collaboratively, they are more likely to model this positive behavior. Library organizations should also work to remove individual reward structures and introduce team-based incentives.[4]

Group members' attitudes can impact the effectiveness of collaboration. Spoilers can include members who push their own agendas and are unwilling to listen to other ideas. A group member who is reluctant to speak up or engage in the group's project can also have a negative effect. A member who argues and finds fault with any idea suggested can play the role of spoiler. Imagine the ineffectiveness of a group of librarians discussing the formation of an instructional team when one member adamantly argues in favor of forming the new group, another member sits back in silence, and a third looks for anything wrong with the idea. It is doubtful the new instructional team will ever be formed. Many of these dysfunctional characteristics are discussed in chapter four, which focuses on toxic behaviors. These types of counterproductive work behaviors make team collaboration challenging or sometimes impossible. Research shows the most effective groups are comprised of members with collaborative attitudes.[5]

A lack of trust is another barrier to collaboration. The exact definition of "trust" is debated by researchers. However, interpersonal trust, which is necessary in a collaborative project, can be cognitive-, affect-, or calculus-based. Cognitive trust is based on past behavior and rational analysis that demonstrates how these previous actions can reflect positively in future behavior. Affect-based trust is based more on the emotional analysis of an individual's "integrity, or goodwill." Finally, calculus-based trust is based on the belief that an individual "intends to perform an action that is beneficial" to the group and organization. Without trust among members of a group, deep and successful collaboration is not possible. Trust is an "enabling condition" and is "indispensable for any strategic alliance."[6]

Another potential challenge to collaboration is distance. A critical facet of effective collaboration takes place when participants see and respond to each other. Nonverbal communications such as eye contact, gestures, and tone of voice play an important part in communication among collaborators. In fact, nonverbal signs are necessary to relay "interpersonal attitudes" in the communication. If collaborating parties cannot be physically present, interaction is hindered. With the emergence of the virtual world, many turn to online collaboration as an option to overcome distance issues. The Association of College and Research Libraries suggests shared wiki pages, institutionally supported web conferencing, using online meeting schedulers, and posting minutes. Many librarians utilize these available technologies to share files, send images and messages, brainstorm, and share ideas on virtual whiteboards, among other methods. Unfortunately, this use of email or cloud sharing, which "lacks visual clues," can depersonalize an exchange. Virtual methods of communication may also limit the exchange of tacit knowledge made possible via the person-to-person collaboration that is "vital for innovation." There is some improvement in the exchange with virtual collaboration that uses visual images and voices so that it is possible to hear inflections and see gestures. However, this method is still not as effective as in-person collaboration which, in addition to being a more robust form of communication exchange, results in higher resiliency and reduced conflict among employees.[7]

Poor synchronization of group members' communication exchanges is another hindrance to collaboration. "When synchronicity and social interaction are combined, it alters the neural system in the brain," and to achieve optimal levels of group work, the individuals should be in synch with each other. In setting up for a synchronous exchange, participants must have the skills necessary to complete a clearly defined goal and set aside a designated time to work together where they have full control over ideas and decisions. Neuroscience has determined that in these synchronized collaborative situations, there is a complimentary positive-to-negative brain charge between parties exchanging information. For example, if a person is talking, the part of the frontal lobe that controls speech is positively charged but the listener's frontal lobe for speech is negatively charged. Instead, the brain of the receiver of information is positively charged in the temporal lobe area for listening. When the proper environment is in place for these types of communication exchanges to occur, group members are in synch with each other and high levels of innovation and collaboration result. However, if any of these factors are missing, group members will fail to reach a synchronized state and thus will not achieve optimum collaboration.[8]

The effects of stress were addressed in chapter three, but are worth mentioning again. Brain activity is impacted by stress. When a person is stressed, the analytical and rigid "left brain" is more active than the creative "right brain." This is a deterrent to collaboration, which often involves more creative, as opposed to analytical, thinking. Thus, stress minimizes brain function in a critical location and individuals are less likely to be effective contributors. A number of mindful approaches to librarianship and meditation techniques, as suggested in *The Mindful Librarian: Connecting the*

Practice of Mindfulness to Librarianship, help combat stress experienced by library staff.[9]

For collaboration to work, the library organization must embrace the team concept and empower its employees to make decisions. Collaborators need to be relatively stress-free and meet in person for at least some part of their work. They must also be focused on a task that is of interest to everyone and find a designated time and adequate place to work together. Lynda Gratton, professor of management practice at the London Business School, calls moments of positive and productive collaboration "hot spots." These comprise four components:

1. Cooperative mindset
2. Boundary spanning

3. Igniting purpose
4. Productive capacity[10]

Gratton states that a combination of excitement about sharing, cooperation, and a common purpose (the first three elements), combined with harnessing group talent and working through conflicts (the fourth element), ignites teams "to work toward goals they never believed achievable." It is at this dynamic level that collaborative efforts deliver stellar results.[11]

UNPRODUCTIVE MEETINGS

Meetings play a huge role in collaboration in organizations, including libraries. The number of meetings held by organizations has been on the rise since the 1960s. Past studies and labor statistics estimate there are currently between 36 and 56 million meetings held in the United States every day. A 2016 survey of the hospitality industry shows upward trends in the number of meetings of all types of industries in North America, Asia, South America, Central America, and Europe. The use of teams in the workplace is rising. Organizations have shifted from being individually centered to employing team-based work to achieve their goals. In his study of the evolution of work in the United States, Adler writes that "the story of work organization in the twentieth century is one of a zig-zag path towards more collaborative interdependence." Libraries, too, have embraced this concept, which is commonplace in public and academic libraries to achieve goals through the use of teams. Teams also bridge separate but intertwined organizations, such as libraries and academic departments or libraries and community partnerships. The use of meetings to facilitate these collaborative gatherings plays a significant role in work life.[12]

Although many meetings are productive and efficient, others are not. A 2001 compilation of studies of US businesses indicated that 33.4 percent of meeting time was unproductive. Statistics on ineffective meetings are similar even in more recent years. Research by Stuart Levine, a renowned international business consultant, indicates 39 percent of business meetings are unproductive. A 2016 online survey of office workers in the United Kingdom indicates that 40 percent of meeting attendees feel they are unnecessary and 30 percent of attendees believe meetings are inefficient and too long. Business meetings in Egypt, the United States, the Gulf States, Europe, and Asia fail to achieve their goals 33 percent of the time. Why is there so ineffective collaboration? There are many factors that inhibit productive meetings, including attendee engagement, meeting relevance, focused agenda, and meeting leadership.[13]

One pitfall of ineffective meetings is the lack of participant engagement. For a meeting to be successful, attendees must be actively involved. Studies indicate that when attendees participate a meeting yields more positive outcomes. In interactive meetings, attendees offer opinions, present information, or brainstorm new ideas. Additionally, meetings with more tasks or fuller agenda have sometimes exhibited higher employee engagement.[14]

Attending a meeting that has no real meaning or significance is an ineffective use of time. Meetings should be relevant to those invited to attend. To be effective, meeting attendees need to have an interest in what is being discussed or in the work to be done. Relevant meetings enable attendees to feel psychologically safe. This means that individuals can contribute and participate without fear that what they may say or do will have a negative impact on their work performance or reputation. Typically, larger meetings may benefit from the contributions of additional members but often encounter communication issues because not all individuals will have a voice. Larger meetings are best used for disseminating information. On a smaller scale, five is the suggested number of particpants for effective meeting groups.[15]

Conducting a meeting without a focused agenda is another pitfall. What is the purpose or objective of the meeting? What needs to be achieved? These concepts should be made clear via a written agenda that is distributed to all attendees. Part of staying focused includes limiting side bar conversations, turning off cell phones, staying on point, and behaving respectfully. If attendees are distracted or the meeting becomes lost in meaningless discussion or deviates from its intended purpose, it will be ineffective.[16]

If the leader of a meeting does not conduct it in an organized and efficient manner, it too will be unproductive. The leader should plan the meeting for a time that is best for attendees. Place is also an important choice. Romano and Nunamaker quote a 3M management team that advised that "the choice of a meeting room has a significant impact on the overall quality of the meeting. Among other things, a meeting room can enhance or inhibit productivity, encourage or discourage communication, promote or stifle creativity, and make participants feel relaxed or tense." Meetings need to start and stop on time. The leader must respect the time commitments of those attending and keep the meeting moving forward even if there are latecomers. Time management has been linked to employee psychological availability (i.e., an employee is capable of accomplishing the work) and meaningfulness (i.e., an employee feels valued). Leaders should also encourage everyone to participate and not allow a few extroverted attendees to dominate the conversation. Encouraging attendees to speak up creates a feeling of psychological safety because they understand that they can freely participate without negative consequences. Leaders must also define the necessary post-meeting steps and assign actions if needed. Following up on these assignments after the meeting concludes keeps group members on task.[17]

WORKPLACE DESIGN

Poor workplace design can contribute to ineffective collaboration. Often little money is spent on employee spaces in organizations such as libraries because of the view that dollars spent should be focused on providing creative spaces for the customers, not staff. Unfortunately, this perspective fails to recognize the negative impact poorly planned workplace design has on the employee's attitude, performance, and collaborative opportunities.

According to Gensler, a leading global design and architecture firm, companies that prioritize workplace design have employees who are more innovative, collaborative, and happier with their management. In the 2016 US Workplace Survey, both nonprofits and government organizations, two work classifications closely associated with many libraries, fell well short in productivity and collaboration. Of the eleven industry groups surveyed, nonprofits and government also ranked last in innovation, a critical component to the success of such organizations, the missions of which are tied closely to improving the public good. Only 30 percent of nonprofits prioritize "both focus and collaboration" (compared to 68 percent of top performing organizations) and only 22 percent of employees have a choice of when and where to work (compared to 38 percent of top-performing organizations). Workspace design can have a positive impact on these low numbers.[18]

Whereas cubicles were ubiquitous in the 1990s, open layouts became popular in the 2000s. Many organizations, including libraries, still utilize open office layouts (e.g., large library circulation workrooms). However, recent studies have shown that this does not provide any more interaction or collaboration than individual office spaces. Additionally, privacy and noise factors can become a distraction for employees. Studies show that proximity and visibility are the critical parts of workplace design needed to facilitate collaboration. The ability to see what coworkers are doing and align or adjust personal behavior based on their feedback is at the heart of working together harmoniously. Along similar lines, the ability to make eye contact is essential to establishing trust, a vital component to effective collaboration.[19]

Successful Collaborative Work

1. Focuses on one area of activity
2. Adjusts to actions of group members
3. Combines individual and group tasks
4. Requires watching collaborator's ongoing actions
5. Uses visible objects to facilitate collaboration[20]

Although libraries offer reading areas with comfortable seating, updated computer labs, study areas, and other design features to create a welcoming space for users, library workers typically have less-than-desirable working conditions. Many library staffers are still operating out of overcrowded office spaces, generic workrooms, small cubicles, or even converted closets. A recent survey of academic libraries in the United States revealed that 39 percent of "their spaces are hindering to their current work." Elliot Felix brought attention to the need to rethink library workspaces: "With all this change occurring and libraries' admirable ethos of putting users first, staff can often be forgotten. This is a mistake. The most effective organizations are the ones that treat staff and customers equally well." Staff are vital to the success of library operations and should not be forgotten when designing workspaces.[21]

Architectural design in the workplace may utilize the space syntax approach developed by Bill Hillier, professor of Architectural and Urban

Morphology at the University of London. It analyzes workspace and its effects on the relationships of those using the space. Through this method of analysis, it has been determined that today's workers thrive in hybrid workspaces—both private and collaborative. Employees can choose which spaces to use to accomplish their work. A suggested division of the work area is 65 to 75 percent individual space to 25 to 35 percent collaborative space. Types of spaces include "assigned and/or shared desks, meeting spaces of varying sizes and atmospheres, phone rooms, booths, quiet areas, consultation spaces, and informal communal space." Community spaces—places to gather for conversation or food—can facilitate collaboration through informal discussion. Consideration should be given to offering standing workstations as well as conventional desks and tables, large flat screens in collaboration areas, and comfortable seating with nearby power connections. This type of workplace design can increase productivity and positively impact collaboration among library workers.[22]

Improvements in library workspaces are not the norm. In a 2015 survey of academic libraries in the United States, only 32 percent of renovation projects impacted employee workspaces. However, some of the hybrid spatial design features that foster collaboration are currently found in some libraries. Workspace at North Carolina State University's Hunt Library mixes private cubicles and a collaboration hub with mixed furniture types and configurations. At UCLA's Powell Library, a living-room space and research consultation spaces are shared by staff and users (although staff areas include large-screen work stations as well as meeting spaces).[23]

Ultimately, workspaces will differ among library organizations, but each should match the needs of the environment. Workspaces should be expanded to include individual private areas as well as unassigned collaborative meeting areas and work stations. Their type and location should be designed to suit the needs of staff, who should be free to choose the areas in which they prefer to work. Design should incorporate the idea that the library staff use the entire building, not just a desk area. Consideration should also be given to the level of exposure to patron areas. Steven Bell writes about achieving the ideal workspace environment: "The key is to create different zones that contribute to an overall ecosystem that lets employees decide the best office location to accomplish their work, whether individually, with a team, when consulting with students or faculty or managing a subordinate." Workspace does have an impact on library staff, and the hybrid workspace model is the best design option to create a positive, collaborative environment.[24]

RESISTANCE TO CHANGE

The study of change and human behavior encompasses many theories. It dates to the 1940s, from the work of Kurt Lewin (considered "the father of social psychology"), whose studies influenced all aspects of management as it is practiced today. Some of Lewin's best-known work focuses on change. He theorized that when individuals felt a need to change (what he refers to as "unfreezing"), they would alter their behavior ("moving"), and then settle into a new norm ("refreezing"). Edgar Schein dissected the unfreezing stage and found that change is facilitated when the forces inhibiting it are reduced in relation to an increase in driving forces. This reduces learning anxiety and increases psychological safety in the individual incurring change. These principles laid the foundation for organizational theory as it is known today. These findings about behavioral change, its methods, causes, and influencing factors, which are rooted in Lewin's early work, lend insight to human behavior in the workplace.[25]

Resistance to change is a common barrier that organizations must overcome. Employees' reluctance to change has often been shown to be the leading cause for change failure. Resistance to change is rooted in both situational and organizational issues. Additionally, the breadth of change impacts responses, because more complex change can be met with resistance. As well, the behavior of individuals impacts resistance to change. Previous chapters of this book have touched on resistance to change as it manifests itself in refusal behaviors or even forms of sabotage. Here the focus is on how it relates to ineffective collaboration.[26]

Research into individual resistance to change identifies a number of causes:

1. Reluctance to lose control
2. Cognitive rigidity
3. Lack of psychological resilience
4. Intolerance to the adjustment period involved in change
5. Preference for low levels of stimulation and novelty
6. Reluctance to give up old habits[27]

In the first case, individuals may resist a change that is forced upon them that they did not initiate. For example, the mere fact a librarian is *assigned* to a work team, rather than given the option of choosing the members of the team, can lay the foundation for individual resistance. Second, cognitively rigid individuals who believe their own methods are the correct ones can be stubborn and refuse to change their thinking. For example, many aspects of libraries have changed dramatically in recent years. Imagine someone resistant to even *considering* new ways to access or classify information. Third, individuals who lack psychological resilience or the ability to adapt to adverse or stressful situations may resist change. A member of a team charged with revamping information literacy instruction must be prepared to encounter barriers and handle increased stress triggered by the changes, but many individuals struggle with this and may resist major program changes. Fourth, with any change there is an adjustment period when things may not run smoothly. Some individuals have difficulty coping with these challenges and therefore resist supporting the change. The fifth identifies individuals who are happy with their own working framework and resist any type of change stimulant that may interfere with how they move through the day. A librarian collaborating on a project to promote electronic resources must ultimately leave the safe haven of the office to conduct outreach visits to other departments and student areas. Although greater use of electronic resources is supported, this type of change in the librarian's work style may result in resistance to the idea. Finally, individuals fall into routines and establish habits. Donald Hebb determined that "neurons that fire together wire together," that is, the process of linking two neurons "makes it more likely that they will be linked in the future" (this is known as Hebb's Law). As neurons respond and link, responses are likely to be repeated at the synaptic level and thus habits are hardwired into the brain, making change possible, but more challenging. Thus, a plan to deviate from these normal routines may meet with resistance.[28]

Shaul Oreg's Categories of Individual Resistance

1. Routine seeking	3. Short-term focus
2. Emotional reaction	4. Cognitive rigidity[29]

In addition to an individual's characteristics, collaboration is impacted by commitment. Employee commitment to change can be categorized as affective commitment, normative commitment, or continuance commitment. These principles can also be applied to a collaborative environment. Affective commitment deals with the positive, emotional ties of the employer to the organization. For instance, a library worker on a team charged to conduct an annual employee work survey may actively contribute if he has a strong, positive feeling about the organization. However, if the worker has had negative experiences while at work, he will be less likely to engage in the collaboration. Normative commitment is rooted in a sense of obligation to the organization. In the work survey team example, individuals may feel they need to participate in the collaboration because it will help the organization as a whole. Finally, continuance commitment reflects the potential social and economic costs of leaving the organization. If participating on the survey team is an assigned part of the position, library staff may feel they must participate or face reprimand or dismissal, and may be reluctant to contribute to the team in a positive way. Overall, those who have a negative emotional organizational attachment, feel a forced obligation to the project, and believe they must participate or be negatively impacted socially and financially, will be less likely to collaborate successfully.[30]

The effectiveness of collaboration can be significantly impacted by individual resistance to change. Psychological and emotional makeup, as well as the ability to handle change and stress, can influence collaboration. The need for control and engrained habits also may inhibit positive group work. Finally, the level of commitment of individuals is rooted in their perceptions of the team and organization as it relates to themselves, which will impact collaboration. If any of these factors are present in a negative way, ineffective collaboration results.

CONCLUSION

Collaboration can be negatively impacted by traditional causes rooted in either organizational or individual attributes. A failure of organizations to promote a culture of collaboration through their leaders and rewards system leads to a lack of collaboration. Stress, distance, and the lack of synchronicity among team members also contribute. Trust is another critical component of a collaborative environment. To be effective, meetings must be conducted properly and purposefully by a leader who understands the dynamics of such gatherings. Libraries must rethink their view of employee workspaces, whose importance has been minimalized by budgets. A reworking of these spaces to include areas for both individual work and group collaboration fosters a positive and productive work environment. Finally, individual resistance to change, which may be based in both emotional and psychological causes, must be acknowledged and addressed to enable collaboration.

NOTES

1. Stephen R. Salmon, "LITA's First Twenty-Five Years: A Brief History," American Library Association, 2017, www.ala.org/lita/about/history/1st25years; Paul S. Adler, "Towards Collaborative Interdependence: A Century of Change in the Organization of Work," in *Balancing the Interests: The Evolution from Industrial Relations to Human Resources and Beyond,* ed. Bruce E. Kaufman, Richard A. Beaumont, and Roy B. Helfgott (Armonk, NY: M. E. Sharp, 2003), 366; Francie C. Davis, "Calling the Shots: Examination of a Self-Managed Team in an Academic Library" (presentation, Association of College and Research Libraries 10th National Conference, Denver, CO, March 15–18, 2001); Adler, "Towards Collaborative Interdependence," 369.

2. Jeffrey D. Ford, Laurie W. Ford, and Angelo D'Amelio, "Resistance to Change: The Rest of the Story," *Academy of Management Review* 33, no. 2 (2008): 368.

3. Dawn Frazier, "School Library Media Collaborations: Benefits and Barriers," *Library Media Connection* 29, no. 3 (2010): 35–36 and Richard Moniz, Jo Henry, and Jo Eshleman, *Fundamentals for the Academic Liaison* (Chicago, IL: Neal Schuman, 2014): 72.

4. Lynda Gratton, "Building Bridges for Success," *Financial Times,* June 29, 1007: 1.

5. Ibid.

6. Bo Bernhard Nielsen, "The Role of Trust in Collaborative Relationships: A Multi-Dimensional Approach," *M@n@gement* 7, no. 4 (2004): 242–45.

7. Geoffrey Beattie, *Visible Thought: The New Psychology of Body Language* (New York, NY: Routledge, 2004), 14; Christy Stevens, "Tips for Conducting Successful Virtual Meetings," Association for College and Research Libraries, 2013, www.ala.org/acrl/aboutacrl/directoryofleadership/sections/is/iswebsite/about/resources/tipsvirtual meetings; Jialin Hardwick, Alistair R. Anderson, and Douglas Cruickshank, "Trust Formation Processes in Innovative Collaborations," *European Journal of Innovation Management* 16, no. 1 (2013): 8; "Barriers to Collaboration," Conscious Business Australia, 2013, http://cbau.com.au/the-barriers-to-collaboration.

8. Richard Moniz, Joe Eshleman, Jo Henry, Howard Slutzky, and Lisa Moniz, *The Mindful Librarian: Connecting the Practice of Mindfulness to Librarianship,* (Waltham, MA: Chandos-Elsevier, 2016), 151; Mihaly Csikszentmihalyi, *FLOW: The Psychology of Optimal Experience* (New York, NY: Harper and Row, 1990), 49; Alan S. Haas, "A Brain Charge Mechanism Modeled in Synchronistic Dyadic Interpersonal Interaction," *NeuroQuantology* 10, no. 3 (2012): 484.

9. "Barriers to Collaboration"; Moniz et al., *The Mindful Librarian.*

10. Lynda Gratton, *Hot Spots: Why Some Teams, Workplaces, and Organizations Buzz with Energy—and Others Don't* (San Francisco, CA: Berrett-Khoper Publishers, Inc., 2007), 21.

11. Ibid., 16.

12. Nicholas C. Romano and Jay F. Nunamaker, "Meeting Analysis: Findings from Research and Practice," in *Proceedings of the 34th Hawaii International Conference on System Sciences (HICSS-34)-Volume 9, January 3–6 2001* (Washington, DC: IEEE Computer Society, 2001): 3; Elise Keith, "55 Million: A Fresh Look at the Number, Effectiveness, and Cost of Meetings in the US," *Lucid Meetings* [blog], December 4, 2015, http://blog.lucidmeetings.com/blog/fresh-look-number-effectiveness-cost-meetings -in-us; "2016 Global Meetings and Events Forecast," *American Express*, 2016, https:// www.amexglobalbusinesstravel.com/wp-content/uploads/2016-ME-LETTER-WEB -oct-17-update.pdf:10; Adler, "Towards Collaborative Interdependence," 354.

13. Romano and Nunamaker, "Meeting Analysis," 8; Stuart Levine, "Boost Productivity with Effective Meetings," *Credit Union Times,* October 29, 2014; "UK Office Workers Spend Two Years of Their Lives Preparing For, and Attending Meetings," *M2 Presswire,* April 26, 2016; Sayed M. Elsayed-Elkhouly and Harold Lazarus, "Business Meetings in North America, Asia, Europe, and the Middle East," *American Journal of Management Development* 1, 4 (1995): 18.

14. Holly Hinkel and Joseph Allen, "Speaking Up and Working Harder: How Participation in Decision-making in Meetings Improves Overall Employee Engagement," *Journal of Psychological Inquiry* 18, no. 1 (2013): 12; Michael Yoerger, John Crowe, and Joseph A. Allen, "Participate or Else!: The Effect of Participation in Decision-Making in Meetings on Employee Engagement," *Psychology Faculty Publications, Paper 120* (2015): 3.

15. Joseph A. Allen and Steven G. Rogelberg, "Manager-Led Group Meetings: A Context for Promoting Employee Engagement," *Group and Organization Management* 38, no. 5 (2013): 545–47; Romano and Nunamaker, "Meeting Analysis," 6.

16. Levine, "Boost Productivity with Effective Meetings."

17. Romano and Nunamaker, "Meeting Analysis," 8; Allen and Rogelberg, "Manager-Led Group Meetings," 545, 547; Levine, "Boost Productivity with Effective Meetings."

18. "Not for Profit 2016 US Workplace Survey, Industry Findings," Gensler, 1–3, www.gensler.com/uploads/document/450/file/gensler_wps_not-for-profit.pdf.

19. Charlie Gullstrom, "Design Frictions," *AI and Society* 27, no. 9 (2012): 93.

20. Ibid., 105.

21. Aliza Leventhal and Bryan Irwin, "The State of Academic Librarian Spaces," *Sasaki,* http://librarysurvey.sasaki.com/; Elliot Felix, "Rethink the Staff Workplace: Library by Design, Spring 2015," *Library Journal,* 2015, 58, http://lj.libraryjournal.com/2015/05/ buildings/lbd/rethink-the-staff-workplace-library-by-design-spring-2015/#_.

22. Felix, "Rethink the Staff Workplace"; Heather Mathias, "Prevent Collaboration Overload Through Design," *The Tennessean,* June 10, 2014.

23. Irwin and Leventhal, "Work/Space"; Steven Bell, "Open vs. Closed: Office Space Design Contributes to the Library Experience," *Designing Better Libraries* [blog], November 25, 2013, http://dbl.lishost.org/blog/2013/11/25/open-or-closed-office-space-design-contributes-to-the-library-experience/#.WFW2DFMrLIU; Felix, "Rethink the Staff Workplace."

24. Steven Bell, "Open vs. Closed."

25. David Coghlan and Teresa Brannick, "Kurt Lewin: The 'Practical Theorist' for the Twenty-First Century," *Irish Journal of Management* 24, no. 2 (2003): 31, 34; Edgar H. Schein, "From Brainwashing to Organization Therapy," in *Handbook of Organization Development*, ed. Thomas G. Cummings (Los Angeles, CA: Sage Publications, 2008): 34, 45.

26. Alexandra Michel, Rune Todnem By, and Bernard Burnes, "The Limitations of Dispositional Resistance in Relation to Organizational Change," *Management Decision* 52, no. 4 (2013): 764–65.

27. Shaul Oreg, "Resistance to Change: Developing an Individual Differences Measure," *Journal of Applied Psychology* 88, no. 4 (2003): 680.

28. Mona Dekoven Fishbane, "Wired to Connect: Neuroscience, Relationships, and Therapy," *Family Process* 46, no. 3 (2007): 397.

29. Oreg, "Resistance to Change," 682.

30. Stephen Jaros, "Meyer and Allen Model of Organizational Commitment: Measurement Issues," *ICFAI Journal of Organizational Behavior* 6, no. 4 (2007): 7.

9

DIFFICULTIES
WITH TEAM COMPOSITION

eturning to some of the ideas expressed in chapter two, which
dealt with dysfunctional organizational culture and its impact on
libraries, we will now analyze team design and teamwork. Poor
communication (the most significant contributor to dysfunction)
is a barrier to collaboration and has significant impact on the creation of
teams and how they perform. Additionally, the pernicious effect of destructive office politics and some of the other workplace cultural dysfunctions
(nepotism, sexism, bullying, etc.) can inhibit work done within teams. These
factors and others damage library teams. A less obvious consideration is
how a lack of diversity can contribute to poor team composition and dysfunctional groups.

It is important to keep in mind that the strength of any team relies not
only on the individual assets of its members, but more importantly, on
the strength of the bonds among members. Although an individual may
not always be able to choose his workplace team or his role within it, the
need to develop trust and a positive mindset about how to be a member of
a team can overcome many hurdles. A positive teamwork mindset helps
to create a foundation for working as part of a group. At first, it may seem
trite to put forth the idea that a simple mindset change paves the way for a
better experience and alleviates some of the hurdles of team composition,
but it is valuable to keep in mind that it is a starting point, not a magic

potion that cures all issues or problems. For example, developing the attributes of a growth mindset can be much more impactful than it may appear at first. The foundations of the growth-mindset concept developed by Carol Dweck are that individuals can learn more effectively when they let go of the idea that capabilities are fixed and that challenges are what help to change mindsets. The real hurdle when attempting to achieve a growth mindset is overcoming engrained ideas of self. In a similar way, developing a team mindset is merely another method to build in a mindful approach to dealing with the messiness and uncertainty while working alongside others. This initial focus on attitude can be a motivator to flip the switch from dysfunctional to functional. Because a positive outlook towards fellow workers is so important to developing confidence in a team member's ability to tackle problems and achieve, the development of a team mindset is crucial.[1]

In addition to exploring positive team mindset, this chapter reviews the types of library teams on which workers can expect to serve, briefly examines some of these teams, addresses the importance of how to compose a team, and finally discusses challenges to teamwork and how to overcome each hindrance. Viewed as a microcosm of all the work that a librarian does with fellow employees (as well as patrons, students, and all those we meet in and outside the library), teamwork allows librarians to develop their interpersonal skills, customer service habits, and provides the opportunity to showcase librarians' value. And most importantly, good teams help to minimize individual dysfunction. Due to this often-overlooked component of teams, and because of the topical nature of libraries and inclusion, this difficulty will be examined closely within this chapter. Ways to create, maintain, and foster teams in the library will be explored. The dysfunctions that affect teams will be discussed and solutions will be put forth. Promisingly, the literature of libraries and teams shows some excellent historical precedent for team-based collaboration and describes continuing success stories. By minimizing dysfunction in library teams, the ideal is to increase these endeavors.

TEAMS IN THE LIBRARY

Just as there can be a myriad of individuals on a team, teams themselves can be characterized in numerous ways. The Types of Teams sidebar shows the result of a cursory search to determine the ways teams are described.

Types of Teams

- department teams
- problem-solving teams
- virtual teams
- cross-functional teams
- self-managed teams
- permanent teams
- temporary teams

- task forces
- committees
- organizations/work forces
- formal teams
- informal teams
- quality teams

In libraries, teams can be comprised of many forms. Although there are numerous resources available when it comes to the general idea of collaboration in libraries, there are fewer sources that focus on library team composition. For example, collaboration from the perspective of working with other departments, organizations, and other libraries are well-mined categories. There is available literature on successful library teams. Yet, considered collectively, strategies for designing how library teams will be defined and built, and how best to motivate for team success, have not been as extensively explored. The thought process that should go into the composition of teams is certainly not to be underestimated, especially when the word "collaboration" is added to the mix and other departments and groups are involved.[2]

A cursory search using keywords such as "partnership," "team," and "collaboration" in conjunction with "library" yields innumerable resources (including whole journals devoted to the topic). Although this chapter focuses mostly on how teams are formed, a brief overview of the history of librarians working with others is valuable here. As libraries have needed to become more and more outreach-focused, this has fostered a greater transition from communities coming to the library to librarians going out into the community. This has required interpersonal skills development because it pertains to the need for librarians to become better at developing relationships. Due to the increasingly networked world in which we live, compounded by advances in technology, librarians have needed to evolve from knowledge workers into relationship workers. This transition has been difficult for some and the struggle associated with this change has led to dysfunction in some libraries.

When looking at workplaces, it is easy to be lured by case studies, articles, and blog posts that address general workplace issues rather than focusing on those that specifically target libraries. This same trap can occur with dysfunction. What in a library (or which aspects of librarianship), would be most pertinent in relation to teamwork and team composition? Beth L. Strecker zeroes in on the confluence of teamwork and libraries in her thesis, "Academic Librarians' Perceptions of Teamwork and Organizational Structure in a Time of Rapid Technological Change." She surmises that "the preference for working in a flat organizational structure was not as strong as the preference for working in teams." Librarians who work in academic public services are well-versed as team members in their liaison and embedded librarian roles. Frontline librarians working directly with patrons must consider their roles from a team-oriented perspective when supporting their communities and as representatives for the library in many ways. The aspects of librarianship that may likely impact team composition are at the core of the history of the profession, that is, the need to prioritize professionalism, and the strong library value system that is in place.[3]

The American Library Association website lists eleven core tenets that promote the value of librarianship. Of these, democracy, diversity, the public good, professionalism, service, and social responsibility appear to play into notions of teamwork. Taking a deeper look at professionalism, there is a focus placed on "professionally qualified personnel who have been educated in graduate programs within institutions of higher education." Perhaps the most important idea here is that a professional librarian needs to focus on "the social needs and goals of library services." Although there are certainly many issues around the concept that going to library school equates to becoming a library professional (see, e.g., *The Politics of Professionalism: A Retro-Progressive Proposal for Librarianship* by Juris Dilevko), librarianship in its ideal state has been shown to be a field that works towards shared goals and has a more unified design and mission than other disciplines, such as information technology and instructional design. (For additional information about how these fields impact each other, see *Librarians and Instructional Designers: Collaboration and Innovation.*). In ideal situations, professional librarians would assess the negative impacts that their own dysfunctions have on team efforts, but this is not always the case. A more detailed look at team design explains why.[4]

CROSS-FUNCTIONAL TEAMS OR CROSS-DYSFUNCTIONAL TEAMS?

Cross-functional teams are comprised of individuals with different (and ideally complimentary) functional expertise. In the academic library environment, there has been a recent move away from subject expertise to functional expertise when updating the liaison (librarian-faculty) role. The main advantage of a cross-functional team is that it can bring together diverse skillsets to work on projects. In an academic library setting, a team with members from public services (for example, reference or instruction), technical services (cataloging, digital services), and possibly library administration not only has a broader representation, but its members can learn more about each other's roles and appreciate how each fits into the bigger picture or composition of the team. A good example of a public library that uses this model is the Denver Public Library. Its presentation at the 2016 Public Library Association Annual Conference, "A Different Way of Doing Business: Cross-Functional Strategic Initiative Teams," showed how the library "recently reorganized, transitioning to a different way of planning and implementing our strategic work. Cross-functional teams were formed and the position of Manager of Innovation and Initiatives was created to help facilitate the process."[5]

In "75% of Cross-Functional Teams Are Dysfunctional," Behnam Tabrizi found that "they fail on at least three of five criteria: 1.) meeting a planned budget; 2.) staying on schedule; 3.) adhering to specifications; 4.) meeting customer expectations; and/or 5.) maintaining alignment with the company's corporate goals." As can be seen time and time again, some of these failures that at first seem disparate can fit under the banner of poor communication. Other team implementations fall prey to this catch-all designation because it is at the core of not understanding unified team goals and function. This lends itself to the idea that whoever is leading the team is most responsible for its direction and achievement. Leadership is the main topic of chapter ten, and although team leadership has some obvious overlap, there are some key differences. The main difference between these roles is that a designated leader may be thought of as existing "outside" of a team and can fall into the trap of not "leading from within." A librarian appointed as team leader who understands and can do the work required of team members is often admired, and fosters a higher level of trust and cooperation.[6]

The dysfunctions that cripple teams are similar to those presented in chapter two—poor communication, minimal collaboration, too much talk and too little action, and lack of diversity. When a team is designed to achieve a specific purpose, it can alleviate some dysfunction because its members share a common goal and have agreed on achievement points. A strong team recognizes its own weaknesses and figures out how to overcome them. The specific way a team is structured is not as important as the development of teamwork components that can lift the team above dysfunction. The individual development and application of a team mindset ideally adds up to a group that is determined to achieve together. Unifying a team around a shared team mindset can be a good starting place.

THE TEAM MINDSET

At face value, what defines a mindset may seem self-evident, but there may be additional layers. Leanne Howard creates an extra dimension by adding in other relevant information about teamwork:

> A mindset is a set of assumptions, methods, or notations held by groups of people that is so established that it creates a powerful incentive within these people to continue to adopt or accept prior behaviors, choices, or tools. Simply put, it is a way of thinking about things that those in a group share or have in common to the point that it becomes a way of life.[7]

Group behavior or group norms also align with this unified-team way of thinking.

The concept of the growth mindset, as set forth and developed by Dweck, makes the important point that a key to change is to recognize the origins of how we think about capacity and ability. Understanding that the reason for personal beliefs about our own ability to achieve (or fail) often is not supported by real evidence but can be mapped to a state of mind that leads to success or lack thereof. Considering potentially dysfunctional fixed perspectives concerning the ability to accomplish something ("I am good at math," "I am bad at completing a research paper," "I am not a team player"), sets an individual on the path of self-reflection. Ideally this will lead to self-discovery—and then, even better, to behavioral change. The primary takeaway from Dweck's ideas is that these notions are not fixed. They can be changed, and the small epiphany that comes with this realization is the path to more personal agency and a flourishing life.

When considering views of teamwork and identifying the efforts needed to work on a team, there are common refrains, many of which are based on team projects in school. Frequently, the general consensus is that when teams are formed responsibility will not be divided evenly, and that one or more team members will have to pull the weight of those who contribute little (or even nothing). This view is often justified and sometimes becomes a self-fulfilling prophecy. Returning to Dweck's concepts, a facet of the growth mindset ideology is the notion that challenges are what help to change mindsets. If leaving preconceived notions of teamwork could alleviate some problems from the very start, perhaps that attitude change could be beneficial. The cynical among us could see this as a trivial ploy—but isn't mindset change at the core of all behavioral growth? For those librarians who teach (and the range of what this includes is broad, from children's librarians reading out loud to reference-desk help to library instruction) a goal is moving someone to a learning threshold. Part of that growth may begin with a learner's dispositional change, which will grant confidence to achieve. Should librarians not attempt to emulate this process with those they wish to help and reconsider how to think about their own dyed-in-the-wool outlooks and habits?

In "Essential Mindsets of the High Performing Team of the 21st Century," Dara Goldberg lays out the key elements of "Empathy, Optimism, Resilience, Reflection, Honesty and Humility" as the qualities that a modern team must possess. She adds:

> Call it frames of mind, thought patterns, how the team thinks, individually and collectively, or the lens through which individual team members observe and experience themselves, each other and the world around them. The team's mindsets drive how team members, and how the team as a whole behaves; the choices they make; the relationships they have and how much they invest in them; the satisfaction they derive; their capacity to fully capitalize on their acquired skills and knowledge and, equally important, their ability to realize their natural talents; and so much more.[8]

In "How to Survive and Thrive in Your First Library Job," Margaret Casado and Alan Wallace present burgeoning librarians with good advice about how to develop a team-focused mindset. These are some of the ideas that they offer:

> To work effectively as a part of a team, the first challenge is literally showing up. You must be flexible enough to work with other colleagues' schedules. Include ample time in your calendar to be available for consultations and impromptu discussions, and make it a priority not to cancel unless you really must. When unavoidable conflicts do come up, let your teammates know as soon as possible, so they can help come up with alternative ways for you to contribute in advance.
>
> As a new staffer, you will likely receive many invitations to participate in committee work. Once there, listening is as important as talking.

Maybe more so: revealing a willingness to learn from more experienced colleagues is sure to be well received, while too many contributions run the risk of looking like showboating or perhaps a lack of interest in others' ideas. Examples from library school may be counterproductive—even if germane, they play up your lack of "real world" experience, so cite them sparingly.[9]

Although some of this advice focuses on fitting in rather than making one's own mark, it does show how developing empathy and recognizing give-and-take are important strategies for navigating teamwork with coworkers. As the importance of building and maintaining relationships becomes more important to librarians, it is valuable to spend time thinking about how to accomplish these goals and work towards positive team outcomes. Books such as *Librarians and Educators Collaborating for Success: The International Perspective* (Libraries Unlimited 2016); *Collaboration and the School Library Media Specialist* (Scarecrow Press 2005); and *Building Bridges: Connecting Faculty, Students, and the College Library* (ALA Editions 2010) are valuable resources.

WHAT DOES IT MEAN TO "COMPOSE" A TEAM?

Words can be both used and interpreted in many intended and unintended ways. Strictly speaking, team composition refers more to the singular members than to the act of creating or designing a team. As defined by Wikipedia, "Team composition refers to the overall mix of characteristics among people in a team, which is a unit of two or more individuals who interact interdependently to achieve a common objective. It is based on the attributes among individuals that comprise the team, in addition to their main objective."[10]

The opportunity to be in control of the makeup of a team can be both empowering and intimidating. Cases where library teams are thoughtfully designed are rare and often amount to volunteer squads or default groupings, especially in smaller libraries. For example, committees are often composed of group members who are chosen from outside the library, randomly constructed, or a combination of volunteers and staff—or a mix of these configurations.

The larger theme of favoritism, and its cousins nepotism, cronyism, and sexism, can arise when personnel choices are considered. Each has the potential to sour teams at their very beginning. This sense of unfairness can occur when certain members of a team are favored over others can create animosity and diminish morale. All of these share similarities, and also have their own unique pernicious effects, which contribute to dysfunction.

Favoritism

The case study "Playing Favorites," which appeared in the March 1, 2009, issue of *Library Journal,* is a good starting point for this discussion. This think piece offers a fictional example of two friends meeting and one mentioning favoritism in the library in which he works. The closing paragraph of the cases truly encapsulates the main point, "Of course, you're always going to like some people better than others. Still, if you're the manager, you can't play favorites, you have to treat everybody equally. Don't you?" In her analysis of this fictional event (titled "Actions, Not Complaints"), Kathyellen Bullard, the assistant director of the Providence Public Library, first weighs the potential for favoritism and balances some of the actions described to give the manager the benefit of the doubt. Moving on to the potential for favoritism, Bullard states that there are signifiers such as performance reviews and speaking to fellow employees that should be considered when identifying favoritism on the part of managers. Bullard finishes by examining the relationships between employees: "But there is a clearly missing ingredient—trust. They must find a way to reestablish that on both sides. And that can only be done if both parties wish it and are willing to communicate with honesty and respect."[11]

Building trust in one another is inarguably the best method to cement firm and lasting relationships. It is the extraordinarily rare relationship that does not encounter interaction that leads to emotional issues. As in all relationships, if there is not a sense of mutual respect and an understanding that it can withstand difficult times, there will always be lingering problems. Even the most communicative and well-meaning relationships encounter hurdles (in and out of the workplace). The advice to "communicate with honesty and respect" is much easier said than done. In addition to the difficulties that can come with the usual hierarchical organizational design, there can be other problems, such as the workplace rumor mill, historical grievances, and highly charged emotional environments.

Addressing charges of favoritism is a difficult endeavor and like most personnel situations, documentation helps to support the case being made. Favoritism (which can be based on cronyism, sexism, or racism) stems from unfair imbalances. If solutions are offered by those who are unaffected, those experiencing the events or painful situations may develop a degree of animosity. All the factors that create a dysfunctional relationship, team, department, or organization can cause participants to become aghast when someone comes in to offer an "easy solution."

Nepotism

Here and in other sections of the book the concept of nepotism needs consideration. When choosing teams, it is often thought that the choices involved are rarely impartial. Nepotism is defined as "the practice among those with power or influence of favoring relatives or friends, especially by giving them jobs." As seen throughout this book, uncivil behavior such as bullying or sexism could at first be thought to be uncommon (even absent) in the library workplace. But like any workplace, libraries are not immune, and incivility through bad-faith behavior (or a combination of behaviors) leads to dysfunction.[12]

Nepotism in workplaces in general has been studied frequently, but the subject of nepotism in libraries is rarely addressed. Certainly, nepotism charges fit into those that are frequently "off the record" and may affect tangential situations such as Board of Trustees or have been a serious problem in the past. Many libraries (particularly public libraries, because of their ties to local government) have nepotism policies in place. Academic libraries are usually covered by the institution's human resources policies. There are some interrelated branches of nepotism, especially when the words "favoritism" or "cronyism" are brought into the discussion. Sexism can be related to favoritism and it can surface when bias is compounded.

The response to the query, "What do you think is the secret to getting hired?" in a question-and-answer post from the blog *Hiring Librarians* is "in my organization, it's to know someone who is involved in hiring, and have a history of being worshipful of the organization. My experience in libraries is that they're rife with nepotism and would rather have incompetent boot-lickers than people who can do the job." This is only one person's experience, but what is interesting about this statement is that it addresses the idea that agreeable employees are preferred over competent ones (and to complete the symmetry, possibly an employee who may not be as conciliatory). Some of the attributes described here could be considered dysfunctional from different points of view. Although competence is certainly important, is that the most desirable characteristic if the employee does not work well with others? This slippery-slope thinking leads to an interesting examination that often reflects on such issues as the personal biases and the comfort level of those who hire. This is a strong factor to consider when examining some of the other "isms" that affect not only hiring, but numerous other decisions regarding fellow employees.[13]

There are obvious human resources ramifications here, further investigation of which is the purview of HR staff. It is easy to place responsibility for the awareness and enforcement of personnel issues on others, but it is a reality that librarians cannot be experts in all topics. This does not absolve library leaders of the need to exemplify high standards and to be forthright and fair when these dysfunctional personnel issues arise. In much the same way that librarians attempt to adhere to ethical standards when dealing with their communities, library leaders must realize that employees' trust grows when the decisions they make are consistently balanced and transparent—as difficult as that may be. (This topic is also addressed in chapter ten.)

Sexism

Because librarianship includes a high percentage of female workers, the first assumption may be that there is less sexism than in other fields. However, this assumption about gender in librarianship does not hold up. There have been problems in the past, and they continue. As recently as a few years ago, there was an incident of sexual harassment of women librarians at a library convention, which was settled out of court. The disproportionate number of males in senior library positions is frequently used as an example of continued sexism in libraries.[14]

According to the AFL-CIO Department for Professional Employees Fact Sheet for 2016:

> Despite the fact that the library profession is predominantly female, a wage gap still exists:
> - In 2014, women working as full-time librarians reported a median annual salary of $48,589, compared to $52,528 for men, a pay gap of 93 percent.
> - The disparity was even more staggering among full-time library technicians where women earned $28,121 per year, compared to men who earned $36,862 per year (a 76 percent gap). However, the margin of error for men's salaries was high, since there were few men in the sample.

- Among librarians with a master's degree working thirty-two hours a week or more in colleges, universities, and professional schools, including junior colleges, women earned 90 percent of what men earned in 2014. Women, on average, were nearly six months older than their male counterparts.[15]

There are pockets of progress, as pointed out by Jessica Olin and Michelle Millet in their recent blog post "Gendered Expectations for Leadership in Libraries":

> Even though there are more women leaders now, we are still not doing it right. Or, more to the point, we are not doing it the way people want us to do it. We do not act like men. This is not, then, parity. It isn't enough to have women in administrative positions and for them to be paid at similar rates, though that's a great start. We want leaders, male or female or people who don't identify in those ways, to be valued for what they each bring to their organizations.[16]

Sexism in libraries is not a new subject. In the article "Feminist Thinking and Librarianship in the 1990s: Issues and Challenges," Sarah M. Pritchard presents a litany of topics that have affected women in libraries:

> Pay equity. Sexual harassment. Child care. Flexible scheduling. Lateral career ladders. Blind refereeing for professional journals. Representative search committees and calls to advertise the full range of salaries for a position. Management development programs for under-represented groups. Health aspects of computer use.[17]

There is much more that can be said about some of the complexities surrounding sexism in the library, particularly around the gendered associations with specific duties and advancement. Sexism, like racism, creates imbalances, foments mistrust, erodes morale and creates a great deal of librarian dysfunction. These can be connected to teams but can also apply to general work relationships. Communication that helps to build trust is the primary way to alleviate these types of problems. (See chapter six, which deals specifically with communication problems.)

Building Trust

For those who genuinely want to help create healthy relationships and trust, the importance of getting to know employees better cannot be overemphasized. Coworker relationships that go beyond the general work environment and allow for more dimensional connections can be tricky to navigate. For every librarian who enjoys getting to know fellow staff and socializing with them, there is someone who wants to keep the relationships as strictly "workplace-only" as possible. In the United States, the amount of time that a person spends at work (or more accurately, on workplace activities, because the work/home balance has been skewed) can be equal to or more than the time spent outside of work. This can lend itself to positive situations where librarians become closer as fellow employees and grow into strong teams with durable relationships. It can also lead to scenarios where the day-to-day stressful realities of the workplace and human emotions find a forum.

In the blog post "Personnel vs. Personal: A Mindset That Can Make a World of Difference," Arron Grow, the associate program director for organizational leadership at the University of Seattle, delineates how leaders should consider those who work for them: "The gist of the matter is this; leaders who treat their staff as property are not effective. Leaders who treat their staff as people are much more effective leaders." He offers three guidelines:

> Learn about your team members: How do good leaders learn about their people? They have conversations with them. Regular, around the water cooler chat about whatever seems natural, off-work activities, family stuff, hobbies, community events—whatever makes sense. The goal is not to become their friend. That has its own set of challenges so minding that boundary is important. The goal is instead to simply learn what's important to them. Knowing this, leaders have a better chance of connecting with their team members to influence as leaders must to be most effective. The age-old adage still applies; people don't care how much you know, until they know how much you care.
>
> Keep team members informed: When information is coming down from *on high* let team members know what that information is. When organizational events are happening, ensure team members know [and] are aware of them. When changes must occur, say as much as can be said. Hint: Because I said so is not an explanation. That may work with a child (and even then only for a time), but it most definitely will not foster engaged, productive team members.

Ask for input: This may seem obvious but my research suggests this is one of the least used tools in the leadership toolbox. When an idea is put before the team, ask team members for their reactions—and mean it! In group settings it can sometimes be difficult to get everyone to open up. No problem, ask team members to provide their input by email. Ask that everyone give input. This practice accomplishes two purposes—you get a more balanced view of things and your team members know that you value their input.[18]

The most important point is that the team mindset requires a great deal of empathy and understanding. It is important to consider other member's roles and ideas in addition to your own. Seeking perspective on the roles of other team members can be an effective way to become more unified.

There are currently many workplace hurdles that make this a much more difficult task than in years past. In the article "The Hidden Toll of Workplace Incivility," Christine Porath writes,

There's no single reason for the trend. Workplace relationships may be fraying as fewer employees work in the office and thus feel more isolated and less respected. Some studies point to growing narcissism among younger workers. Globalization may be causing cultural clashes that bubble beneath the surface. And, in the digital age, messages are prone to communication gaps and misunderstanding—and, unfortunately, putdowns are easier when not delivered face to face.[19]

Team communication is multifaceted. Communication styles are significant, as are the oft-heard refrains of those who feel as though they are not "in the loop." Spending time talking to fellow team members not only helps to develop trust and spread empathy, but also helps to connect communication silos.

Diverse Teams

Librarians have always been interested in providing access to information to all. In recent years, however, the lack of diversity in the profession—and how it is perceived by the diverse communities served—has been questioned. Additionally, collections built by librarians who do not represent a wide range of different backgrounds and viewpoints has caused many librarians to wonder if they are meeting the goal of serving all community members.

As pointed out in the AFL-CIO Department for Professional Employees Fact Sheet, library teams comprised primarily of white women may have a difficult time representing diverse communities. It is much easier to call for diversity than to work for it. It is better to present opportunities than to force teams that appear diverse, the outcome of having dissimilar aspects of members' team should be a goal of group composition.

In the post "Why Diversity Matters: A Roundtable Discussion on Racial and Ethnic Diversity in Librarianship," six academic librarians discuss this. Juleah Swanson writes, "I think diversity matters because, right now, it allows us the opportunity to reinvent our organizational and professional culture into something that is not reliant on homogeneity of people and ideas, but rather looks toward what we bring to the future of higher education." The current need to address diversity has helped librarians rally around a new shared value. An excellent view of how teams with diverse members should be composed is "The Zen of Multidisciplinary Team Recommendation" by Anwitaman Datta, Jackson Tan Teck Yong, and Stefano Braghin. These authors present a diversity recommendation framework, which they call "SWAT" (Social Web Application for Team Recommendation). They consider this tool as a method to analyze the diverse aspects of teams.[20]

Fortunately, as the push for diversity within librarianship gains traction, the resulting advances will create more diverse teams. Although it will require considerable work to achieve this goal, many librarians are creating awareness and designing education to increase awareness.

AGILE TEAMS

One response to dysfunctional teams that has recently gained traction in the workplace has occasionally been adopted by libraries. This is the concept of the agile whole-team approach. This approach began in the software development field. It "describes a set of principles . . . under which requirements and solutions evolve through the collaborative effort of self-organizing cross-functional teams." The agile approach breaks up a problem or issue into smaller, more manageable parts and then tackles the work in incremental and iterative sections: "The Agile movement seeks alternatives to traditional project management. Agile approaches help teams respond to unpredictability through incremental, iterative work cadences and empirical feedback. Agilists propose alternatives to waterfall, or traditional sequential development."[21]

Although it comes in different flavors and the nomenclature varies, Leanne Howard's article "What Does It Mean to Have an Agile Mindset?" sums up this approach:

> To me, an agile mindset is "There is no failure, only feedback." It's about taking everything as lessons, adjusting actions according to the feedback, and proceeding toward desired outcomes, resulting in continuous improvement.
>
> The ideal is for everyone to have what the team decides is its collective agile mindset, but that all starts with the individual. I have worked with some great people who I think embody this mindset. They attack their work with a positive attitude, providing suggestions to overcome obstacles. They ask questions to understand what is in the best interests of the business, often coming up with innovative solutions as they experiment. They have realistic and practical attitudes focused on helping the team succeed.
>
> When looking for people to be part of my agile teams, these are the mindsets I look for. It is difficult to change people's intrinsic personalities and ways of thinking, so it is important to get the right selection of people for your team.[22]

Note the emphasis here on the importance of mindset development, as well as team composition and collective agreement about goals and norms. Agile teams are successful because they work towards short-term attainable goals (which must meet deadlines) that help to build momentum. Paring down some of the bloat that can be associated with group work helps to refocus on team efficiency.

THE ART OF COMPOSING A TEAM

The organizational design of the library in which you work, specifically the roles assigned to the librarians, impacts numerous aspects of your job. Similarly, the composition of the jobs for which coworkers are responsible affects day-to-day life. Fortunately, librarians share library values, codes of ethics, and numerous other professional guidelines that provide concrete guidance on how to behave. This commonality among librarians helps to form bonds that can align them. As the next example will illustrate, these can also be agreed-upon norms.

"What Google Learned from Its Quest to Build the Perfect Team" is an enlightening read that can lend valuable insight into library team composition. In the article, Charles Duhigg details Project Aristotle, an effort Google created to optimize teams that focused on ways to compose the best teams. The study eventually revealed that "understanding and influencing group norms were the keys to improving Google's teams." For this study, group norms are the

> behavioral standards and unwritten rules that govern how we function when we gather: one team may come to a consensus that avoiding agreement is more valuable than debate; another team might develop a culture that encourages vigorous arguments and spurns groupthink. Norms can be unspoken or openly acknowledged, but their influence is often profound. Team members may behave in certain ways as individuals—they may chafe against authority or prefer working independently—but when they gather, the group's norms typically override individual proclivities and encourage deference to the team.[23]

Note how the word "function" opens this passage, and also the assertion that agreed-upon terminology creates more unified teams. (The benefits of agreed-upon missions and goals as they pertain to leadership is a focus of chapter ten).

CONCLUSION

Dysfunctional roots bear rotten fruit. This analogy can represent the way in which teams can be corrupted by individual problems. Even more damaging is the lack of thought that goes into designing teams for cohesion, efficiency, and effectiveness. For some librarians, thinking in business terms or adhering to business principles may seem foreign, but it may be helpful to look towards that field because it is well-versed in composing teams. It is not necessary to adhere to these ideas strictly—they can be altered to reflect library values.

Librarianship is a field in which great value is placed on human resources and collective achievement, so these resources need to be at their functional best. Increasingly, focus is moving away from the importance placed on the "things" offered within a library (the collection, electronic resources, etc.) because of ever-increasing external competition. Strong relationships are built on mutual respect, and they create strong library teams that in turn send a message to library communities that their efficiency and achievements should be acknowledged. The most functional teams are combinations of the most functional individual units; however, carefully composed teams (even those that include some dysfunction) can provide good models for good librarian behavior.

NOTES

1. Carol Dweck, *Mindset,* 2010, http://mindsetonline.com/whatisit/themindsets/index.html.
2. Bobby Smiley, "Deeply Embedded Subject Librarians: An Interview with Brandon Locke and Kristen Mapes," February 10, 2016, http://acrl.ala.org/dh/2016/02/10/deeply-embedded-subject-librarians-an-interview-with-brandon-locke-and-kristen-mapes/; Amanda Visconti, "Service +/- collaboration for digital humanities in the library" (a DH job talk), February 28, 2016, http://literaturegeek.com/2016/02/28/DHjobtalk; Laura Soito, "Freeing Knowledge: Approaches to Foster Collaboration Between Academic Libraries and the Wikipedia Community," *Collaborative Librarianship,* 9, no. 2; Maxine Melling and Margaret Weaver, editors, *Collaboration in Libraries and Learning Environments,* (London, United Kingdom: Facet Publishing. 2012); Georgia Institute of Technology, H. Milton Stewart School of Industrial and Systems Engineering. *Senior Design Team Instrumental in Successful Georgia Tech Library Move to New LSC.* https://www.isye.gatech.edu/featured-stories/senior-design-team-instrumental-successful-georgia-tech-library-move-new-lsc; North Carolina State University Libraries, *Library Stories,* https://www.lib.ncsu.edu/stories; Association of College and Research Libraries, AASL/ACRL Task Force on the Educational Role of Libraries. *Blueprint for Collaboration,* www.ala.org/acrl/publications/whitepapers/acrlaaslblueprint.
3. Beth L. Strecker, "Academic Librarians' Perceptions of Teamwork and Organizational Structure in a Time of Rapid Technological Change "(doctoral dissertation, East Carolina University, 2010), retrieved from the Scholarship. (http://hdl.handle.net/10342/3186.)
4. American Library Association, "Core Values of Librarianship," June 29, 2004, www.ala.org/advocacy/intfreedom/statementspols/corevalues; Juris Dilevko, "The Politics of Professionalism: A Retro-Progressive Proposal for Librarianship" (Sacramento, CA: Library Juice Press, 2009); Joe Eshleman, Richard Moniz, Karen Mann, and Kristen Eshleman, *Librarians and Instructional Designers: Collaboration and Innovation* (Chicago, IL: Neal Schuman, 2016).
5. Anne Kemmerling, "A Different Way of Doing Business: Cross-Functional Strategic Initiative Teams," presented at Public Library Association Conference, April 8, 2016.

6. Behnam Tabrizi, "75% of Cross-Functional Teams Are Dysfunctional," *Harvard Business Review,* June 23, 2015, https://hbr.org/2015/06/75-of-cross-functional-teams-are -dysfunctional.

7. Leanne Howard, "What Does It Mean to Have an Agile Mindset?," Agile Connection, April 2015, http://athena.ecs.csus.edu/~buckley/CSc190/What%20Does%20It%20 Mean%20to%20Have%20an%20Agile%20Mindset.pdf.

8. Dara Goldberg, "Essential Mindsets of the High Performing Team of the 21st Century," April 21, 2016, http://switchandshift.com/mindsets-high-performing-teams.

9. M. Casado and A. Wallace, "How to Survive and Thrive in Your First Library Job," *Library Journal* 138, no. 18 (2013): 49.

10. "Team Composition," Wikipedia, The Free Encyclopedia, 2017. https://en.wikipedia .org/wiki/Team_composition.

11. Michael Rogers, "Playing Favorites," *Library Journal* 134, no. 4 (2009), 40 and Kathyellen Bullard, "Actions, Not Complaints," *Library Journal* 134, no. 4 (2009).

12. "Nepotism," Dictionary.com, http://dictionary.reference.com/browse/.

13. Emily Weak, "My Experience in Libraries Is That They're Rife with Nepotism," *Hiring Librarians* [blog], https://hiringlibrarians.com/2014/12/14/my-experience-in-libraries -is-that-theyre-rife-with-nepotism/.

14. Lisa Peet, "Update: Librarians Embroiled in Lawsuit Alleging Sexual Harassment," *Library Journal,* March 25, 2015.

15. "Library Workers: Facts and Figures Fact Sheet 2016," AFL-CIO Department for Professional Employees, http http://dpeaflcio.org/programs-publications/issue-fact -sheets/library-workers-facts-figures/.

16. Jessica Olin and Michelle Millet, "Gendered Expectations for Leadership in Libraries," *In the Library with the Lead Pipe* [blog], www.inthelibrarywiththeleadpipe.org/2015/ libleadgender/.

17. Sarah M. Pritchard, "Feminist Thinking and Librarianship in the 1990s: Issues and Challenges," *Feminist Research in Librarianship,* 1999, http://libr.org/ftf/femthink .htm.

18. Arron Grow, "Personnel vs Personal: A Mindset That Can Make a World of Difference," *City U News,* City University of Seattle, November 17, 2015. www.cityu.edu/ blog/personnel-vs-personal/.

19. Christine Porath, "The Hidden Toll of Workplace Incivility," *McKinsey Quarterly* (December 2016), www.mckinsey.com/business-functions/organization/our-insights/ the-hidden-toll-of-workplace-incivility.

20. Juleah Swanson, "Why Diversity Matters: A Roundtable Discussion on Racial and Ethnic Diversity in Librarianship," *In the Library with a Lead Pipe* [blog], www.inthelibrary withtheleadpipe.org/2015/why-diversity-matters-a-roundtable-discussion-on-racial -and-ethnic-diversity-in-librarianship/; Dave Anwitaman Datta, Jackson Tan Teck Yong, and Stefano Braghin, *The Zen of Multidisciplinary Team Recommendation,* https://arxiv.org/abs/1303.0646.

21. "Agile Software Development," Wikipedia, The Free Encyclopedia, 2017, https://en.wikipedia.org/wiki/Agile_software_development/; "The Agile Movement," *Agile Methodology: Understanding Agile Methodology*, http://agilemethodology.org/.

22. Howard, "What Does It Mean to Have an Agile Mindset?"

23. Charles Duhigg, "What Google Learned from Its Quest to Build the Perfect Team," *The New York Times Magazine* (February 25, 2016), https://www.nytimes.com/2016/02/28/magazine/what-google-learned-from-its-quest-to-build-the-perfect-team.html?_r=0.

10

LEADING AWAY FROM LIBRARY DYSFUNCTION

C onfronted with an unstable environment subject to continual change, libraries and librarians must learn to live with a certain amount of dysfunction. This does not mean that dysfunction cannot be minimized. There was a more constant and stable history in which the definitive function of the library was a given. This led to a present that demonstrates how libraries can adapt and transform. The constantly evolving world of technological challenges will continue to add to the dysfunction within libraries, but it can be offset by following a clear vision. This persistent change must be met with a leadership style that is aware, prepared, and vocal about the challenges ahead. Library leaders must meet the reality of the ever-evolving impacts of technology (as well as societal changes) with strategies that point to both defined and purposeful librarian roles and insure a sense of stability for librarians. Otherwise, dysfunction will continue to grow in an environment of imbalance and instability. This chapter provides balanced ideas that illustrate a middle way through the polarities that affect libraries and lead to librarian dysfunction.

As a response to continual change, library leaders should focus on the messages they send to librarians and members of their library community. These have great significance because they characterize how librarians are perceived. Regarding the academic realm, in "The Evolution of Teaching and Learning Professions" (from the Educause series *Seven Things You Should*

Know About...), Joshua Kim, the director of digital learning initiatives at Dartmouth College, makes a critical point. His conceptually driven focus on the semantics used for the "higher education teaching and learning support professional" (i.e., academic librarians) is excellent advice for all library leaders when thinking about how to portray staff:

> How might the profession of a "higher education teaching and learning support professional" change and evolve over the next three years? This question is instructive in the words we use to discuss our work. Many times, we still use the word "support" in talking about what we do. Over the next three years [the authors] hope to see this word disappear from the vocabulary we use to describe our work. "Support" connotes a hierarchy that doesn't recognize that staff are valuable assets who play an important role in postsecondary education. We need to find a new language that promotes the ethos of service and servant leadership, within the context of describing ourselves as non-faculty educators and alternative academics.[1]

Because the words we use to describe ourselves and the way librarians are perceived are crucial to what we want to achieve, moving away from the hard and fast designator of all librarians providing "support" should be reconsidered by library leadership. Although the idea of support is embedded into some of the core concepts of librarianship, without a change of mindset about how librarians are perceived, greater change cannot occur, and dependencies that contribute to dysfunction will only grow. It cannot be overstated that a focused and meaningful role for the librarian is paramount. The idea of librarians as leaders of change is continuing to gain more adherents, especially as the importance of accessing and properly using information continues to be pervasive in our daily lives. In addition, librarians were, and continue to be, at the forefront when promoting the use of open-access resources. These are two areas that have shown that librarians can change and can lead. Often, librarians are leaders but are not recognized as such.

"The Ithaka S+R Library Survey 2016 examines strategy and leadership issues from the perspective of academic library deans and directors. [The] project aims to provide academic librarians and higher education leaders with information about chief librarians' visions and the opportunities and challenges they face in leading their organizations." In this report, key findings underscore that this is a transitional time in academic libraries, where there is a refocus on the importance of the educational role of librarians as well as concern about the perceptions of librarians, and a lack of alignment with their institutions. The report has three key findings:

1. Library directors anticipate increased resource allocation towards services and predict the most growth for positions related to teaching and research support.
2. Library directors are deeply committed to supporting student success, yet many find it difficult to articulate these contributions.
3. Library directors are pursuing strategic directions with a decreasing sense of support from their institutions.[2]

These summaries demonstrate that library leaders who strive to present librarians in a new light face both challenges and opportunities. Time and again, librarians struggle with the quandary of how to present themselves— as both support staff and leaders—a difficulty that will need to be resolved by library leaders. Clear messaging is a start.

It is important to recognize that a false binary need not apply when we refer to "support" and "leader." A concept such as "servant leadership" may be applied, whereby "the servant-leader shares power, puts the needs of others first and helps people develop and perform as highly as possible." Kim's advice alludes to this. This approach could be applied, at minimum, on a case-by-case basis (if not in the broader sense of how libraries are viewed within a community). It is important to realize that leaders serve those who they lead, but there is also an unfortunate perception outside of the library that relegates librarians to a fixed role that denies them "leader status." Although supporting and leading can coexist, the perception of librarians as people who are in a support role can confine them to that role and is a potential barrier to leadership as it is classically understood. Once more, this impasse complicates moving forward and contributes to dysfunction.[3]

A blog post by Mark Ray, a former teaching librarian and current chief digital officer for the Vancouver [WA] Public Schools, writes in "The Future Ready are Among Us,"

> As schools seek to improve and innovate, there will be a need for exper-
> tise and leadership beyond principals and district personnel. Speaking
> from experience as a district administrator, the digital shift is too vast
> and fast for district leaders to effectively identify and curate innovative
> tools and practices for their schools.[4]

This is a direct call for librarians to lead others in the school systems; those who Ray feels may not be as qualified as librarians to accept technological changes.

Ray, as a leader for Future Ready Librarians, sees that librarians can be in front rather than behind, particularly in the digital environment. The Future Ready Librarians initiative came out of the Alliance for Excellent Education's 2014 report, *Leading In and Beyond the Library*, by Mary Ann Wolf, Rachel Jones, and Daniel Gilbert. This document begins with a comment from Steven T. Webb that parallels Kim's earlier idea to change the librarian mindset (and the words used to define what the librarian does) as a step on a path towards leadership:

> Ultimately, a successful digital transformation requires a ubiquitous leadership, creating a culture in which everyone can act with focus and coherency around our strategic vision. We must leverage leadership by creating the context and conditions for our team to take enlightened risks. Our teacher librarians have re-invented their role in our schools, serving as "digital mavens" to support colleagues in new and innovative ways as we scale our twenty first century flexible learning environments. Teacher librarians are an essential piece of our transformation professional development.[5]

This new focus on role changing and culture shifts also affects public libraries. As an example,

> The Aspen Institute, in partnership with the International City/County Management Association (ICMA), and the Public Library Association (PLA), released Local Libraries Advancing Community Goals, 2016, a report detailing results of a nationwide survey of nearly 2,000 chief administrative offices of local governments focused on the *evolving role of public libraries in advancing community goals* [emphasis added].[6]

Likewise, the 2014 report *Rising to the Challenge: Re-Envisioning Public Libraries* lists four strategies for success: aligning library services in support of community goals, providing access to content in all formats, ensuring the long-term sustainability of public libraries, and cultivating leadership. On this last relevant pathway, "vision is a critical component of leadership." The authors continue:

Every community needs a vision and a strategic plan for how to work with the public library to directly align the library and its work with the community's educational, economic and other key goals. It must have input from all stakeholder groups in the community. Key steps in building community leadership to support the public library include improving communications with community leaders, developing community champions, strengthening intersections with diverse communities and communities of color, reaching out to and engaging with young-professional organizations and demonstrating the collective impact of partners working together.[7]

Reaching out to the community is a hallmark of public libraries, and the needs of their communities can be more varied than those of academic or school libraries. This can occur in public libraries that serve extremely diverse communities, for example, in a larger urban environment. Although there is not as much focus here on reestablishing librarian roles as in the other library types, the need to include all groups and reach out to build strong connections to diverse communities foreshadows a point made later in this chapter around the need for critical librarianship.

Library leadership can work on two levels, the larger scale (sometimes referred to as "macro") and the smaller scale (the "micro"). When libraries are viewed in this dualistic way, a global and local dichotomy may result, particularly when community becomes part of the equation. Public, academic, and school media libraries are generally concerned with their own local community (as it may be defined) and special libraries appear to have a focused community as their default. Despite this, there is always the larger issue of "libraries with a capital 'L,'" sometimes more broadly considered as "library as concept" or "library as values." There are individual cases of librarian dysfunction and as documented throughout this book, each has its own set of causes, influences, effects, and so on. Many of the chapters analyze these and offer solutions. This chapter takes a "top down" approach and points out ways in which library leadership can address both larger (macro) and then, smaller (micro) dysfunctions.

The goal of this book is to shine a spotlight on the problems that prevent libraries and librarians from achieving their shared goals. As with all dysfunction, a first step is recognition. Once it is confirmed that the individual library is not operating properly, it is up to leaders to address the issues to optimize functionality. Unfortunately, libraries can have a difficult time measuring what it means to "operate properly" or "malfunction." This is especially true from the business perspective due to the "nonprofit" nature of libraries. Despite this, this chapter also explores what constitutes a functioning library and attempts to present the case to library leaders. This book speaks to a time when leadership will not be satisfied by merely functioning but, rather, actively minimizing dysfunction. The focus also promotes environments where librarians are considered change agents who occupy the lead position when someone in their community needs help with information.

Library directors and lead personnel need to be confident of their answer when asked, "where are we going, leader?" To answer that question properly, library leaders must plan for the impact of continuing technology changes and create clear and concise messaging about library goals for library staff and the community. A facet of the messaging goal is to work towards developing librarians who welcome change and show initiative. Although supporting the library community is a valuable librarian role, libraries need more innovation and collaboration. Placing more emphasis on these attributes will create more leaders and portray the library as moving forward rather than falling behind.

Three Messages Library Leaders Can Use to Battle Dysfunction:

- the importance of modeling within the library what the library wants to give to its community (which is dictated by what the community wants from its library)
- clear and consistent communication to all the members of the library regarding the way in which library goals will be met
- clear and consistent communication to all the members of the library whether the goals have (or have not) been accomplished within a selected amount of time

---

DYSFUNCTIONAL DESIGN

A type of dysfunction is embedded in the design of what it means to be a library leader. If looked at from the librarian's perspective, which has at its core an embedded service mindset, leadership for the librarian may be at odds with the need to serve. This could be considered a contradictory or dysfunctional design. As previously mentioned, although an artificial polarity does not need to exist, a conflict is present in some form. Librarians are so driven by a service mentality that they may not be able to fully come to terms with this issue, and can attempt to find semantic ways around it, for example, by gravitating to the idea of service leadership or embracing the concept of leading from behind. One approach to this problem is to ask, "what does it mean to be a library leader?" Would a comparison of leaders in other fields with library leaders show similarities or differences? Another way to move beyond the library perspective is to look towards other models and organizational designs in other disciplines for clues to break the artificial polarity between service and leadership.

Dysfunction is not a given. It develops and spreads when given room to fester. Library leaders must attempt to find ways to minimize the origins and growth of dysfunction by avoiding the creation of library environments that foster it. Sometimes, it is too late. This is hard work. The role of the librarian as designed, with its particular conflicts and instabilities, can breed dysfunction. It is therefore necessary to overcome this specific challenge. As shown in this chapter, the unstable conditions that create anxiety for librarians are manifold. One of the greatest is the conundrum of how to preserve librarians' values in a time of great technological change. Many of these "change" quandaries, taken together, contribute to the cumulative effect that creates a library environment that produces or enculturates dysfunctional librarians. Library leaders need to refocus on creating initiatives and strategies that zero in on direction and purpose to minimize dysfunction. As some libraries have slowly lost their own concepts of how they function, dysfunction moves in to influence how librarians perceive themselves.

When pondering the word "dysfunctional," consider what it means to function (or to be functional)? What does it mean for a library (or librarian) to be functional? This question can lead one down several paths. There is the larger, general conceptual sense of what libraries are for, as well as individual cases for each library (and in turn, each librarian). This type of global/local dichotomy affects libraries in a unique manner. Exploring the functions of a library lends insight into how libraries are viewed within their communities, and leads to a careful examination of the history of libraries and how they function.

At one point in time, questioning the value that libraries provided and how they functioned was not a pertinent or pressing query, especially considered in general terms. Libraries were places to go to find written collections of information that could be accessed and shared; this was the main assessment of a functional library. The public services librarians who helped patrons find, access, and possibly borrow the information that the librarians had curated provided a great deal of their functionality. According to the standards outlined at that time, dysfunctional librarians would not have been able to satisfy these relatively basic duties. Because there was little outside "competition," libraries had a type of "functional monopoly." To drive this point home, consider journalism, another field that has suffered a similar fate. Today more than ever, the news media's role as mediator and gatekeeper of civic discourse is being questioned. Jeffrey Rutenbeck, American University's dean of its school of communication, voiced what many are feeling when he observed in a recent Knight Foundation report, "Journalism has had the luxury of not having to ask itself the existential question of why anyone should pay any attention to us at all."[8]

The historical relationship between libraries and publishers, while still a dependent one from the point of view of libraries, was more symbiotic than confrontational. As time went on and computer use started to gain momentum, the functional value of libraries began to be questioned and reciprocal dependencies lessened, especially in relationships with database vendors, in which the suppliers held more power. Libraries became more dependent on information technology staff and departments, and librarian expertise waned to some extent. This growth of dependency on electronic resources by the library created new dysfunctions that were not formerly present because libraries now had less functional control. Put another way, libraries of the past had greater self-sufficiency and agency because their direction was clear. As time went on, this clear-cut self-direction lessened. Libraries have continued to find themselves beholden to many, and it can sometimes be difficult to clarify if the relationships are dysfunctional dependencies or fit a better design of mutual support to gain collective goals. As an example of direction combined with dependency, although library instruction can sometimes be the pinnacle of librarian-faculty collaboration, it can also inspire numerous laments (and articles) contending that "librarians are invisible "and "don't count."

Combining a continual loss of function with more dependencies has led to another form of library dysfunction. Although this book has documented numerous "individual" types of dysfunctional behavior such as poor communication, sexism, nepotism, bullying, and others, this chapter concentrates on how leaders can create libraries that help to minimize this dysfunctional dependency from the top, with the expectation that new visions and initiatives for librarians may alleviate problems. A key point here is that these campaigns to minimize dysfunction must be exceedingly clear in their goals and must provide straightforward and achievable action items for each librarian. Furthermore, library leaders need to make the difficult decisions that create demarcations for those who will perform the stated goals when given the agency to do so, and decide who has aligned with the goals of the library (the functional librarian) and who has not (the dysfunctional ex-librarian). As in most cases involving inflexibility and change, this is easier said than done.

Another definition of functional is "capable of a particular function or use—performing or capable of performing." From the historical perspective of a librarian who is not able to perform (especially basic job requirements), it would seem the rare case that a librarian with a Master's Degree in Library and Information Science would not be able to fulfill basic job requirements. Certainly, the possibility that library schools have fallen behind when training future librarians for the profession is an ongoing point of discussion in the field. This manifests in other ways as well. For example, there continues to be debates around the staffing of libraries and who is most qualified. This generally pertains to the professional/paraprofessional conversation.[9]

In *Academic Librarianship Today*, the chapter titled "Recruitment, Retention, Diversity, and Professional Development," by Marta Brunner and Jennifer Rosario addresses the professional/paraprofessional situation as follows:

> The role of the paraprofessional—which historically demanded only "routine" tasks in libraries, such as copy cataloging, initial acquisitions work, and physical processing—has grown to include original cataloging, metadata creation, management of electronic resources, and other higher-level tasks. This trend extends into the leadership ranks, with the management of the technical services department. But it may also be a natural shift because librarians find their own duties changing to require more outreach, instruction, and assessment, all duties that take them out of the library and into the classroom and data lab.[10]

One point to keep in mind is the effect that budgets have on the impact of staffing choices. In the article "The Library Paraprofessional Movement and the Deprofessionalization of Librarianship," Rory Litwin addresses the conflict directly and concludes,

> to be fair and to lend the issue a degree of complexity that is very much owed to it, "library administrators" as a group are also mostly professional librarians and therefore occupy a dual class position within their institutions. Perhaps their identities and ways of thinking are often shaped more by their status as library professionals than as managers. The conflict should therefore be seen not so much as a conflict between individuals as a conflict between roles, with library administrators, as librarians, often occupying a difficult position.[11]

Another interesting view of library professionalism was put forth by Juris Dilevko, who believes that academic librarians lose sight of their core principles when obsessing over professionalism, and are beholden to their institutions, which are increasingly becoming corporatized. In his book *The Politics of Professionalism: A Retro-Progressive Proposal for Librarianship,* Dilenko puts forth new ways for librarians to perceive themselves by bypassing library school and concentrating on their knowledge expertise, and to set themselves apart through more focused skill sets:

> Anyone wishing to work in an academic, research, or public library must independently pass a series of essay-type subject-specific examinations in about ten to fifteen fields or areas of the arts, social sciences, and sciences. In addition, he or she must be able to read and speak at least one non-English language fluently, as well as attend courses about various aspects of the operation of libraries at regional summer institutes.[12]

This excerpt show yet another way in which librarians' work is questioned and the numerous ways in which librarians can feel pressured and become dysfunctional in their working roles.

Another example of a formerly static position that has seen upheaval in libraries and may be to blame for creating dysfunction in some librarians is the myth of neutrality in libraries. Librarians have in the past prided themselves on being able to minimize bias when building collections and helping patrons find information. In one sense, this concept may be somewhat apocryphal, because the idea that libraries were (or can be) "neutral" is more idealistic than practical. Many current librarians feel as though this is impossible to achieve. In some cases, it has inhibited the ability to represent true library ideals, and is especially pernicious when creating value for librarians. In "The Myth of Library Neutrality," Candise Branum points out that "this idea of the librarian as a neutral medium takes away the powerfulness of the lived experiences and learned knowledge of librarians."[13]

Librarians have become more interested in social justice and ensuring that their communities are evenly and comprehensively represented in the library. Social justice is an extremely appealing method to retain librarian values and move forward. It is focused on ethics and does not tip the scales into an arena that is driven solely by money. It is "people-focused." Open access also fulfills the need for direction, which is one reason why it has such widespread support from librarians.

These discussions raise further questions such as "how do you define any deficient librarian, one who is not doing his library job, and what are the repercussions when this occurs?" Would such a librarian be a "dysfunctional librarian?" These questions emphasize the focus on "librarian dysfunction" as opposed to general "workplace or staff dysfunction." Put differently, is there something unique in the field of librarianship that contributes to dysfunction, and if so, can that specific dysfunction be minimized? The answer to this question, based on the internal and external oppositional quandaries set forth in this chapter, appears to be "yes."

Although there are many fields currently trying to keep up with the onslaught of technological change, librarians have the added burden of questioning whether they are "being true to their roots, or core values." Education finds itself similarly taxed, yet appears to have more resources to deal with this issue. Librarians often seem to second-guess themselves about not moving quickly enough, which can lead to hand-wringing when they feel as though they are moving away from historical values.

As an example of how *not* to lead and how self-reflection and constant questioning can lead to stasis and standstill, consider the recent disagreement about the guiding document for information literacy in libraries and library instruction. The Association of College and Research Libraries website explains that the *Information Literacy Competency Standards for Higher Education* (originally approved in 2000) were rescinded by the ACRL Board of Directors on June 25, 2016, at the 2016 ALA Annual Conference in Orlando, Florida, which means they are no longer in force. These standards have been replaced by *Framework for Information Literacy for Higher Education,* which was filed in February of 2015. Controversy arose for several reasons, one of which emerged due to uncertainty (which, again, helps to add to stress and dysfunction) about which professional guidelines to follow during a time when both documents were available. Many librarians felt as though ACRL should have been clearer about the decision and the timeline for the transition from one document to another. Additionally, many librarians felt allegiance to the *Standards* and had built strong programs around its design. Indecision marked this event, and though there were certainly legitimate reasons for the delay, the results were damaging. It can be a fine line between allowing input and nuanced discussion and "cutting the cord."[14]

Librarians have often painted themselves into a corner when trying to come to consensus about direction and shared goals. The overarching library principles and guidelines from the history of librarianship are often stretched because technology rapidly changes the environments of library work. For example, libraries have needed to cordon off space for quiet areas due to the demand for "noisier" group spaces, makerspaces, and the need to reach out to different communities such as young adults. These types of changes to physical library space are much different from the silent spaces of the past. It can be cathartic to explore the numerous pressures that can arise when librarians feel as though they are in a bind. The historical need to be organized and precise when creating a collection may hinder librarians when ambiguity is part of a decision-making process. Ethical standards protecting patrons are continually endangered by the desire to "predict" events that support sustainability, especially in relation to budget concerns. These conceptual conundrums can yield a long list, and seemingly everywhere librarians turn, they are confronted by allegiance to historical antecedents clashing with change pressures.

The same structure that evoked allegiances to database vendors also led to competition among search engines; those who control search engines; and how information is designed, accessed, and monetized. One option is for libraries is to consider a move to monetization, but this unswervingly opposes many cherished library values, particularly patron protection. Especially in academic libraries, there is a concern that education has moved away from the former ideal where the creation of responsible citizens is a priority and has become instead another avenue for profit-making. Despite the allure, monetizing library services may not be the most sustainable design because it will diminish one of the features that sets libraries apart from money-making ventures and could lead to libraries losing in a competitive business environment.

What makes libraries unique is that they are typically not profit-driven, and their work is based on access (sharing) and support (giving). Once more, librarians may be conflicted when called upon to be leaders, especially in a capitalistic arena. Another way to leverage the unique values that libraries espouse is to publicize them. For example, in a technology-driven world that is often impersonal, libraries could emphasize the aspects that make them humane and unique institutions.

One tangential topic here that currently plagues libraries is the continual need to prove value. The administrative requests and money-driven obsession with providing value can cause stress and dysfunction. It can be especially troubling to try to find an answer that stops the questioning. This is not to say that assessment, strategic plans, goals, and all the various statistics that support library values have no value. The point here is to question the design of continual "value questioning" and to find a correct balance between showing that the services and support that libraries provide is efficient and valuable and obsessing over quantitative numbers and the doomsday predictions about the future of the library. When asked to demonstrate worth, it can be important to determine who is asking, and why, to get an idea of the "satisfactory" answer to the question "what is your value?" There needs to be something in place that satisfies the question of library value or it will never be answered satisfactorily. Too often, librarians are tasked with providing a satisfactory answer to support their value and then told that there is a "correct" way to prove their own value. That is not shown within their response. This can be frustrating and lead to a great deal of dysfunction.

It can be useful for librarians to emphasize that their own ethical and idealistic librarianship ideals provide value to their communities. Examples such as Ranganathan's Five Laws of Library Science and the American Library Association's Core Values of Librarianship provide guidance for librarians to show ethical value to their communities through such ideals as equal access to information and patron protection. These are, however, not easily measurable in a quantifiable or monetary sense. Again, this is not to say that this obviates reflecting on value or that assessment is not worthwhile.

One way for libraries to prove value that has gained more and more support, especially in relation to the pervasiveness of technology, is focusing on the human aspects of libraries. Libraries are becoming more human-centered and are moving to differentiate themselves from tech companies or other institutions that are less concerned with the "personal touch." In the *Guardian* article "World Book Day: Without Libraries We Are Less Human and More Profoundly Alone," as Nicola Davies bemoans the lack of public support for British libraries, she weaves her childhood recollections of library collections and realizes that

> Librarians are far more than stackers and catalogers. They are creative curators of their book collections. They review and renew their flocks of books, adjusting what they have to fit their readers, highlighting certain sections and topics to reflect the world. They are on hand to guide and encourage, to foster relationships between books and people. Subtly, quietly, inexorably, they weave individuals into a community . . . This book habitat does not happen on its own—it is created by librarians. Librarians are the keystone of good libraries . . . Without librarians and the libraries, they make we are less alive, less human, more profoundly alone.[15]

Note here how Davies relates the importance of human-centered interactions and human communities.

As libraries put more emphasis on programs that support mindfulness, health issues, community support, and personal librarians, they prove that "values are library value." Values are not measurable, but they do have impact. Critical librarianship "includes the development of critical thinking, information literacy, and lifelong learning skills in students, as well as engagement with diversity, information ethics, access to information, commodification of information, labor, academic freedom, human rights, engaged citizenry, and neoliberalism." Concentrating on moving the library forward by critically examining how it relates to and represents its community is a good way to replace the lost "functionality" in libraries. Because libraries need to show value and librarians need ethical, focused goals, investing in the future of our community (and not focusing all our effort only on its members' information needs) helps to minimize the current dysfunctional sense librarians have of themselves.[16]

THE DYSFUNCTIONAL LIBRARY LEADER

In the chapter entitled "Ineffective (bad!) Leadership" from the book *Making a Difference: Leadership and Academic Libraries,* Donald E. Riggs points out that the focus on leadership in the library field is relatively new. Since Riggs's book was published in 2006, the literature has focused more on the topic of library leadership. Riggs concludes, "Little on bad leadership can be found in the literature; a possible rational for this omission is based on the 'immaturity' of the study of leadership . . . An intellectual approach to library leadership requires an understanding of effective and ineffective leaders."[17]

Riggs does an excellent job of shining a spotlight on dysfunctional patterns that lead to library leadership errors. These patterns include conflict avoidance, mistreatment of staff, micromanagement, inaccessibility, non-communication, passive-aggressiveness, and irrational behavior. Each of these have been addressed in his book, and although it can be helpful to address each individually, considering the factor that seemed to arise repeatedly in the authors' qualitative research may have greater impact. The single topic that came up most often was communication. Many of the dysfunctions that this book addresses seem to have grown out of an absence of focused intent, and thus allowed dysfunction to fester. In other words, if a group of librarians do not understand the core daily mission they are trying to achieve because it is not communicated well, dysfunction moves in through the cracks. This is important. Core missions must become mantras and, in most cases, the core missions of libraries are a combination of historical library values combined with the needs of the community. Each idea, initiative, and dysfunction should be met with the query, "How does this help us achieve our core mission?"[18]

Carol A. Brey-Casiano, director of the El Paso, Texas, public library system, states, "I have always believed that the mark of a good leader is one who can articulate a vision for his or her organization and then motivate others to share and accomplish that vision." Library leaders who do not examine aspects of leadership that may fall into the category of bad practice or lack a coherent vision have failed to be self-reflective and are not constantly striving for their libraries' better future. Has a library leader shown the capability to prove value to those outside of the library and clearly communicate the vision for her library? Once again, someone designated as a library leader who does not find a way to communicate to staff the vision for his library is contributing to dysfunction. If library directors or supervisors are not sure whether the staff they manage and lead know what the library's goals are and how to achieve them, they likely work in dysfunctional library environments. And most importantly, if the staff does not represent a diverse group of backgrounds, ideas, experiences and other factors (e.g., age, gender, race, and sexual orientation, especially as these characteristics reflect the community served), then a current core goal of critical librarianship is not being met. At one point in the history of libraries an admirable conceptual goal was equal access to information for all. And while this goal was mostly met, as society evolved it began to seem as if libraries had not been quite able to fulfill all their ideals, especially the goal of breaking through all systemic barriers.[19]

Allowing lengthy (or even short) conversations in the library is yet another sign of changing times. This is nothing new, but whereas in the past the entire library was quiet, it has now morphed into quiet spaces *within* the library. Although this change treads upon stereotypes, there continues to be a push for librarians to be more outgoing and personable and to spend time creating and nurturing relationships. Similarly, library leaders have been asked to improve their emotional intelligence. Because we have learned that poor communication contributes to dysfunction, a library leader should try to speak frequently with librarians.

In a post from the popular and influential library blog *In the Library with the Lead Pipe,* "Nothing Tweetable: A Conversation on How to 'Librarian' at the End of Times," when Joshua Finnell and Lareese Hall broach the question, "Why do we care about libraries?" they receive the response, "I suppose, like you, I complain about libraries because I see the unlimited potential and it never ceases to amaze me how much of it is squandered." Certainly, many librarians appear to have idealized viewpoints about libraries and librarianship, and when confronted with some of the dysfunctions documented here find themselves disappointed or disillusioned. This discussion is a good example of how conversations reveal hidden and often unseen contributions and unspoken ideas. A true library leader is akin to a good coach, who knows the best attributes of staff and tries to get to know the players. A leader who devotes effort to fellow employees will minimize dysfunction.[20]

Lareese Hall makes a perceptive observation that aligns with the overarching ideas presented in this chapter. Although she puts more emphasis on collections, her summary of how loss of control is a direct line to uncertainty could serve as a coda for this chapter. Her contention that instability breeds fear, and for our purposes, dysfunction, is explained as follows:

> We create distinctions because it is easier to manage the uncertainty of our very human existence. It is a kind of control. Control is a mechanism for managing fear. How we define that fear is entirely our own, but having control is one way to manage the total weight of that reality. Libraries (and people who work in them) like to control things.[21]

This need for control is a direct irritant for dysfunction. When things go awry (as they are prone to do), a librarian subject to the tyranny of control will not react well and may certainly become dysfunctional.

Hall quickly offers a strategy to avoid this: "I see collaboration as a way to let go of control (and fear). I spend a good deal of time getting to know people wherever I work, and in those introductory conversations projects or ideas emerge." Daily face-to-face communication with all employees whenever possible alleviates many attributes of dysfunction. It shows empathy, bridges to often buried ideas, allows librarians to show off their agency, and sheds light on dysfunction. As with all these suggestions, it is up to library leaders to begin these discussions and then act.[22]

Some of the contributors to library dysfunction were discussed at the beginning of this chapter. Leadership is difficult and taxing work. As Steven Bell points out in "Toxic Leaders, Toxic Workers: Learning to Cope,"

> There are no easy answers or solutions in these situations. Advice is abundant and cheap and not always of value. Fixing the toxic workplace starts with library leaders. Whether they cause it or stand by while it happens, their behavior allows the culture of incivility to exist. It is on the shoulders of those who lead to model civility and root out dysfunction.[23]

THE FUNCTIONAL LIBRARY

The measurement of a functional library can differ according to the type of library. Providing for the community's needs is tantamount. Public libraries might encounter smaller communities within the larger, whose needs create function: reading events for children, media spaces for young adults, and classes about topics like starting a business for the adult community. Similarly, a school library works with different grade levels. The special library may have a wide variety of communities to serve. Despite numerous groups coming to the library, the central function can be folded into a general definition. A well-written library mission can help to focus on a library's primary function.

The academic library's main function is to support its parent organization's institutional objectives, but those libraries also have various communities. As the name suggests, academic libraries are involved in providing support for research and educational activities in universities, institutions, and other academic organizations. It involves content development, acquisition, technical services, providing institutional repositories, interlibrary loan, and document-delivery services. Some academic libraries branch out to establish writing centers and centers for information literacy.

We must pivot so that we can grapple with leadership and dysfunction in a positive manner instead of fixating on what is wrong. A good current model is the Massachusetts Institute of Technology (MIT) libraries' approach to leadership. Chris Bourg, the director of libraries, set the tone for leadership in a recent blog post about machine learning:

> One of the things I think is important for library leaders is that we look at fundamental changes outside of knowledge management and consider their implications for libraries and the work we do. I think looking outside of changes in our own field is essential if we want to be active, effective leaders who don't merely respond to change, but who create and shape the change we believe is needed in libraries and archives.[24]

The focus here is on keeping up with change, but the importance of creating and shaping change is a template for how to move away from dysfunction. A renewed leadership call to influence change moves libraries away from dependencies (and the insecurities associated with them) and creates a better sense of direction. In a nutshell, a great deal of dysfunction can occur when there is a lack of agency. Libraries must continue to recognize that remaining in a continued position of "support" is a zero-sum game.

Especially in relation to academic libraries' ability to influence change on their campuses, no progress will be made until the administration and faculty demonstrates the kind of respect for librarians that creates partnerships rather than unbalanced relationships. (This is explored in more detail later in this chapter when discussing the design of better library leaders.)

For now, let's return to Chris Bourg's statements and parse more of what she wrote. This strategy of creating and shaping the future for libraries leverages communication towards change as a fulcrum to alleviate some of the problems and issues that plague librarianship. Another crucial theme revolves around the keyword "outside," as she employs the phrases "look at fundamental changes outside" and "looking outside of changes in our own field." Bourg uses the strategy of turning to other fields and professions (especially the technological impact on knowledge management, in this case, artificial intelligence) to connect to current changes. This strategy works well to address direction, promote agency, and alleviate dysfunction.

As mentioned earlier in this chapter, there are levels of libraries. They can be considered in a broad, conceptual way or from the more provincial "my local library" perspective. The larger model may be connected through a library association, for example, the leadership tools of a large organization such as the American Library Association, or any others (see the list of Library Associations Around the World at www.ala.org/offices/iro/intlassocorgconf/libraryassociations). Here library leadership could be conceptualized as externally focused on a larger community rather than on a smaller local library community.

This book has skewed towards those dysfunctions that are primarily behavior-based. Although chapters 2 and 5 did place more emphasis on the design of library culture and the workplace, many of the other chapters dealt with those behaviors that define and contribute to dysfunctional librarians. Chapters 9 and 10 looked at design, but rather that of teams and leaders, so there is some balance here. What this division points to is a type of chicken-and-egg theory as it relates to dysfunction in libraries. Does dysfunction begin with the individual librarian or is leadership responsible for creating and fostering inoperable libraries? This question usually leads to further questions. The bottom line is that the problem-solving burden ultimately rests on the shoulders of library leaders.

One entry point into leadership may eventually depend on the previously posed question, "Where are we going, leader?" There are macro and micro answers for each library leader. This chapter does not presume to answer contextual questions, but will attempt to show how libraries can get a general sense of how to get to where they want to go. Therefore, we must first focus on local matters. Because this book is primarily interested in dysfunction, we will not reiterate challenges but instead work in a more positive direction. This book has illustrated that, simply put, good communication makes good leaders and poor communication creates and adds to dysfunction.

MIT's approach to library leadership models a local/global strategy. Although it can be frustrating, even a bit demoralizing, to compare your organization directly against a library that may have more resources, it can also be illuminating and beneficial. The point of investigating other libraries' missions and strategic initiatives is not to imitate them, but to discover what might apply to your individual library. This is a good way to stay local while reaching out for larger ideas that affect the library profession (and the world we live in).

In October of 2016, MIT came out with a directional document put together by its Future of Libraries Task Force. It assessed the information landscape and explained that a way forward was for libraries to work from a local/global ideology, with even greater emphasis on global service:

> For the MIT Libraries, the better world we seek is one in which there is abundant, equitable, meaningful access to knowledge and to the products of the full life cycle of research. Enduring global access to knowledge requires sustainable models for ensuring that past and present knowledge is available long into the future. Moreover, access to knowledge must be fluid, interactive, contextualized, participatory, programmable, and comprehensive in order to fully enable citizens and scholars to integrate across disciplines, timescales, geographies, languages, and cultures. The Task Force asserts that the MIT Libraries should be leaders in developing those models, and in advancing more radically open systems for the discovery, use, and stewardship of information and knowledge.[25]

Again, not all libraries have access to the many resources that MIT does, but other libraries may want to explore how the MIT Libraries plan to become "leaders in developing those models." Connecting to the goal of diminishing dysfunction, a report like this aligns with the type of action that moves an organization away from focusing on some of the drivers that can create dysfunction and leave it to fester. As discussed throughout this book, dysfunction cannot be ignored, but it is often the case that library supervisors are reluctant to deal with it head on. Therefore, a solution would be to design and develop plans that do not allow dysfunction to develop and grow. This an important point, because although it can be helpful to document and analyze librarian dysfunction, without implementing means to combat it, it will endure. Leadership that shows practical ways to admit to, anticipate, and address dysfunction is poised to make advances.[26]

One caveat needed here is that there must be an attempt to boil down the most highly prioritized goal into a sentence of very few words so that it can constantly be used to evaluate initiatives and actions. In the case of an academic library, if the primary goal of the library could be paraphrased as "we help students accomplish their academic work," then anything that the librarians do should be put up against this litmus test. As a method to recognize some of the various instances of dysfunctional behavior documented in this book, it is quite easy to ask questions that relate to this prioritized goal, for example, "How do social media efforts help students accomplish their academic work?" Of course, there is always the possibility that an extremely tenuous connection could be made. A librarian could say "we can publicize that we have additional hours during exam week, which helps students accomplish their academic work." This then moves the conversation to a discussion where prioritizing specific goals and outcomes is even more crucial.

THE OUTWARDLY FOCUSED LIBRARY LEADER

Perhaps one element of dysfunction, especially as it relates to many of the problems the authors have documented, can also be traced to a type of inwardly focused mindset. Issues such as bullying, nepotism, and others can be said to emanate to some extent from situations where there is either too much time when work is not prioritized, or when "down time" allows for negative events to fester. Those who are given time to ruminate on dysfunction can amplify it. This should not lead to the trite suggestion that "hard work erases dysfunction," but merely points out that too much time spent away from service or leadership provides the opportunity to gravitate towards negativity and to become overly introspective. The concept of looking "outward" seems quite pedestrian, but considering that libraries in the past were more internally focused, in the current environment it makes sense to focus attention outward.

An outward focus allows visionary library leaders to push boundaries and create new perceptions of librarians in their communities. When librarians are seen at social or sporting events, at a nightclub, or in unexpected places (this may sometimes be anywhere outside the library), they are given new context—regardless of whether they provide on-site library services or just show up.

The following list provides some benefits of moving towards an outwardly focused viewpoint:

- It creates a unified purpose. (This is a single matter that is at the crux of dysfunctional complaints. There should be a focus on communication and consistency is key.)
- It enables placing priority on professional development.
- It helps the library's community to understand the function and value of librarians.
- It creates an environment that is "bigger picture" (versus one that is personality driven).

Similar to how repeating an easy-to-recall prioritized library goal (i.e., a "mantra") enables a concentrated way to evaluate librarians' work, an external focus helps to distance library leaders from internal dysfunctions. This does not mean they will be allowed to ignore or dismiss dysfunctional actions or librarians, but it may help to put certain dysfunctions into perspective.

Generative leadership is an approach that aligns with the goal of looking outward. It relies on forward thinking and is focused on growth and change. As explained in the blog post "The 4 C's of Generative Leadership," "the role of the generative leader is to lead and take accountability for the collective learning of their organization. Their function is to challenge people to recognize the lenses through which they view the organization and any personal biases or influences they hold that may impact thinking."[27]

What distinguishes generative leadership is an emphasis on creation, which includes the creation of more leaders. Generating change through several tactics, the generative leader

> recognizes that organizations are dynamic, living systems, and, to create new constructs and possibilities, this leader puts into action collaborative decision-making and idea-generating models, recognizing that every individual is an integral element to the living system. Central to this endeavor is creating environments where innovation is not only encouraged but is a driving factor in everything one does at the institution. For an educational organization, meaningful learning is the focus of innovation.[28]

Looking at how librarians would prefer to be perceived outside of the library is an effective exercise. A library leader (e.g., a library director) might want to consider how he envisions the library and how its librarians will be viewed outside of the library. This type of public relations-campaign refreshes the library's vision and creates a shared sense of community.

The primary drivers that can create dysfunction stem from a general sense of insecurity, for example, not having a deep understanding of purpose (or function), insecurity about change, and dependencies that diminish personal and collective library agency. What is interesting is that historically, none of these issues were as evident or pressing in the past.

Another persistent theme in this book is that library leadership has the opportunity and responsibility to recognize and address dysfunction. Although there appear to be innumerable cases where leadership has failed to do this, the main goal of this chapter is to posit examples and ideas that can help leaders accomplish this important part of their work. Rather than dredging up instances of mistakes and improper behavior when dealing with dysfunctional librarians, our goal is to focus on the creation of a positive framework for leaders. To some extent this approach bypasses those leaders who are themselves dysfunctional; therefore, that subject will be considered separately.

To bookend this chapter, we revisit the concept of the outwardly focused librarian leader. Although at first this idea could be viewed negatively (e.g., as when it could imply that a library leader does not pay much attention to her fellow librarians), it means the direct opposite and has positive conotations. Allowing the community that a library serves to understand the function and value of the librarians, and connecting librarians with that community, is a great form of advocacy that can minimize dysfunction. As described below, advocacy is essential for a fully functional library.

The added pressures of the continued questioning about the value of libraries and their worth in an increasingly technologically driven environment make it difficult for libraries to see their way to a stable future. One conversation the authors had when writing this book focused on how to shed light on the harmful habits that keep libraries (and librarians) from moving forward. From a pedantic point of view, what does it mean to move forward? This may initially seem to be a somewhat innocuous question, but it could be at the heart of the matter. Once more, it is especially important that a library leader can say, "this is where we are going." Providing that direction confidently requires a firm grasp of the larger issues affecting libraries globally and the local ones impacting an individual library. Dysfunctional problems can be met head-on instead of being swept under the rug when there is clear direction, because librarians who do not align with the library's mission can be quickly identified when they do not contribute to the function of the library.

DESIGNING TODAY'S FUNCTIONAL LIBRARY

A thought experiment can shed light on the multiple problems in libraries that stem from antiquated thinking or legacy systems. Attempting to think dispassionately about how to design a library that would be both useful and valuable in today's (and future) environments will clarify what librarians should be working towards (and away from). Stepping back to assess this situation and looking holistically at this idea can lead to insight about specific library dysfunction. The thought experiment would be proposed like this: "What would a library that impacts its community in a positive way and stays aligned with the goals of librarianship look like? How would its leaders act? And what would the librarians do in this library?"

Based on what we have learned, this library would be active and community-centered. All librarians would have a concise understanding of their roles and how they fit in with the library's common commitment to its community. The librarians would be well-versed in understanding how agency is a core principle for identifying any responsibilities, tasks, or initiatives that do not contribute to the library's succinct mission. All library leaders would be responsible for communicating face-to-face with each employee and asking daily if the employee's personal goals are being met. Again, this activity is a difficult mission, and agency must always be a priority. All idealistic notions must be tempered with the realities of everyday burdens and circumstances that cannot be controlled. Leaders already know this.

There are, of course, libraries that manage to meet several of these wish list targets. Note the pattern throughout this chapter. In the past, libraries had a clear path to their function. Changes outside the library forced librarians to confront those changes. The lack of purpose in work combined with the fear of future instability led to loss of direction. These elements of a shaky environment combined into a breeding ground for dysfunction. But there are always ways forward. The Knight Foundation published "Developing Clarity: Innovating in Library Systems" in March of 2017. This public library–focused report attempts to "understand the state of innovation capability and culture of urban libraries." It presents numerous rallying points, one of which is that "all urban library systems have the immediate opportunity to articulate and communicate clearly to staff, funders and patrons the particular problems they have prioritized for innovation (versus sustaining and improving existing offerings and operations)." This ability to beyond dysfunction and concentrate on where libraries need to go is a great reminder of the importance of direction and goals.

CONCLUSION

Returning once more to the question that led off this chapter, "Where are we going, leader?" we can answer "away from dysfunction." All the suggestions to counter the challenges that have been presented in this chapter have common solutions. Prepare for and embrace technological change, create clear library messaging, reevaluate librarian roles to minimize service focus and maximize innovation, and support the library community—all of which must be consistently communicated. As has been shown throughout this book, dysfunction stems primarily from a lack of good communication. Librarians who are confused about their roles or are not in sync with the goals of their library will not be functional. It is up to library leaders to impress upon those who do not understand their function the importance of communication.

Certainly, this is easier said than done, and daily dysfunction wears down even the most energetic and idealistic librarians. Still, without clearly communicating with their leaders, how can librarians move forward in a positive way? We know that librarians feel most comfortable and are at their best when they have a good sense of their function and meaning. When that meaningful function is unclear, dysfunction occurs. Some librarians can find their own personal meaning within such environments, but these disparate directions do not lead to a whole library. The profession finds itself in a situation that calls for new professional models to accompany the models for teaching and learning that are now being invented. This evolution requires new leadership skills to help guide the cultural shifts associated with the transformative dimensions of our work. Communication skills appear to be of the utmost importance at this time.

As stated in the beginning of this book, all librarians must strive to improve themselves and to diminish their own dysfunctional qualities. As humans and as librarians, we are all works in progress. Leaders need to recognize this and lend a helping hand to communicate the dysfunctions that block librarians' progress. Library leaders can help libraries and librarians move forward only if they are able to identify dysfunction, map out functional directions, and communicate solutions.

NOTES

1. "The Evolution of Teaching and Learning Professions," *Seven Things You Should Know About the Evolution of Teaching and Learning Professions*, Educause, https://library .educause.edu/~/media/files/library/2017/3/eli7142.pdf.:2.

2. Christine Wolff-Eisenberg, US Library Survey 2016, Ithaka S+R, https://doi.org/ 10.18665/sr.303066, 3–4.

3. Greenleaf Center for Servant Leadership, 2016, https://www.greenleaf.org/what -is-servant-leadership/.

4. Mark Ray, "The Future Ready are Among Us," *Seen,* March 3, 2017, www.seen magazine.us/Articles/Article-Detail/ArticleId/6131/THE-FUTURE-READY-ARE -AMONG-US.

5. "Leading In and Beyond the Library," The Alliance for Excellent Education, http:// a114ed.org/reports-factsheets/leading-in-and-beyond-the-library/.

6. Amy Garmer, "The Role of Libraries in Advancing Community Goals," The Aspen Institute Dialogue on Public Libraries, www.libraryvision.org/the_role_of_libraries _in_advancing_community_goals.

7. Amy Garmer, "Rising to the Challenge: Re-Envisioning Public Libraries," *Report of the Aspen Institute Dialogue on Public Libraries—The Role of Libraries in Advancing Community Goals*, http://d3n8a8pr07vhmx.cloudfront.net/themes/5660b272ebad 645c44000001/attachments/original/1452193779/AspenLibrariesReport.pdf? 1452193779: XI–XII.

8. Rich Grundy, "What the News Media Can Learn from Librarians?," *Columbia Journalism Review*, October 24, 2016, www.cjr.org/innovations/librarians_journalism _lessons.php.

9. "Functional," Dictionary.com, www.dictionary.com/browse/functional?s=t.

10. Marta Brunner and Jennifer Osario, "Recruitment, Retention, Diversity, and Professional Development," in Todd Gilman, ed., *Academic Librarianship Today,* (Lanham, MD: Rowman and Littlefield, 2017), 147.

11. Rory Litwin, "The Library Paraprofessional Movement and the Deprofessionalization of Librarianship," *Progressive Librarian* 33 (Summer/Fall 2009): 59-60, www.libraryjuicepress.com/docs/deprofessionalization.pdf.

12. Juris Dilevko, *The Politics of Professionalism: A Retro-Progressive Proposal for Librarianship* (Library Juice Press, 2009), http://libraryjuicepress.com/dilevko-professionalism .php.

13. Candise Branum, "The Myth of Library Neutrality" [blog post], May 14, 2014, https:// candisebranum.wordpress.com/2014/05/15/the-myth-of-library-neutrality/.

14. Association of College and Research Libraries, "Standards for Proficiencies for Instruction Librarians and Coordinators," June 24, 2007.

15. Nicola Davies, "World Book Day: Without Libraries We Are Less Human and More Profoundly Alone," *The Guardian,* March 2, 2017, https://www.theguardian.com/

voluntary-sector-network/2017/mar/02/without-libraries-and-librarians-we-are-less
-human-and-more-profoundly-alone.

16. Kenny Garcia, "Keeping Up With . . . Critical Librarianship," Association of College and Research Libraries, www.ala.org/acrl/publications/keeping_up_with/critlib.

17. Donald E. Riggs, "Ineffective (bad!) Leadership," in *Making a Difference: Leadership and Academic Libraries* (Boulder, CO: Libraries Unlimited, 2006) ed. Peter Hernon and Nancy Rossiter, 187.

18. Ibid., 185.

19. Carol A. Brey-Casiano, "Leadership Qualities for Future Library Leaders: Carol's 10 Steps to Being a Great Library Leader" [blog post], October 24, 2016, www.library .illinois.edu/mortenson/book/10_brey-cassiano.pdf.

20. Joshua Finnell and Lareese Hall, "Nothing Tweetable: A Conversation or How To 'Librarian' at the End of Times," *In the Library with the Lead Pipe I* [blog], March 8, 2017, http://inthelibrarywiththeleadpipe.org/2017/nothing-tweetable-a-conversation-or-how -to-librarian-at-the-end-of-times?platform=hootsuite.

21. Ibid.

22. Ibid.

23. Steven Bell, "Toxic Leaders, Toxic Workers: Learning to Cope | Leading From the Library," *Library Journal,* June 24, 2015, http://lj.libraryjournal.com/2015/06/opinion/ leading-from-the-library/toxic-leaders-toxic-workers-learning-to-cope-leading-from -the-library/.

24. Chris Bourg, "What Happens to Libraries and Librarians when Machines Can Read All the Books?," *Feral Librarian* [blog], March 14, 2017, https://chrisbourg.wordpress .com/2017/03/16/what-happens-to-libraries-and-librarians-when-machines-can-read -all-the-books/.

25. MIT Ad Hoc Task Force on the Future of Libraries, https://www.pubpub.org/pub/ future-of-libraries.

26. Ibid.

27. Susan Taylor, "The 4 C's of Generative Leadership: What Is Dialogue?," March 14, 2016,whatisdialogue.com/4-cs-generative-leadership/.

28. Jill Channing, "The Benefits of Generative Leadership in Community Colleges," *Higher Learning Commission, 2015Annual Conference,* http://cop.hlcommission.org/ Leadership/channing2015.html.

CONCLUSION

When the authors first began to discuss this book in earnest it became clear that we did not want just to go down the standard library-management path. After lengthy debate, we decided to write a book that explores the biggest problems faced in libraries (especially by managers). Along the way we quickly realized that *all* librarians can benefit from this type of information. The idea was to gather background on these matters and then provide some solutions. The problems and solutions were to be supported by facts and scholarship rather than mere opinion or personal experience. The 4,186 librarians who responded to our survey helped immensely by giving vivid, first-hand information about the kinds of problems and concerns that we planned to explore. The multitude of studies we gathered, in addition to our original research, also helped develop a context and, in many cases, provided solutions, or at minimum, constructive ways to frame problems.

You, the reader, have travelled a difficult path to get to the end of this text. The problems discussed were complex, and then you had to relate them to your own experiences. We set out to address major problems, and hope that dealing with these kinds of issues on a daily basis is not the norm in most of our libraries. That said, we can see from the information presented here and confirmed by our own research that many librarians do face significant problems and are anxious to find new methods to address them. For many, even those who have since overcome challenging circumstances, scars remain. If civility is to be the norm, then we must challenge ourselves to address the hard problems that can arise in any library workplace. It is important that we do not bury our heads in the sand but instead take action to make lives better for ourselves, our coworkers, and the patrons that we serve.

This book started where we hope to have it end—with you, a sense of optimism, and a catalyst for further sharing and discussion. At the outset, we made the case that until we find some inner peace and balance, it will be hard to solve the problems that we face. Emotional Intelligence and similar concepts were explored in detail, and it was revealed that librarians exhibit a bit less confidence in social skills than in other components of EI. This is something to consider moving forward in a world where communication is critical. These skills determine how healthy our libraries will be both internally and externally. How can we develop our skills and help others around us to develop their emotional intelligence?

Organizational culture was another topic covered in depth. Although chapter two is dedicated to this topic, it permeates the whole book. The survey we used indicated that 53 percent of librarians found themselves working within a significantly dysfunctional culture at least part of the time. It is important to keep in mind that dysfunctional culture may be a combination of reality and perception. We had no way, after all, to quiz others we may know personally about shared problems. That is why we collected our data anonymously, so we cannot say "although this person noted severe dysfunction at X Public Library, six other respondents indicated that the culture was not by and large dysfunctional." Two key issues were emphasized most strongly by survey participants. One is that leadership is incredibly important when setting the tone for a culture. Dictatorial—or even worse, weak—leaders are a big problem, especially when they look the other way when encountering bullying, sexism, cronyism, or any number of factors. Second, poor communication can derail a culture. When people feel they are being lied to or left out of the loop they are not going to give their best.

At one point, we debated about the need for a focused chapter on civility. The argument against including such a chapter prompted the question, "Is this not what the whole book is about anyway?" Luckily, the view that this stands as a separate issue prevailed, and therefore we examined civility in its most basic sense. Many of the other topics covered in this book are especially heinous (e.g., mobbing). But the chapter on civility reminds us that merely avoiding harming others is not adequate. For our libraries to be effective we need to treat one another with respect and dignity. Managers need to model and instill this behavior. Training needs to address it. It needs to be ingrained deeply within our expectations of the culture and of each other.

Although civility is our goal, we need to recognize that even in a relatively non-dysfunctional library conflict will arise. The discussion on conflict noted that, in some ways, the absence of conflict can in itself be a major problem. Libraries need librarians with competing ideas and perspectives. They need to be more diverse. That said, there should be mechanisms and training in place for handling differences. Although disagreements over tasks may not be as emotional as interpersonal conflicts, each requires strong leadership with a certain degree of skill in managing conflict. These same leaders, in conjunction with other library staff, need to build a culture that creates trust and fosters civil disagreement followed by a coming together around shared values and goals.

Much of this book covered problems such as bullying, mobbing, harassment, and other especially deviant and corrosive behaviors. Our survey revealed that, while all these may not be pervasive, there are still a significant number of library staff who are being bullied, or to a lesser extent, mobbed. There are staff who are experiencing harassment and similar problems that can turn dysfunction from a problem into a nightmare. Again, it cannot be emphasized enough how strong, sensitive leadership is needed to handle these types of issues. Nobody should be placed in the circumstance of not being able to be successful at work, much less be afraid of the workplace itself.

The latter chapters attacked this last point straight on. Genuine, motivated, and authentic leadership is needed in libraries. Administrators do not need to be perfect, but rather must be willing to learn from their mistakes and grow while also facilitating the growth of those who report to them. They must cherish diversity. They must develop high-functioning teams that work together by utilizing and accounting for individuals' strengths, weaknesses, skill sets, and different perspectives in order to come together and build better services. A functional library relies on transparency in communication so that all parties are incorporated into real discussion and decision-making. It has strong leaders who model appropriate behaviors and step in immediately when any staff feel bullied, harassed, or marginalized. The leaders and librarians in functional libraries know their own strengths and weaknesses. They work towards building a culture of trust and respect. They care about the development of their staff. Finally, they do not fear, but rather embrace, change as the new way of doing business.

We thought it would be helpful to share some of the best ideas that came from librarians who shared their thoughts on our survey. Of the 4,168 librarians who responded to our survey, 1,758 provided answers to the question "Do you have any suggestions for creating a more civil library workplace?" They were all expressive. We cannot share all the responses, but we would like to close with a handful:

> There's a very delicate balance between creating an accommodating, supportive space for the staff and creating consistent, functional, and fair personnel policies. To do so, I think that library administration and staff need to have constant, honest communication that lends to visible results.

It has to come from the top down, and be emphasized in training, in staff meetings, etc. Especially it has to be demonstrated by supervisors as well as other workers, both in customer interactions and in interactions between colleagues.

Be truthful yet considerate to others.

1. Assume no negative intent for small/first time transgressions 2. Listen to others 3. Try to find out what the other person's true concern is.

Listen carefully to one another and take ownership of mistakes and/ or actions.

More openness about what people do. Things can silo or become territorial very quickly. All employee groups must recognize the value in others' work.

Listen with empathy. Be consistent. Care about others.

ABOUT THE AUTHORS

JO HENRY serves as a librarian with the Charlotte Mecklenburg Library. Previously, she was the information services librarian at South Piedmont Community College. Ms. Henry obtained a Master of Library and Information Studies from the University of North Carolina Greensboro and a Master of Public Administration from Georgia Southern University. She has published in *Public Services Quarterly*, *Library Review*, *Community and Junior College Libraries*, and *College and Research Library News*, and has presented at the Metrolina Information Literacy Conference, the North Carolina Library Association Conference, and the ALA Annual Conference. She currently serves on the Metrolina Library Association board. Ms. Henry is coauthor of *The Mindful Librarian: Connecting the Practice of Mindfulness to Librarianship* (2016), *Fundamentals for the Academic Liaison* (2014), and *The Personal Librarian: Enhancing the Student Experience* (2014).

JOE ESHLEMAN received his Master of Library and Information Science degree from the University of North Carolina at Greensboro in 2007. He was an instruction librarian at Johnson & Wales University Library–Charlotte from 2008 to 2015. During this time, he taught numerous library instruction sessions. Mr. Eshleman completed the Association of College and Research Libraries' Immersion Program, an intensive program of training and education for instruction librarians, in 2009. He is a coauthor of *The Mindful Librarian: Connecting the Practice of Mindfulness to Librarianship*, *Librarians and Instructional Designers: Collaboration and Innovation*, *Fundamentals for the Academic Liaison* (with Richard Moniz and Jo Henry) and a contributor to *The Personal Librarian: Enhancing the Student Experience*. He has presented on numerous occasions, including the American Library Association Conference, the Lilly Conference on College and University Teaching, the Teaching Professor Technology Conference, and the First National Personal Librarian and First Year Experience Library Conference.

RICHARD MONIZ, EdD, served as the director of library services for Johnson & Wales University's Miami campus from 1997 to 2004 and has been the director of library services at Johnson & Wales University's Charlotte campus since 2004. He has previously served as head of information technology services for Johnson & Wales in Miami and while teaching classes on subjects such as computer science, world history, US history, and American government. Since 2006, he has taught for the MLIS program at the University of North Carolina at Greensboro. Dr. Moniz has published widely. He is sole author of the 2010 textbook *Practical and Effective Management of Libraries,* coauthor of *Fundamentals for the Academic Liaison,* coauthor and coeditor of *The Personal Librarian: Enhancing the Student Experience,* coauthor of *The Mindful Librarian: Connecting the Practice of Mindfulness to Librarianship,* and coauthor of *Librarians and Instructional Designers: Collaboration and Innovation.* He is actively engaged in the profession serving as a facilitator, presenter, and keynote speaker on multiple occasions and has held a number of committee and board responsibilities within ALA LLAMA, ACRL CLS, and the Metrolina Library Association, in addition to other nonprofit organizations.

INDEX

C

Cain, Jeff, 100
calculus-based trust, 127
Carr, Adrian, 74
Carton, Andrew, 117, 119
Casado, Margaret, 147
cataloger role and possible dysfunctions and
  remedies, 14
cell phone use as organizational deviance, 75
Chan, Darius, 113
change
  establishing a culture of, 18–19, 31–33
  individual resistance to, 134–136
channels of communication, 94–96
Charlotte Mecklenburg (NC) Library, 26
Chen, Chao, 32, 100
Chittock, Sharon, 12
*Choosing Civility: The Twenty-Five Rules of
  Considerate Conduct* (Forni), 37, 43
Christian, Linda, 12
civil behavior, tips for modeling, 46–47
Civility, Respect and Engagement in the
  Workplace (CREW), 45
Civility in America poll, 40, 41, 75
civility in the work environment, lack of. *See*
  incivility in the work environment
code of ethics and incivility in the work
  environment, 39
Coggburn, Jerrell, 110, 118
cognitive bias, 85–86
cognitive trust, 127
collaboration
  components needed for, 129
  historical overview of collaboration in
    libraries, 125
  incivility in the work environment and, 44
  ineffective. *See* ineffective collaboration
  in organizational culture, lack of, 26
*Collaboration and the School Library Media
  Specialist* (Doll), 148
College and Research Libraries News, 19
communication apprehension, 96–98
communication in the workplace
  active listening, 99, 101–102
  authenticity and, 103
  barriers to, 96–102
  channels of communication, 94–96
  digital communications, lack of empathy
    in, 100
  dismissiveness and, 101
  distrust and, 103

empathy and, 100–101
employee engagement and, 102
gossip and, 80–82
impact of, 102–104
introverted personalities and, 98
nonverbal actions and, 101
organizational culture and, 21–22
overview, 94
passive (mindless) listening and, 98–99
shyness and, 97
strategies for, 104
team composition and, 153–154
communication theory, 93–94
complaining as counterproductive behavior, 65
compromising as strategy for conflict
  management, 111, 113
confirmation bias, 84
conflict management
  approaches to, 110–113
  avoiding as strategy for, 111–112
  compromising as strategy for, 111, 113
  cultural differences and, 114–116
  dominating as strategy for, 111, 112
  guidelines for, 119–120
  healthy, 118–119
  integrating as strategy for, 111, 112–113
  obliging as strategy for, 111, 112
  overview, 109–110
  personality differences and, 113–114
  situational, 117–118
  theories on, 110–113
  unhealthy, 118–119
conversations as approach for
  counterproductive work behaviors, 67
Cook, Robert, 20
core mission, library leadership and, 174–175
Core Values of Librarianship (American
  Library Association), 173
Counterproductive Work Behavior Checklist
  (CWB-C), 64
counterproductive work behaviors (CWB)
  incivility in the work environment and,
    42
  overview, 64–67
Covey, Steven, 6, 8
cross-functional teams, 144–146
cross-lateral communication, 95
Crumpton, Michael, 6–7
cultural differences and conflict management,
  114–116
cyberbullying, 54–55